Kenyan
Capitalists,
the State,
and Development

Kenyan Capitalists, the State, and Development

by
David Himbara

Lynne Rienner Publishers • Boulder & London

Published in the United States of America in 1994 by
Lynne Rienner Publishers, Inc.
1800 30th Street, Boulder, Colorado 80301

and in the United Kingdom by
Lynne Rienner Publishers, Inc.
3 Henrietta Street, Covent Garden, London WC2E 8LU

Library of Congress Cataloging-in-Publication Data
Himbara, David,
        Kenyan capitalists, the state, and development / David Himbara.
        Includes bibliographical references and index.
        ISBN 1-55587-430-4 (alk. paper)
        1. Capitalism—Kenya. 2. East Indian—Kenya. 3. Businessmen—
Kenya. 4. Kenya—Economic policy. I. Title.
HC865.H56   1994
338.96762—dc20   93-14453
                                                    CIP

British Cataloguing in Publication Data
A Cataloguing in Publication record for this book
is available from the British Library.

Printed and bound in the United States of America

        The paper used in this publication meets the requirements
⊗ of the American National Standard for Permanence of
        Paper for Printed Library Materials Z39.48-1984

Contents

Tables and Figures

Tables

Figures

Abbreviations

ACCEA	Association of Chambers of Commerce of East Africa
AFC	Agricultural Finance Corporation
APIEA	Association for the Promotion of Industries in East Africa
CDC	Colonial Development Corporation
DFCK	Development Finance Company of Kenya
EABS	East African Building Society
EAC	East African Community
EAI	East Africa Industries
EARC	East African Railway Corporation
EPZs	Export Promotion Zones
FICCEA	Federation of Indian Chambers of Commerce of Eastern Africa
GEMA	Gikuyu Emba Meru Association
IBEAC	Imperial British East Africa Company
IBRD	International Bank for Reconstruction and Development
ICDC	Industrial and Commercial Development Corporation
ICM	Intergovernmental Committee for Migration
IDA	International Development Association
IDB	Industrial Development Bank
ILO	International Labour Office
JLBs	Joint Loan Boards
KAM	Kenya Association of Manufacturers
KANU	Kenya African National Union
KCC	Kenya Co-operative Creameries
KENATCO	Kenya National Transport Company
KETA	Kenya External Trading Authority
KFA	Kenya Farmers' Association
KIE	Kenya Industrial Estates

K-Map	Kenya Management Assistance Programme
KNA	Kenya National Archives
KNCCI	Kenya National Chamber of Commerce and Industry
KNTC	Kenya National Trading Corporation
MCI	Ministry of Commerce and Industry
MNC	Multinational Corporation
MUB	Manufacturing Under Bond
PTA	Preferential Trading Area
UNDP	United Nations Development Programme
UNIDO	United Nations Industrial Development Organisation

Preface

This book began as an inquiry into Kenyan capitalism, a subject that seemed to be confused by the tendency to omit from consideration nonblack domestic capitalists, in particular Kenyans of Indian extraction, on the basis that they constitute "Asian capital." My objective was, therefore, to redress this misconception by incorporating all homegrown economic activity, thereby establishing a more accurate picture of the extent and role of the Kenyan domestic bourgeoisie in different fields of specialization. Such an exercise permits a more accurate analysis of Kenya's potential to emerge from the ranks of economically backward and low-income countries.

Once in the field, however, a number of factors changed the original plans and scope of the project. First, during most of the research period, Kenya's agricultural sector was in a state that rendered it inappropriate as a subject for survey. The headlines in the local media at the time[1] suggest the then-prevailing environment in agriculture: "Whither coffee and tea?"; "Riotous Murang'a tea farmers destroy 2,400 kilos of tea"; "Workers dump tea leaves at factory"; "Leaders irked by uprooting of coffee"; "Coffee farming on verge of collapse." Further, most of the sectoral state regulatory agencies, including the Kenya Tea Development Authority (KTDA) and the Kenya Coffee Growers' Association (KCGA), were either under official investigation themselves or were not functioning at all.[2] Similarly, Kenya Co-operative Creameries (KCC) was under investigation for accumulating large losses and failing to pay farmers.[3] Both the Kenya Meat Commission (KMC) and the Uplands Bacon Company (UBC) had effectively collapsed, and efforts to revive them did not succeed at the time.[4] The case of the National Cereals and Produce Board (NCPB) was most remarkable. Not only did the NCPB consistently fail to pay farmers (while the produce it collected from them either spoiled in transit or failed to reach the market), it could not account for its finances. A report tabled in the National Assembly in October 1989 indicated that the NCPB had accumulated a KShs10 billion debt, which the government had written off in January 1988 "to lengthen the board's life and give it a new lease of life." The NCPB incurred an additional loss of roughly KShs3 billion by the following year.[5]

A second factor also changed the scope of the project: it soon became evident that no recent data were to be had for agriculture-related activities. The Central Bureau of Statistics (CBS) indicated in 1988 that a comprehensive economic survey was last attempted in 1974, and that that exercise was limited to manufacturing. Moreover,

> there has been only one more report published in 1977, which was itself a supplement to that produced in 1974. . . . It is regretted that the coverage . . . is still restricted to the manufacturing sector only. . . . Even within the manufacturing sector, the list of firms is not exhaustive.[6]

The unavailability of reliable and recent data was further confirmed in 1989, when the Kenyan government acknowledged that "in the past, non-Kenyan consultants have been called upon to do a one-time analysis of selected industries. As a result, the country has been unable to retain such data and information for effective institutional capacity building."[7]

In the case of manufacturing activity, the impoverished nature of official data was compensated for by other sources, including those of the Kenyan Association of Manufacturers (KAM), a private organization. It turned out that the KAM had undertaken a series of studies relating to Kenyan industries.[8] The KAM's subsections, i.e., textile, chemical, steel-aluminum, pharmaceutical, automobile component, capital, machine tools, and agro-manufacturing, also publish periodic internal reports on their own sectors, in addition to the minutes of meetings. Manufacturing was studied in 1988 by the United Nations Industrial Development Organisation (UNIDO). For historical background, valuable material covering the 1940s up to the early 1960s could be drawn from the Kenya National Archives (KNA).

It was from these assorted sources that I selected two hundred potential enterprises for study (out of the KAM's approximately six hundred members), eventually succeeding in distributing 120 questionnaires and recovering one hundred completed ones (see a sample of the questionnaire in the Appendix). The firms studied were not randomly selected, but were chosen on the basis of the following considerations: (1) various subsectors of the manufacturing sector had to be included in the sample so as to ascertain the composition of Kenya's industrial base; (2) most large firms had to be included so as to evaluate their role in extending and deepening Kenya's industrialization process; (3) a reasonable geographical representation was sought, so as to get an insight into the role of Kenyan industries in facilitating national policies such as job creation, rural industrialization, and the decentralization of industry away from the major centers of Nairobi and Mombasa; (4) a representative range of products was sought, so as to grasp the capacity of the Kenyan economy to overcome, or to lessen, foreign exchange and balance of payments difficulties. The sample eventually adopted was biased toward medium- and large-scale firms (i.e., with fifty employees or more).[9]

The potential flaw in not choosing a more "scientific" sample was that African and local European members of Kenya's bourgeoisie might be concentrated in small but important sectors and could, therefore, be missed, biasing the study in favor of Kenyan Indians. Local Europeans, as shown in Chapter 3, were almost never an important force and were decisively defeated by Indian commercial and industrial capitalists during the colonial period. The place of Kenyan Africans has also been recently summarized by the Kenyan government in a candid concession in regard to its past policies of Localization-Africanization-Kenyanization-Indigenization. The government's *Development Plan 1989–1993* (page 153) states categorically that "although after more than two decades of independence considerable progress has been made in the Kenyanisation, . . . most [black] Kenyans are still unable to participate in the ownership and control of large-scale industrial and commercial enterprises."

Development Plan 1989–1993 further acknowledges that various schemes, including those under the auspices of the Industrial and Commercial Development Corporation (ICDC), failed to achieve even modest success in fostering African capitalism. The report says (page 161) that "many businesses transferred in this process from non-indigenous to indigenous businessmen reverted to the former through 'back door' transactions." Nevertheless, a number of African-owned manufacturing firms were traced and scrutinized (including those companies that had been used as evidence of the national bourgeoisie in the existing research on Kenya) in an attempt to determine in more detail what went wrong.

Finally, while such admissions by the state generally confirmed one of my hypotheses, namely that relative development success in Kenya was mainly due to Kenyan Indian capitalists (as far as the domestic bourgeoisie was concerned), another of my hypotheses was being seriously undermined: namely, the notion that Kenyan success was equally to be explained by the competence of the postcolonial state. It is in this context that a factor unforeseen prior to my field work came into the picture and had to be evaluated: the substantial role of international development institutions that are actively bolstering and reconstructing some elements of the Kenyan state apparatus.

* * *

I hope that I have been able to present a coherent account, but more importantly, I trust that I have used the evidence gathered from the assorted sources as objectively as possible. Many will vehemently disagree with my account; others, interested in "pure" theories, will be disappointed. The obsession with theoretical frameworks has tended to produce abstract discourses that either dismiss the possibility of peripheral transformation or grossly overstate its actual or potential accomplishments in order to "prove" their respective approaches right. These exchanges confuse rather than explain the issues at stake, as the Kenyan case demonstrates. This book is less concerned with finding the model that fits. Rather, it seeks to tell the Kenyan story, and indeed that of East African commercial and industrial development, and to show how and why it was East Africans of Indian descent that came to play a leading role.

The explanation for this does not require hairsplitting theoretical arguments. East African Indians were simply first in the field, having played a merchant role in East African coastal trading enclaves for several centuries. The poor performance of white settlers and African businessmen has to do with their belated entry into commerce and industry and their marked reliance on the state apparatus for technical and financial support. In this sense, I hope I may contribute to redirecting studies of commercial and industrial development in East Africa and sub-Saharan Africa in general, and perhaps provoke some Africans and Africanists into pursuing deeper and more historically, theoretically, and empirically integrated investigations of their own.

Several institutions and many individuals contributed to the successful completion of the book. I cannot thank them enough, nor can I list them all. The International Development Research Centre (IDRC), Ottawa, supported me financially. Queen's University provided me with an intellectual context. The University of Nairobi's Institute for Development Studies enabled me to conduct research by affiliating me as a research associate. The Kenyan Association of Manufacturers allowed me the use of their library and key documents, and this source proved to be one of the most valuable. For this I thank Mr. Silas Ita, who was chief executive of the KAM, and his successor, Mr. John Kuria. Mr. Kuria's insights and kindness saved me valuable time. His staff, especially Ms. Cecilia Mbabu, were helpful. Finally I thank the Kenya National Archives for granting me permission to use their research facilities; the assistance of its staff, in particular Mr. Richard Ambani and Mr. Peterson Nthiwa, was very much appreciated. The Ministry of Commerce also allowed me to use their library resources.

Among the many colleagues who have helped me, Professor Colin Leys must be mentioned first. I am especially grateful to Professor Leys for his endless generosity and his intellectual guidance throughout my stay at Queen's University and in the course of this work and beyond. Professor Leys's ever-critical probing combined with supportive supervision make him a rare teacher and colleague. Although the final product will most likely not satisfy him, he has taught me a great deal and saved me from errors time and again.

Professor Bruce Berman's suggestions at the various stages of this work were also very valuable. His kindness to my family and myself will always be remembered. Without Professor Lee Lorch's fatherly and comradely attention, my academic life would have been much less rewarding. Professor Judith Hellman had an impact on my earlier, but important, scholarly evolution. Professor Abbie Bakan has been very kind and helpful. Among other contributors to the completion of this work were owners and business executives in Kenyan companies who completed my questionnaires and allowed me interviews and visits to their plants. Without their generosity in sharing their time, this study would not have been possible. The Mwendwa and Chandaria families helped me very generously, sparing their valuable time to discuss with me some historical and contemporary realities of Kenya. The kindness of my dearest friend Susan Anderson of Queen's International Centre I cannot forget. Members of the African-Caribbean Discussion Group, especially Mitalene Fletcher, Deanna Brown, and Godwin Friday, provided constructive criticism and companionship that helped steer this work toward a more fruitful terrain. My friends at UNICEF's Nairobi office, especially Ms. Debra Ash, provided a friendly but challenging environment in which to discuss my research as it progressed.

The individuals named above will not agree with all of what I have written; I must, therefore, absolve them from any responsibility for either the views or the errors the book contains. Nonetheless, I am grateful to them all.

Finally, I thank my partner, Fazela Haniff, who shared my academic trials and tribulations, including the long periods spent apart. Her tolerance of lapses in the performance of my domestic responsibilities made a profound difference. The delivery of our daughter, Dillea Himbara, extended the writing time considerably; we would not have it any other way. The memory of my mother, Didilli Musanabera Nyirabushishi, with her accommodating but unyielding philosophy of "never quit," inspired Fazela and myself to press on and meet the challenges entailed in this work.

Notes

1. *Industrial Review,* December 1989; *Daily Nation,* 15 November 1989; *Kenya Times,* 6 November 1989; *Kenya Times,* 10 November 1989; *Daily Nation,* 6 November 1989.

2. On the KTDA's inconsistencies, see *Kenya Times,* 12 October 1989.

Besides KCGA's shortcomings, it was suggested that the government's decision to dissolve it had political motives, as the state sought "to reduce the influence of mass-based autonomous farmers' organisations." *Weekly Review,* 7 April 1989.

3. *Weekly Review,* 2 June 1989.

4. For President Moi's proposals to revive the KMC, see the *Financial Review,* 3 August 1987. For the UBC's revival, see *Kenya Times,* 23 August 1989.

5. *Kenya Times,* 27 October 1989.

6. Republic of Kenya, *Directory of Industries,* 1988, p. i.

7. Republic of Kenya, *Development Plan 1989–1993,* p. 146.

8. KAM's numerous reports include lists of members, industrial maps, export surveys, and assessments of government policies. See Bibliography.

9. In opting to study medium- and large-scale firms, I followed Indu Chandaria. His study of Kenyan industrialists in 1963 remains exemplary and my questionnaire was adapted from his. See Chandaria, "Entrepreneurship," 1963. The 1988 UNIDO study was not based on specific field surveys and acknowledges the limitations of relying on national data: "The presentation of up-to-date information on sub-sectoral manufacturing trends is usually constrained by incomplete national data." See UNIDO, *Kenya,* 1988, p. i.

Introduction:
A Test of Two Arguments

The 1980s and early 1990s witnessed, almost worldwide, radical initiatives aimed at safeguarding and intensifying national economic performance in a more competitive world. Examples abound of programs contrived to stimulate productivity and to engender a more enabling economic environment in national, regional, and international contexts. In Western Europe, a strategy for forming a larger and more dynamic economic bloc set the stage for strengthening the European Economic Community by attempting to transform it into a closer political alliance. A more surprising and less expected change was in Eastern European countries and the former Soviet Union. There, state-run economies were discarded for private enterprise and competitive politics. In the Americas, the United States–Canada Free Trade Agreement—with Mexico as a projected participant in the larger North American Free Trade Agreement (NAFTA)—became operative; and the goal of forming a common market between Brazil and Argentina by 1999 was shifted to 1994. There was the further intent of involving other South American countries. By far more spectacular changes occurred in Asia, where, besides Japan, the newly industrialized countries (NICs) of South Korea, Taiwan, Singapore, and Hong Kong graduated into the industrial league on the basis of high value-added international exports. Following in the footsteps of the NICs were the so-called rapidly industrializing countries (RICs)—ASEAN countries (especially Malaysia, Indonesia, Thailand), coastal China, and India: their transformation was driven both by exports and large internal markets. Finally, during this period novelty economic experiments, notably the conversion of debt into portfolio or foreign direct investments, gained momentum in some countries with notable success, particularly in Latin America.[1]

In contrast to the recognition in all these cases of the need for new social, economic, and political strategies, the agenda in sub-Saharan Africa remained curiously unchanged. Most African countries remained

1

engrossed in crises that consisted of every conceivable malaise. Where populations were not threatened by starvation, disease, or war, dissipation of the economic infrastructure amidst astonishingly widespread corruption became the norm. Even where there was a realization of the dire need for some form of economic cooperation, for example the formation of the Preferential Trade Area (PTA) incorporating many sub-Saharan African countries, myopic preoccupations rendered such attempts largely ineffective.

It was largely due to these circumstances that sub-Saharan Africa became increasingly marginalized during the 1980s and early 1990s, as indicated, for example, by the region's share of international trade and foreign direct investment. Sub-Saharan African exports in all world trade fell from 2.5 percent in 1970 to 1.7 percent in 1985.[2] Further, the structure of the region's exports remained the same as in the late 1950s and early 1960s, with a marked overreliance on primary commodities that accounted for over 90 percent of export earnings.[3] In regard to foreign direct investment, most of it was concentrated in the industrially advanced countries, in excess of $572 billion in 1989. Developing countries' share amounted to $32 billion in 1990. Of this amount, the Asian region took in 61 percent, or $18 billion, with Latin America and the Caribbean receiving 32 percent. Investments in Africa (excluding South Africa) were valued at a mere 7 percent. Even more revealing was the fact that sub-Saharan Africa received on the average "less than $0.5 billion per year during the second half of the 1980s—roughly what Papua New Guinea alone attracted during the same period."[4] These alarmingly low inflows of foreign direct investments, combined with the absence of productive domestic capitalists, saw the region's real income and related social and economic indicators drop in catastrophic proportions. It was estimated, for instance, that the number of underemployed persons in sub-Saharan Africa increased from 63.6 million to 95 million in the same period, while that of the openly unemployed rose from 9.7 million in 1983 to 22 million in 1985 (or nearly 40 percent of the labor force).[5] Joan Robinson's famous expression that "the misery of being exploited by capitalists is nothing compared to the misery of not being exploited at all" was being validated by the sub-Saharan African conditions.[6]

One of the few countries that appeared to be an exception to the wretched condition of sub-Saharan Africa was Kenya. With its avowedly private enterprise strategy, Kenya was successful in avoiding the devastating social, economic, and political breakdowns that became hallmarks of the region. This stability allowed since 1964 an environment in which to formulate and administer development plans and other policies. That Kenya experienced some measure of sustained economic development is suggested by a comparison of selected orthodox economic indicators in leading sub-Saharan African countries. As is shown in Table 1, the trend in gross domestic investment was upward from 1965 to 1980 in Kenya,

Nigeria, and Cote d'Ivoire, while the general downturn experienced in the 1980–1986 period was less drastic for Kenya. The significance of Kenya's performance against that of Nigeria and Cote d'Ivoire, as illustrated in tables 1 and 2, was further emphasized by the fact that during the mid-1980s the latter two were categorized by the World Bank as "middle income economies," while Kenya was in the ranks of "low income economies."[7] An additional suggestion of Kenya's better performance was that both Nigeria and Cote d'Ivoire, but not yet Kenya, were enlisted into the newly created category of "highly indebted countries" and thus had less of their national income available for domestic investment due to larger interest and amortization payments on their foreign debt in the late 1980s.

Another indication of Kenya's accomplishments is that, despite its classification as a low income economy, it has an industrial base matched by few in the region. In this regard, a 1988 United Nations Industrial Development Organization (UNIDO) report stated that the Kenyan economy is

> one of the most industrialized in East Africa. . . . Kenyan GNP *per capita* has grown at an annual average rate of 2 per cent over the period 1965–1985. During this period average *per capita* income has been negative in Uganda (–2.6 per cent), Zambia (–1.6 per cent). . . . Zimbabwe, Tanzanian and Sudanese GNP per capita income has remained stagnant during 1965–1985. Kenya is thus the most dynamic and thriving national economy of East Africa.[8]

Table 1   Gross Domestic Investment as Percentage of GNP

Country	1965–1973	1973–1980	1980–1986
Kenya	22.6	29.2	25.5
Nigeria	17.5	22.1	14.5
Cote d'Ivoire	22.8	29.2	20.5

Table 2   Annual Growth Rates in Kenya, Nigeria, and Côte d'Ivoire

Country	Manufacturing		Service		Agriculture	
	1965–1980	1980–1986	1965–1980	1980–1986	1965–1980	1980–1986
Kenya	10.5	4.1	6.4	4.2	4.9	2.8
Nigeria	14.6	1.0	8.2	0.0	1.7	1.4
Cote d'Ivoire	9.1	0.0	9.4	-.05	3.3	0.8

Source: The World Bank, *World Development Report*, Washington D.C., 1988.

Another observer arrived at a similar conclusion two years later: "Kenya does have a competitive edge. It is well placed to become a manufacturing and service hub for East and Central Africa. It has the best port, the best trade, the best roads, the best climate, the best communications network, the best international reputation and the most vigorous free-market tradition in East Africa."[9] The 1988 UNIDO report showed another suggestive feature of the Kenyan case: while the public sector investment stagnated in the 1980s in almost all sub-Saharan African countries, the result was not as catastrophic in Kenya due to the cushioning provided by a dynamic private sector. Kenya's 12 percent average annual increase in gross fixed capital formation during 1985–1987 was "sustained almost entirely by the private sector," making the country's gross capital formation as a proportion of the GDP "one of the highest levels in sub-Saharan Africa."[10]

It was encouraging but impressionistic conclusions such as these that made me, like many others, interested in Kenya as a subject for research. It was appealing to investigate those phenomena that have made Kenya different; factors which, if explored, could contribute to the literature on Kenya and also shed light on prospects for economic development in Africa and other developing areas. Put differently, by inquiring into general conditions under which favorable environment for development evolved in Kenya, one should be able to get a better understanding of what enhances or impedes the process.

Once the project was envisaged, two hypotheses were derived from the existing literature to explain why Kenya appeared to be an exception to general degeneration in the region: two elements were seen as fundamental in spearheading the drive towards economic, social, and political transformation—the Kenyan capitalist class and the state. It was proposed that the relative success in Kenya was partly due to the presence of competent indigenous entrepreneurs who pioneered and continually transformed Kenya's commerce and industry. The role of such a class was the subject of a well-known discussion reviewed in more detail in Chapter 1. Two schools of thought, orthodox Marxism and neoliberalism, maintain that Kenyan developmental success was attributable to the existence of an exceptionally strong African bourgeoisie, especially among the Kikuyu. This bourgeoisie's origins pre-dated colonialism. The same social forces were responsible for the effectiveness of the postcolonial Kenyan state. Opponents of this view, who operated mainly in a dependency perspective, stressed, on the contrary, the small scale of the African bourgeoisie, and the dependence of the Kenyan state on foreign capital.

This discussion was inadequate in assessing Kenya. A more fruitful approach required an inquiry into the productive capacity of the entire homegrown capitalist class, reflective of Kenya's multiracial character. Such an approach would demonstrate, it was hypothesized, that commercial and industrial development was largely pioneered by local capitalists of Indian descent since the founding, in the modern sense, of the countries of the region. This approach would further show that black Kenyan capitalists, who constituted the central focus of much of the existing literature, were almost nonexistent. An overwhelming majority in this category crossed over from the civil service during the 1960s—a transition that was sustained by legislative directives and erratic state subsidies. Such a pattern of accumulation confined this section of the Kenyan bourgeoisie to a dependent status, with dubious prospects of survival if left to its own devices (either by a shift in policy or a change in regime).

In regard to the Kenyan state, the hypothesis, also drawn from the existing literature, was that it was unusually competent, a reflection of a "productive culture" engendered in the colonial state by its orientation to a settler class of capital. The application of the term *competence* to the state alluded to its ability not only to safeguard the accomplishments of the colonial era but also to initiate and implement appropriate policies that promoted further capital accumulation and development.

A study based on these hypotheses was carried out from April 1989 to April 1990, and from December 1992 to January 1993 to update the original research. In the case of the capitalist class, three strategies were utilized in the field work. First, use of the Kenyan National Archives: this was indispensable for exploring the activities and patterns of accumulation that formed the basis of Kenya's commercial and industrial development. Second, for the contemporary period, questionnaires and interviews were distributed to owners and managers of manufacturing enterprises to acquire data on such issues as levels of capital investment, types of industrial activity, the number of employees, and linkages to other sectors. Third, scrutiny of the records of organizations such as KAM and the Kenya National Chamber of Commerce and Industry (KNCCI) was essential for studying the collective organizational capacity of Kenyan capitalists. A fourth research technique resulted from the need to hand-deliver questionnaires to industrialists or their managing directors on plant sites. This proved to be extremely rewarding in supplementing the principal means of research. It permitted the collection of additional documents from individual enterprises and afforded an opportunity to become acquainted with industrial activity through tours and discussion.

Research on the Kenyan state followed a similar pattern. The archives provided valuable historical material on the nature and role of the Kenyan state up to 1963. For the contemporary era, interviews with selected ministries and key state agencies were conducted. In addition, assorted government documents were surveyed. For debates in the Kenyan National Assembly on key policy issues, the official records of the National Assembly from the 1950s to 1992 were extensively sampled. Policy pronouncements, such as development plans from 1964 to 1993, were studied and assessed; findings of government commissions initiated to assess the extent of the implementation of development targets were scrutinized. In this regard, documents such as the *Review of Statutory Boards* (1979), the *Working Party on Government Expenditures Report* (1982), and annual reports from the controller, the auditor general, and the Public Accounts Committee from the 1960s to 1992 were most useful for investigating outcomes of policy pronouncement in development plans. Besides these, annual reports of key state corporations such as the Industrial and Commercial Development Corporation (ICDC) were examined. And for the structure of the civil service as a whole, there were reports of three major commissions: the 1971 Commission of Inquiry on Public Service Structure and Remuneration, the Civil Service Review Committee, 1979–1980, and the Civil Services Salaries Review Committee (*Sessional Paper No. 3 of 1985*). Together with documents, position papers, and minute books of Kenyan commercial and industrial organizations, and editorials in local papers, these reasonably diverse sources offered a relatively clear view of the workings of the Kenyan state.

Research findings substantiated the hypothesis on Kenyan capitalists but invalidated that on the state.

In the case of Kenyan capitalists of Indian descent, their role in commercial and industrial development was found to be greater even than the author had imagined. It was found that they spearheaded the industrialization process from the 1940s onwards. For the black segment of the Kenyan capitalist class, it was confirmed that they remained numerically and strategically inconsequential, severely limited in operation, having sprung after independence mainly from the senior ranks of the civil service, the top echelons of state corporations, and politically connected circles. Moreover the national development agencies created to counter such shortcomings as lack of capital and skills on the part of Africans barely functioned. Political power and legislation could not imbue this section of Kenyan business with entrepreneurial skills, nor could it create a competent state machinery to sustain a program that could nurture them. Kenya's relatively better commercial and industrial performance, therefore, had very little to do with this segment of domestic capital.

The failure of the state to intervene effectively to create and support a black business class was, moreover, only one aspect of a more general weakness of the state. Contrary to my original hypothesis and the existing literature that informed it, the postcolonial Kenyan state proved not to be a factor that explains Kenya's relatively strong record of economic growth. The dissipation of skilled personnel (British and local Indians) led in the mid-1960s to a loss of effectiveness and in some cases to total collapse of some critical elements of the country's administrative regime. In effect, the disintegration of the state apparatus continues. Particularly revealing is the condition of the former East African Common Services Organisation (EACSO), the development institutions created during the postcolonial period, and the principal ministries, such as commerce and industry, and finance. The research found that the public sector hardly operates at all for its official purpose. Indeed the whole state apparatus could appropriately be described as a set of institutions for the aggrandizement of those who oversee its units.

The above findings led to the view that lack of historical perspective coupled with an impoverished comparative framework in the existing literature results in a misreading of Kenyan realities. To reverse prevailing misconceptions, an elementary chronology of Kenya's stages of development must be constructed to provide a point of departure to grasp its particular trajectory. How did commerce and trade emerge in Kenya? How did the internal market form? And, most importantly, how and when were merchant activities transformed into industrial capital and to what ends? What was the role of the state in marshalling and mediating contending racial fractions of capital before and after independence? In addressing these questions, this book establishes that the present Kenyan bourgeoisie essentially originated from Indian merchant activities based on the East African coast. On the one hand, these served the transocean trade between Europe and the Indian subcontinent and, on the other hand, the hinterland trade before the colonial period. These forces were augmented by wage workers and administrative cadres associated with the building of the Uganda Railway. The colonial state had to turn to India for a labor force precisely because local productive relations were such that there was no "free" labor to be had: the need for wages, not to speak of a disciplined labor force, still had to be created.

Coastal merchant activities explain the Indian creation and control of the internal market and why they were not successfully challenged even by white settlers who, as is often claimed, controlled the state throughout the colonial period. It was, therefore, natural that it was from within the Indian segment of Kenyan and East African societies that the commercial and industrial bourgeoisie emerged, given its historical experience and role. Among the glaring shortcomings in the literature on East African capitalism is the fact that this segment of domestic capital has been largely left out: it is said to have represented "Asian" capital.

In the case of the Kenyan state, highly instrumentalist conceptions depict it as, during the colonial period, either a tool of the British bourgeoisie or of local European settlers, and, after independence, an instrument of the African bourgeoisie. A more complex picture emerges in this book. It is shown that during and after World War II, a space was created between the imperial center and the colony that compelled the Kenyan state and local business groups together to seek local solutions to development problems. This development recalls Andre Gunder Frank's observation that when Latin America's link to the world metropolis was disrupted by the Depression and by World War II, it experienced the "largest independent industrialisation drive since the post independence 1830s and 1840s."[11] In the Kenyan case, a series of events thereafter saw the state between 1947 and 1963 becoming more and more a national capitalist state that actively fostered commercial and industrial development in a way that was not in the cards previously, nor since independence. The state of this period became, in effect, ambitious and complex, incorporating the Kenyan administrative regime and East African supranational apparatus that coordinated Kenya, Uganda, and Tanganyika. As shown in various sections of this book, it would be extremely difficult to reduce the actions of the state to a single interest, least of all to the metropolitan bourgeoisie or local European settlers. It becomes clear, however, that the strategic commercial and industrial position of the East African Indian bourgeoisie rendered them the principal beneficiaries of the enabling policies adopted by the state after World War II, notwithstanding the fact that they were the least influential in politics. The role of the state was to decline when, during the postcolonial period, it became highly personalized, autocratic, and counterproductive, with most elements quickly unravelling, leading to profound contradiction. There was on the one hand a commercial and industrial bourgeoisie with the capacity to place the country on a far more promising path of development. But on the other hand, the state failed to provide policy mechanisms to utilize available technical skills and resources.

Some notes on the organization of this book: Part I traces the development of commerce and industry in Kenya; Part II gives more attention to the role of the state in this process. In Chapter 1, there is a critical assessment of the existing research. A reinterpretation of the Kenyan development process is outlined, highlighting key historical moments in the rise of the Kenyan bourgeoisie and the state. African capitalists, who have occupied center stage in most writing, are shown to be, at best, a bourgeoisie-in-formation. The thesis that they used the state to accumulate and move into all sectors of the economy is shown to be essentially false. The already noted confusion regarding the domestic bourgeoisie is also dealt with, demonstrating the fact that by focusing on "African" capitalists, the existing writing generally failed to grasp the principal roles of the homegrown capitalists of Indian descent. This confusion is reflected in the terminology used, especially the local code word *Asian*. The term *Asian capital* should refer to multinational corporations from Asia (of which there are many in Kenya), and not to industrialists from within the East African Indian community whose ancestors came from the Indian subcontinent. The Indian community is, therefore, indigenous and African, in the sense that the duration of their presence in East Africa spans several generations, and their commercial and industrial activities were formed within East Africa.[12] Finally, the concept of the Kenyan state as a rational and coherent instrument of a single class is found to be particularly misleading.

Chapter 2 explores the conditions that enabled the rise of an Indian commercial and industrial bourgeoisie in Kenya and East Africa, despite the fact that the Indian community has historically had limited direct influence in the politics of Kenya. The conditions that permitted this success and the various patterns of accumulation followed by some groups are highlighted by tracing, especially, how they made the transition from merchant to industrial capitalism. Drawing on case studies, the chapter focuses on the sources and means of the initial accumulation of capital, and on the sectors of their concentration in industrial production. The role of business organizations before and after independence is also scrutinized, as is the role of mediation by the state. It becomes evident that the most conducive environment for Kenyan Indian capitalists to accumulate and move into the more challenging industrial niches was from the 1940s to 1964. Thereafter, the climate changed quickly, mainly as a result of a contradictory policy. On the one hand, the national development plan called for a policy of encouraging domestic and foreign capital to invest in modern manufacturing plants to enhance Kenya's productive capacity in the larger East African market. On the other hand, the goal was to enable black Kenyans to acquire a commercial and industrial niche through either a coerced acquisition of existing (mainly local Indian) businesses, or by compelling large-scale domestic and foreign manufacturing concerns to appoint African distributors of their goods.

Most manufacturers saw this policy as a deterrent to the deepening of their operations and a threat to their investments in an already poor political and economic climate, especially in the wake of the weakening and eventual collapse of the East African Common Market in the late 1970s. In fact, large-scale foreign capital investment declined during this period, with some of the larger multinational corporations divesting altogether in the early and mid-1980s. As for the Kenyan Indian capitalists, not being as mobile they adopted a different defense; a remarkable number shifted into more complex industrial sectors, where larger scales of capital and management requirements placed them beyond the reach of the Africanization drive. Thus, Africanization, in effect, fortified their significance in Kenya's development process, notwithstanding occasional attacks on their role from official circles.[13]

Chapter 3 examines the case of the African capitalists and shows that they still play a very modest role, notwithstanding various state schemes initiated in the colonial and postcolonial period to foster them. It is established that, contrary to the popular belief that the colonial state hindered their rise, it promoted it through a number of specialized credit and educational schemes, but with poor results. It is also illustrated that postcolonial policy aimed at promoting this segment was flawed in a number of ways. The informal, or *jua kali,* sector and small-scale industries that had been already subject to policy and support mechanisms since the 1940s were ignored in preference to the coerced takeover of existing non-African businesses. The Africanization attempts failed, reflecting the fact that those who acquired businesses possessed neither the skills nor capital to hold their own in the market place. The state agencies created to support them suffered the same fate. The failure of this policy saw the state revert to the pre-1964 strategy of nurturing African capitalism by concentrating on those elements with experience mainly drawn from the informal sector, an approach that was repeatedly called for by a number of international development institutions through the 1970s and 1980s.

The nature and impact of the Kenyan state in commercial and industrial development are more fully addressed in Part II. The rise of that section of the Kenyan state apparatus responsible for commerce and industry is outlined. Key moments are highlighted—such as the initial phase, during the colonial period, when vital infrastructures and an institutional framework were installed, and the transition from the colonial to the independence era. The 1940s and 1950s are shown in Chapter 4 to have been something of an industrial revolution, under the leadership of the Ministry of Commerce and Industry and associated authorities. The early transition period from the colonial period (between 1964 and 1971—Chapter 5) is shown to have been regressive—one from which the country has yet to recover, mainly on account of the loss of specialist administrative personnel. The implications of this transition are studied, as are factors that account for an investment environment that has facilitated Kenya's capital accumulation (relative to its sluggish sub-Saharan neighbors), but that has also circumscribed the successful implementation of state-led plans. This latter factor is contrasted with implementation in the Asian developmentalist states, and a more recent case closer to Kenya—Mauritius.

Success Story or Disaster?

With such findings, namely, on the one hand, a highly industrious capitalist class, but on the other hand an inept state that obstructs the deepening of the development process, the question arose: What then explains Kenya's development success relative to other sub-Saharan African countries? An adequate answer lies beyond the scope of this book, but this question nonetheless helps to underscore the questionability of the comparative framework in existing research that led to an overstatement of the Kenyan case. In effect, inasmuch as Kenya's development record is "impressive by African standards," as shown in tables 1 and 2, it can also be construed as a disaster when assessed from the standpoint of its own potential and the

Table 3   Manufacturing Exports of Kenya, Mauritius, and Botswana ($US million)

Country	1965	1980	1987
Kenya	14	210	164
Mauritius	0	125	486
Botswana	1	353	641

Source: World Bank 1989.

level of development it had already attained by the early 1960s, or if it is examined in relation to countries outside sub-Saharan Africa. As J.B. Wanjui aptly remarks, Kenya's success as measured by African standards is bound to mislead:

> When outsiders wish to praise Kenyans for their economic and social achievements, they most often do so by noting that Kenya is considerably more advanced than other African countries. Since we all know that the economic and political performance of most African states has been dismal, this comment sharply qualifies the accolade as, at best, faint praise and avoids the greater question of how we Kenyans would measure up to the optimum standards applied to non-African societies. . . .Until we dare compare our performance with the successful nations of the world, instead [of] with failures, we have no . . . cause for self-congratulation. By world standards no economy in Africa is performing as it should. Acknowledgement of this reality, regardless of its toll on national pride, must no longer be postponed.[14]

Wanjui's point is all the more important when the Kenyan case is contrasted with the more recent African success stories of Mauritius and Botswana. As indicated in Table 3, Kenya was already fairly industrialized with substantial manufacturing exports in the mid-1960s. By comparison, both Mauritius and Botswana were monocommodity economies with almost no manufacturing sector to speak of until the 1970s when the two implemented export-processing industrialization strategies. By the late 1980s, both countries had not only overtaken Kenya but had more than doubled their manufacturing export performance. Kenya's performance meantime actually declined. It is worth noting that when Mauritius and Botswana were making a breakthrough in export-processing industrialization in the 1970s, the Kenyan bourgeoisie and elements of the international development institutions were pressing the Kenyatta government to adopt similar plans. Such plans have appeared in almost every Kenyan development plan since the early 1970s. However, not only did the Kenyan state fail to implement these plans, it actively participated in the demise of the East African Common Market that had previously absorbed most of its products. Kenya's industrial capacity, installed during the 1950s and early 1960s to serve East Africa, now had to be reoriented to the Kenyan market alone. Overcapacity remains a major problem for the Kenyan bourgeoisie. It was mainly on account of this obstacle that some multinationals left the Kenyan market altogether, contributing significantly to the decline of the country's manufacturing sector.

Insofar as Kenya did do better than most other African countries, an explanation for this would probably include at least the following factors. First, Kenya had, at independence, a more sophisticated institutional infrastructure than any of its neighbors: Nairobi was a regional and international center; the country's port facilities at Mombasa were of regional and international importance, rendering Kenya not only the leading partner state in the East African Community (EAC) but a critical transit point for most countries of east and central Africa, including Rwanda, Burundi, Zaire, and Sudan; and many headquarters of the supranational state organizations were based in Kenya. Second, the scale of foreign investment in Kenya expanded from the 1950s, only to decline sharply in the wake of the collapse of the East African Common Market in the late 1970s. The Kenyan Indian bourgeoisie filled the gap (a factor that contrasts with disastrous results in Uganda where local Indians were expelled, and in Tanzania where their industries nationalized). Third, the *jua kali* sector, a sphere in which potential African entrepreneurs have been gathering momentum, supplemented the formal sector, despite official neglect and hostility to them as shown in Chapter 3 and later chapters. Fourth, Kenya's relatively diversified economy enabled it to cope with price declines in any one export commodity (at least until the mid-1980s), and tourism, with its related activities, replaced agriculture as the single most important earner of foreign exchange. A fifth significant factor was the scale of foreign aid to Kenya and the remarkable direct role of the donor community in administering it. This practice had become routine since early independence days: it began with the high profile of the British state (through the Commonwealth Development Corporation) and continued with the World Bank in the transfer of the agricultural sector from white settlers to Africans.[15] In effect, following a decline in the ability of Kenya's institutions to execute elementary administrative tasks, or produce technical personnel to perform them, external agencies set up shop in the country in an attempt to reverse this. So thanks to these factors—the presence of a dynamic domestic Indian commercial and industrial bourgeoisie, a growing *jua kali* sector, a substantial foreign investment, a formerly remunerative agricultural sector, and an expatriate administrative cadre—the Kenyan state appeared, to outsiders, as an effective and visionary planner on a continent in chaos. This was far from being the case.

Not only did international aid to Kenya increase steadily after the mid-1960s, it was *pledged ahead*—ahead of the fiscal period it was intended for. This enabled the Kenyan government to incorporate the aid into its budgetary projections and plans. The minister for finance, George Saitoti, could declare in 1989: "In light of the sound economic policies which Kenya has been pursuing, foreign donors have pledged to assist us with an amount equivalent to Kenyan Pounds 971.1 million the next fiscal year."[16] Most of the aid package was also in the form of grants and concessionary loans. Thus, for example, in the fiscal year 1985/86, 13 percent of the Kenyan government's budget (i.e., KShs4 billion) came from aid, of which 49 percent was in grants and 51 percent was in concessionary loans.[17] In the fiscal year 1986/87 the proportion of aid in the Kenyan national budget was 18 percent (i.e., KShs7 billion), 45 percent of it in the form of grants.[18] By 1989/90, donor "contributions" to the budget had jumped to over 28 percent (i.e., KShs19.4 billion), of which 40 percent was in grants.[19] However, in an exercise designed to force the Moi regime to curb corruption and initiate economic and political reforms, the donor governments suspended their annual practice of pledging aid to Kenya in November 1991 and instead called for a series of structural adjustments (Chapter 6). These included reduction of the civil service and privatization of the largely ineffective parastatal sector. The suspension of aid was still in force in early 1993, notwithstanding the introduction of multipartyism in December 1992. The donor community maintained that the Kenyan government had not made enough progress in the implementation of structural adjustments.[20] With the country in acute need of aid, but with a government unwilling to undertake the reforms demanded by its traditional donor supporters, the so-called Kenyan economic miracle was no more; the once "prosperous paradise amid the chaos of the Horn of Africa" was fast becoming "a shambles."[21]

In conclusion, I must repeat that this book has a specific focus, arising from its original goals and the limitations encountered in the field. It does not claim to explain the reasons for Kenya's apparent development successes relative to other African countries. It claims to test two of the main arguments that have been advanced hitherto to explain those successes. Its contribution to the explanation of Kenya's development record is as much negative as positive. It does contend, however, that it is only on the basis of a historical and empirical approach, such as it adopts, that an adequate explanation of Kenyan development can be hoped for, and useful lessons be drawn for other countries.[22]

Notes

1. United Nations, 1990.
2. World Bank, 1989, p. 19.

1

Perspectives on Kenyan Development

The main contending perspectives on Kenyan capitalism have generally followed cyclical trends in the broader development field. Neoliberal writing inspired by classical political economics set the tone in the 1950s and the early 1960s. The thesis was that the insertion of colonies into the world economy, and the subsequent presence of multinational investments in them as independent nations, placed them on a healthy course.[1] This combination of factors, it was maintained, facilitated the rise of local entrepreneurial classes and modern governmental institutions destined to play roles similar to their counterparts in Western industrial societies.

From the mid-1960s through the 1970s a new trend set in, advancing opposing theses. Dependency theorists, though they accentuated different features, shared the notion that development at the periphery was forestalled by the colonial legacy. This, they said, created a nonproductive bourgeoisie and a comprador state that merely superintended the transfer of any national economic surplus to imperial centers.[2] By the mid-1970s, however, some adjustments to the dependency framework were being made. A number of authors argued that not all local capitalists and states could be conceptualized as subordinates of international capital in all peripheral countries and at all times. Further, an alliance between some local capitalists and international capital did not rule out the emergence of a relatively independent segment of local capital, or of a relatively autonomous local state, oriented to national development. Such an assortment of forces, it was urged, had already overseen considerable transformation in some peripheral countries.[3]

By the late 1970s and early 1980s, the principal current in the development discourse was once more closer to where it had been in the 1950s; the revisionist dependency propositions had given way to questioning the value of the framework itself and to a rejuvenation of some of the neoliberal themes of the 1950s, this time advanced by authors inspired by orthodox Marxism.[4] Observations by Dudley Seers and Alain Lipietz that

17

a convergence had taken place within the contending doctrines, notwith-standing their conflicting epistemological foundations, were on the mark.[5]

In the sub-Saharan African case, however, the discussion during the 1980s and the 1990s remained in a stalemate, still reflecting a propensity to either dismiss or exaggerate the possibility of capitalist transformation, depending on the theoretical framework adopted. The *dependentistas* depicted African capitalist classes and states as agents for foreign interests, while orthodox Marxists and neoliberal writers maintained the reverse: that vigorous African capitalist classes and coherent states in a vanguard role were a fact. From a dependency perspective, for example, Samir Amin asserted that African underdevelopment was the result of its "inte-gration into the world capitalist system as an exploited and dominated periphery, fulfilling specific functions in the process of accumulation at the centre of system." In order to overcome this structural impediment, according to Amin, Africans have to adopt a "strategy of delinking, that is to refuse the imperatives of the international division of labour."[6] From an orthodox Marxist position, John Sender and Sheila Smith maintained that African postcolonial states were highly successful in promoting "the development of capitalism and the consolidation of an indigenous bour-geoisie." An indication of the latter was the fact that African capitalists were able "to intervene and maximise forward, backward and fiscal linkages."[7] Far from hindering African development, foreign capital led to "an extremely favourable environment for the development of indige-nous capitalist classes"—through, for example, technical and managerial careers.[8]

This debate must surely be transcended: sub-Saharan African condi-tions of the 1980s and the early 1990s readily belie the above extraordi-narily innocent and repetitive views. It is abundantly clear that the region neither became a site of increased productive interest for multinational investments, nor gave rise to social forces attempting a steadfast national development strategy, as the two perspectives would have it. On the contrary, the region generally became marginalized, as shown in the Introduction.

The literature on Kenya illustrates how fruitless such discussions became, and how, in effect, they confused rather than clarified the issues. The dependency writers[9] depicted the Kenyan African bourgeoisie and the state as agents of foreign capital, while neoclassical scholars[10] and orthodox Marxist authors[11] saw them as constituting a transforming bour-geoisie, especially Kikuyu accumulators whose roots were purportedly traceable to precolonial primitive accumulation and long-distance trade. However, not only was the debate[12] speculative and the information used in it too impressionistic to establish clearly the origin and the contempo-rary extent of Kenyan capitalism: the Kenyan and East African Indian merchant and the industrial bourgeoisie, who spearheaded the accumulation process in almost all historical phases, were bypassed almost entirely. Equally, if not more problematic, was the analysis of the Kenyan state. This remained trapped into a question of whether the state is an instrument of foreign capital or of the local African bourgeoisie, a preoccupation that overshadowed more fundamental problems. Without a deeper study to establish the state's actual history and contemporary condition, the disintegration, and indeed the collapse, of some its vital elements, especially the East African supranational state institutions that had historically played a leading role in Kenyan and East African development, was effectively obscured. The reality was that the postcolonial Kenyan state conformed in the main to the prevailing pattern of predatory, corrupt, and counterproductive African states.[13] The ramification of the role of international financial institutions in reconstructing elements of the Kenyan state, if known, was not incorporated into the analysis of contemporary Kenyan circumstances.

In light of these theoretical and substantive shortcomings, the discussion on Kenya is subject to the criticisms of the general development discussion of the 1970s and the 1980s: namely, that the contending perspectives largely failed to shed light on real countries, but recapitulated what Aidan Foster-Carter termed "dependency predictions of doom" against "neoclassical pipedreams."[14] Albert Hirschman saw the discussion as constituting "compulsive and mindless theorising" hindering more informed appraisals of the highly diverse experiences in developing areas.[15] Perhaps a more devastating critique came from Lipietz, who characterized the debates as amounting to "a collection of labels to stick on real nations and actual existing international relations without first analyzing them carefully."[16] In his 1991 reassessment of the Kenya debate, Leys, too, objected to the contending perspectives, noting that both dependency and its orthodox Marxist critique were too deterministic to make a meaningful contribution. For this to occur, he noted, both sides need "to abandon their untenable assumptions and converge around a programme of enquiry in . . . the long-term economic implications of what is happening *in any given country.*"[17]

With these scholars, I would argue that, moreover, since neoliberal, orthodox Marxism and modified dependency perspectives now converge on the belief that there is no reason why a particular region or country should remain underdeveloped (or remain successful once developed for that matter), the task now is to conduct deeper research to enable us to draw conclusions from particular historical experiences.

In what follows, an alternative analysis of Kenyan capitalism is outlined, highlighting the critical stages in the rise and role of Kenyan capitalists and the state. A more comprehensive account of both appears in subsequent chapters. In the case of the bourgeoisie, all homegrown elements are sketched, not just Africans. The state is outlined in a way that refrains from the instrumentalist reductionism that is so prevalent in much of the existing writing, most of which has oversimplified a rich and complex interplay of forces and historical events.

Origin and Role of Kenyan African Capitalists

Both orthodox Marxism and neoliberal writings on Kenya, as previously noted, locate original African capitalists in the precolonial period, especially in the area of local and long-distance trade. However, the suggested degree of this development is supported neither by economic historians nor by contemporary research. In Victorian writings on British activities, Kenya is portrayed as lacking economic activities in excess of social subsistence needs and therefore also lacking a widespread trading culture. McDermitt reported: "The districts intervening between the coast and the lake regions, owing to the present economic condition of the country, are comparatively useless, and must so continue until the process of development has realised their latent resources."[18] It will also be recalled that the Imperial British East Africa Company (IBEAC) collapsed partly due to lack of a substantial economic activity, a factor that contributed to its failure to attract British capital to the area (unlike the case of West Africa). Robinson and Gallagher write that "Business men were unmoved by tall stories of its bright commercial prospects. Investors refused to sustain the Chartered Company or to build a Uganda railway without a Treasury guarantee which Parliament would not give."[19]

Apart from its geopolitical value[20] to imperial Britain, the region's commercial worth remained in question.[21] Part of the dilemma faced by colonial administrators, as later historians indicate, is that most precolonial East African societies were based on subsistence economies in which people produced foodstuffs and goods principally for their own consumption. According to Van Zwanenberg and King, some exceptions included "the lacustrine kingdoms of Uganda where governments were concerned to control trade and market-places so that the state could reap some benefit from the trade."[22] But in the case of the East African "acephalous societies"—in future Kenya—accumulation was still

> a social investment, maintaining and expanding social relationships and, in a situation where famine and disease were likely to occur, it acted as an insurance against the future. . . . In general, therefore, we can say trade could not have led to rapid technical change in the nineteenth century, although it was important for comparatively slow dispersion of technical goods over wide areas. Trade was concerned with social accumulation within the confines of existing technical knowledge.[23]

Van Zwanenberg and King are not alone in drawing this conclusion. Isaria Kimambo states that as "we move into the eighteenth and nineteenth centuries some internal trade, especially that of the Akamba, Mijekenda and Kikuyu, became a means of accumulating wealth, but since it was small and still restricted to cattle and foodstuffs this trade did not lead to any qualitative, or quantitative, economic and technological change."[24] Leakey concurs that the extent of agricultural surplus and the scale of markets for it was still rudimentary:

> The big, organised markets for internal trade that are such a feature of present day Kikuyu life did not come into existence in South Kikuyu until the time of the great famine of 1898–1899. . . . As far as agricultural produce was concerned, every family grew what it needed, and if some accident—such as the destruction of a crop by wild animals or birds—resulted in a family being short of its requirements, they would obtain what they wanted by private barter with other families.[25]

Van Zwanenberg and King share this view of African trade.[26]

According to Godfrey Muriuki, it is the Akamba that came the closest to becoming a commercial agency between the coast and the hinterland. They were renowned hunters, an occupation that enabled them to control the ivory trade, the principal commercial activity of the day.[27] It would appear from the above that the precolonial origin of the African businessmen in Kenya has to be put into a proper perspective.[28]

Post-1963: Overstatement of Value and Scale

Just as the precolonial and colonial roots of African businessmen have been overstated, so is their capacity in the postcolonial period. Part of this confusion is due in part to a simplistic approach. Thus, Swainson attempted to show the rise of a national bourgeoisie, and of an interventionist state acting on their behalf, on the basis of two African cases:

> Using detailed analysis of data from two case studies, evidence is provided of the growth of indigenous capitalist enterprise in Kenya. A local capitalist class is developing, originally based on merchant capital and gradually moving into manufacturing. Far from this class being "auxiliary" . . . to international capital, it has used its connection with the Kenyan state successfully to establish itself in direct competition with foreign firms.[29]

The author further asserts that "African firms gradually increased as a proportion of new private firms being formed in Kenya and in 1972, 310 African firms exceeded for the first time the 249 formed by the Asian community. This reflected an increasing amount of merchant capital accumulation taking corporate forms."[30] Her source for these assertions was the registrar of companies, about which the author remarks that this "kind of information is available through published reports of the Registrar of Companies or can be looked up in the official Company Registry office in most African countries."[31] It is difficult to see how a capitalist class can be established on the basis of two cases, or from such records as those of the registrar of companies.

As already indicated in the Preface, most official data are highly suspect by self-admission, and must be supplemented by other sources. At any rate, it is not the number of companies but rather, their value, an aspect that can be assessed only by looking at their patterns of accumulation, and the source of their original capital, to establish their productive potential and, therefore, to assess their significance in the national economy. It is worthwhile to note that the more detailed studies at hand do not share the above views. The work of Marris and Somerset, who highlighted the novice state of African businessmen (admittedly some years earlier), is considered in Chapter 3. Writing at the end of the 1970s, Kitching also found that Kenyan African businessmen were still essentially a petite bourgeoisie. He aptly remarked that it is the state that defines "the position of the richest Africans in Kenya, and the total absence of such access which defines the poorest."[32] Kitching wondered whether such a "state petite bourgeoisie . . . will attempt to convert itself into a fully developed bourgeoisie."[33] A detailed analysis of their attempts at transforming themselves into a productive bourgeoisie based on the purchasing of labor power is found in Chapter 3, which traces their patterns of accumulation from the 1940s to 1993. It becomes clear that they remain, at best, a bourgeoisie-in-formation.

The Indian Bourgeoisie in Kenya and East Africa

Remarkably, the homegrown Indian merchant activity is rarely given the central importance it deserves. This is in spite of the fact it introduced a money economy to East Africa, extended it and converted it into large-scale commercial activity in the early phase of the twentieth century, and transformed it into industrial capital after World War II. One of the insights of earlier writings (before the dependency–orthodox Marxist debate) was a recognition of the importance of this segment of domestic capital.

Examples of development observers sensitive to this role include Peter Bauer, who argued that immigrant communities (e.g., Indians in East Africa, Chinese in Malaysia, Levantines in West Africa, and Jews in South Africa) tended to become more successful in business and played leading roles in economic development because they were often excluded from noncommercial activities, among other things.[34] Paul Kennedy makes a similar point when he writes that the vulnerability of these ethnic minorities operating in an alien environment gave them every reason "to maintain a degree of internal solidarity." This led to considerable success during the 1950s, when sections of "the Indian and Levantine commercial communities, in East and West Africa, respectively . . . transferred capital into manufacturing,"[35] Indu Chandaria's thesis on "The Development of Entrepreneurship in Kenya"[36] sought to illustrate the central role played by local Indian capitalists in Kenya's industrialization process during the 1950s; Leys's earlier work also acknowledged the fact that East African Indians, by the 1950s, had evolved to become a potential indigenous industrial bourgeoisie.[37] Robin Murray's essay on "The Chandarias: The Development of a Kenyan Multinational" analyzed patterns followed by one of the most successful East African Indian industrialists whose activities became internationalized.[38]

Unfortunately, this direction in the study of Kenyan capitalism gave way to an academic obsession with the emerging African segment, and to classifying local Indians as "Asian capital," a practice that continued into the late 1980s. Thus, in his 1989 study of the glass manufacturing industry in Kenya, Peter Coughlin misleadingly asserts that "The Kenya Glass Ltd. was started in Mombasa in 1946 by the Madhvani Group out of India."[39] In this case, since the Madhvani family is not black, its enterprises are transferred to a foreign category.[40] A similar approach is found in Swainson, who writes that "The development of an indigenous manufacturing sector during the 1970s has been a logical outcome of the conversion of merchant capital into productive capital."[41] Apart from the fact that she does not establish the existence of African merchant activities, let alone their conversion into productive capital as indicated below, she assumes that indigenous manufacturing began in the 1970s because this was a period when black Kenyans appeared to be entering the sector. In this way, she effectively glosses over the history of domestic capital accumulation from coastal-based merchant activity and its spread inland in the early 1900s, differentiation within the commercial Indian bourgeoisie, and the subsequent emergence of an industrial bourgeoisie from the 1940s onwards.

The approach and conclusions drawn by Coughlin and Swainson are obviously misleading. The Madhvani Group is not "out of India" but is one of the leading East African business families. Its members pioneered numerous enterprises in commerce and industry since the early 1900s, as is illustrated in more detail in Chapter 2. Ironically, in the 1950s, one of the early sources of competition to local East African Indian manufacturing companies was India, a development that led the former to seek protection from the Kenyan state, and the creation of East Africa–wide agencies to promote industrial development (more in chapters 2 and 4). The numerous protests in the 1950s against international Indian trade by local East African Indian capitalists included the following presentation from Kaluworks, a leading local group:

> We have been engaged in the manufacture of Karais [washing basins]
> since 1938 and the productive capacity of our plant is more than sufficient
> to provide the total requirements for East Africa in this article. . . .
> Unfortunately we are now facing competition from overseas, chiefly
> India, and the market is being flooded with Karais of inferior quality.[42]

Berman's treatment of Kenya's industrial development after World War II reflects a similar bias. He maintains that this was a period when "international manufacturing capital, mostly from the metropole, was firmly established in Kenya," an activity that "was reinforced by metropolitan pressures to encourage industrial investment and protect the position of British capital in the colony." More importantly, he continues: "the metropolitan state, through the Colonial Development Corporation, intervened to assume the role of finance capital and encourage British industrial investment."[43] As for local Indians, Berman maintains, just as

> the Kenya Government preferred large mercantile firms or organized
> marketing monopolies over small traders, so its introduction of industrial
> licensing reveals a preference for European (large-scale) versus Asian
> (small-scale) developers. . . . [T]he system of industrial licensing sought
> in part to forestall this development [of Indian bourgeoisie].[44]

To illustrate how the imperial and colonial states facilitated metropolitan capital at the expense of the local Indian bourgeoisie, Berman uses the example of East Africa Industries (EAI),[45] a formerly local state investment board whose principal ownership passed over to a British multinational corporation (MNC), Uniliver, at the invitation of the Colonial Development Corporation (CDC), an arm of the imperial state; this intervention, according to Berman, turned the EAI into a viable venture within a year after Uniliver took over its management and control in 1954.[46]

This account raises both theoretical and empirical questions. Theoretically, it involves a rather instrumentalist concept of the state, and indeed, a dependency position, where the powers of the state and the metropolitan bourgeoisie loom large, determining almost every aspect of colonial investment patterns, a perspective that Berman appropriately rejected elsewhere in his book.[47] His account is also apt to mislead. The metropolitan state may indeed have intended to intervene "to assume the role of finance capital and encourage British industrial investment," but the outcome was considerably different. The various industrial schemes introduced in the 1940s and 1950s were, in fact, largely taken advantage of by domestic Indian capitalists, because they were the ones already in position to do so, as official documents consistently confirmed. Large Indian industrial groups such the Chandarias could be described in 1949 as "undoubtedly enterprising and have started a number of different enterprises . . . and appear to have very considerable financial resources."[48]

Three years later, family members of the same industrial group were described by the Ministry of Commerce and Industry as "the most enterprising industrialists in the colony, who have not only pioneered in the establishment . . . of successful industrial undertakings but [are] always planning for further expansion and development to meet the general needs of East Africa."[49] More detailed cases of leading Indian industrial groups are found in the next chapter.

It must also be emphasized that CDC financing schemes did not exclude emerging Indian industrial groups. The case of the Steel Corporation of East Africa, part of the Madhvani Group, is shown in more detail in Part II, in connection with state stimulation of the productivity of the East African bourgeoisie. The case of the Uniliver-controlled EAI is particularly problematic for Berman's position: the EAI consistently failed to compete successfully with East African Indian companies up to the early 1960s, and its appeals to the Kenyan state for special treatment to help it resist the challenge were flatly turned down (see Chapter 3). Eventually the EAI did manage to become viable, but not because it was given special status by the colonial administration.

The establishment of the origin of capitalism in Kenya calls for a different approach. It must begin at the beginning, with the Indian merchants, based on the coast of East Africa, who initially—for centuries—served the transit route between Europe and the Far East. Then, after the 1840s, they linked and controlled hinterland trade. With direct British intervention in East Africa, and especially in the wake of the building of the Uganda Railway from the late 1890s, these coastal merchants and new Indian traders followed the railway inland,[50] and with them came widespread use of money (namely Indian rupees)[51] and extensive use of imported consumer goods by Africans. Given such a prominent precolonial role, it is not surprising "to find that Indian dukas rapidly spread out throughout Kenya."[52] Mangat states that

> The petty Indian merchants were the real founders of commercial enterprise in the interior of East Africa—and helped to create trade, first in a small way and then in a large way, in areas where none existed previously. With considerable fortitude and perseverance, they pioneered the establishment of dukas, of local trading centres and Indian bazaars in different districts; and by introducing the local populations to a variety of imported goods and later the rupee currency, they provided an incentive to greater local production as well as the transition from a barter- to a money-based economy.[53]

For a more detailed review of the early phases of East African capitalism and the process through which some large commercial houses converted themselves into industrial capital after the Second World War see Chapter 3.

"The State Is Not a Unity"

There does not appear to have been any serious attempt to study the evolution of development policies and the extent of their implementation in Kenya beyond a cursory and abstract conceptualization of the state—the state seen either as an instrument of local capitalist classes, or as an instrument of the alliance between local compradors and international capital. Kitching criticized the participants in the Kenya debate in this regard when he aptly noted that "a great deal of dubious inference from highly partial information is being dignified as theory (ies) of the state."[54] He offered an alternative and, in my view, a more realistic conception of the Kenyan state:

> The state is not 'it'—that is, it is not a unity. . . . The state in Kenya is a mess, in short, and it is so because it is embedded in a society and economy undergoing continual conflicts between nascent forms of national capital, different fractions of transnational capital, and . . . between different social strata, ethnic and regional groupings, and so forth, within the indigenous population.[55]

Numerous factors are seldom accounted for: The contradictions between the state's various components, the conflicts between the competing ethnic and regional groupings in their attempts at "winner take all," the extent of the disintegration of some of its key units, and the extensive involvement of international financial institutions in reconstructing some of them—all these must be considered. Five important stages in the workings of the Kenyan state can be distinguished.

1. The 1963–1969 period can be seen as a period of accumulation of presidential powers and the establishment of the Kikuyu hegemony, or more specifically, the domination of political affairs by the Kikuyu from the Kiambu region and the corresponding marginalization of other ethnic groups. This period of transition from colonial rule to independence was characterized by numerous constitutional changes that transferred powers and duties from state institutions to the president and his inner Kiambu subgroup (see Chapter 5 for more detail). The period saw the emergence of a one-party state: the opposition party, Kenya African Democratic Union (KADU) was absorbed in 1964; the Kenya Peoples Union (KPU) was banned in 1969, trade unions were restricted (trade union leadership was appointed by the president after 1966); and major state institutions were monopolized by the Kikuyu (and in particular by the Kiambu subgroup). Almost all the important national executive posts (attorney general, finance, commerce and industry) and the state corporations (Central Bank, Kenya Commercial Bank, Industrial and Commercial Development Corporation) passed into Kikuyu hands. As Peter Anyang' Nyong'o points out, with the establishment of new parastatals

there was a tendency for the president to staff top posts predominantly with people of Kikuyu origin. . . . The more Kenyatta came under attack because of the favours he was seen to be granting to his clansmen, the more the Agikuyu bourgeoisie as a whole, whipping up popular support within Kikuyuland, banded together in defence of his presidency.[56]

But contrary to Leys's earlier arguments and Swainson's thesis, this accumulation of political and economic power in Kikuyu hands turned out not to be a sign of strength but one of weakness, especially in the post-Kenyatta era. But first. . . .

2. The next major phase was from 1970 to 1977 when the Kikuyu governing elite further consolidated its control of the state. An example of the group's political domination is the rise of Gikuyu Embu Meru Association (GEMA), an ethnic investment company and political agency for the Kikuyu and associated ethnic groups. GEMA was to become powerful to the point of almost supplanting the national party, the Kenya African National Union (KANU). A local observer wrote:

> Those who are not MPs are top civil servants or top executives. Looking at the leadership, we see that the majority are also KANU leaders. It is here that one fails to distinguish GEMA from KANU. If not checked, GEMA is going to wear KANU armour very soon . . . and if a tribal organisation replaced a national political party, it is anybody's guess as to what would follow.[57]

The leading personalities in GEMA were a *Who's Who* of the heads of state corporations, national ministries, and Kikuyu MPs (see Chapter 4). An additional indication that GEMA became a vehicle for ensuring the domination of national affairs by the Kikuyu ethnic group became manifest in the events around the death of J.M. Kariuki (a Kikuyu from Murang'a) in 1975, and the "change-the-constitution conspiracy" of 1976. In the case of Kariuki's death, GEMA went on a counteroffensive assault against Parliament and the select committee set up to probe official involvement by attempting to discredit members of the committee. In regard to the conspiracy, GEMA became the leading force calling for an amendment of the constitution to bar the incumbent vice president, Daniel arap Moi, a non-Kikuyu, from automatically succeeding the president.[58] The same period also witnessed the demise of the supranational state. Various institutions of the East African Common Services Organisation (EACSO)—which formerly had played crucial roles in national development—collapsed in 1977 after almost two decades of mismanagement and indifference. Their replacements barely function (see Chapter 5).

3. The 1978–1985 period saw the transition to the Moi presidency and the initial tentative steps in dismantling the Kikuyu hegemony. Among the first tasks for the Moi government was, predictably, to disband all

"tribal" organizations, a move primarily directed at GEMA, under the guise of seeking national unity. Few senior members of GEMA—which essentially meant the leading Kikuyu politician-businessmen—survived in the political or economic realm. The case of Charles Njonjo was indicative of this development. The once powerful attorney general was retired from political life after being accused of conducting himself "in a manner prejudicial to the security of the state, the position of the head of the state, the image of the president and the constitutionally established government of the republic of Kenya."[59] Almost all Kikuyu heads of state corporations and national ministries were systematically replaced by Kalenjin.

4. From the mid-1980s to 1990 a further consolidation of the Kalenjin in state institutions occurred. In 1988, the influential Kikuyu politician and vice president, Mr. Mwai Kibaki, was removed. He had served in the original Kenyatta cabinet in such key ministries as finance and commerce and industry. He was replaced by Mr. Josephat Karanja, another Kikuyu politician who did not have ties with the old guard of the Kenyatta era. Mr. Karanja was himself unceremoniously dropped a year later and replaced by a non-Kikuyu politician, Professor George Saitoti, a Masai. For the first time in postcolonial history, the Kikuyu were excluded from all key national posts—the presidency, vice presidency, finance, and defense. All these were now in the hands of the Kalenjin or their "small tribe" associates. Meanwhile a number of constitutional amendments virtually consolidated presidential powers by removing them from the organs of state, a lesson well learned by the Moi regime from its predecessor. This time these changes were aimed at the Kikuyu elite who had helped set up the practice. By this time the Kikuyu elite's position was being compared to that of the Luo during the 1960s. The former, according to some local observers, find themselves

> in the position that faced Luo leaders in the 1960s. . . . The [Luo] region was ostracised and condemned to the national periphery as the bedrock of anti-establishment politics. . . . Luo leaders faced a double-edged sword. They could stand with the establishment, and face the danger of being rejected as traitors by their own people. Or they could opt to stand with the people, and face the risk of being identified as anti-establishment people—cruel choice.[60]

5. Finally, from 1990 onwards, more bold and open challenges to the Moi presidency became widespread, as exemplified by the call for multiparty politics by two powerful Kikuyu politician-businessmen, Mr. Kenneth Matiba and Mr. Charles Rubia, who had earlier been expelled from KANU. The imprisonment of the two did not end the matter. Other "intermediaries" were at work. In the aftermath of neutralizing the Kikuyu political machine in the 1980s, the church (i.e., the National

Christian Council of Kenya [NCCK]) and elements in the Law Society of Kenya constituted the only vocal "opposition" forces—a constituency that increasingly became supported by the international community. Even the World Bank, a body not known for progressive politics, acknowledged the role of intermediaries who exerted pressure on public officials "for better performance and greater accountability. The National Christian Council of Kenya has played this role for some time," said a World Bank report. "The intermediary role can be politically controversial, yet it is essential."[61] The combined internal and external pressure forced President Moi to allow multipartyism, something he had vehemently objected to, citing "African traditions."

> Over the years we have put in place a system of government responsive to the wishes of our people, based on time-honoured African traditions of consensus. . . . Now we are being told by a few, in words and actions that echo their foreign masters, that we must adopt completely alien systems of government dictated to us by outsiders. We are threatened that if we do not bend to the dictates of foreigners and their hirelings amongst us, we shall perish—perish because they shall see to it that we perish . . . ; [we] are ready to stand up as a united people against any attempt by foreigners, directly or through their proxies in Kenya, to impose their will upon this nation.[62]

The general elections held in December 1992 did not dislodge KANU and President Moi from power, although the combined vote of the opposition, ethnically fragmented, was larger than his.

How Long Does a Revolution Take?

In this analysis of Kenyan capitalism, both the overly optimistic conceptions—"the emergence of the African national bourgeoisie"—and the dependency, pessimistic approach—reducing all domestic capitalists to foreign proxies—are equally rejected. Instead, a chronology of development is constructed to help steer the discussion to a proper footing, demonstrating the fact that neither African businessmen nor the postcolonial state have taken a definite form in Kenya.

This is where "historical time" comes in—a concept that has been called "the very plasma in which events are immersed, and the field within which they become intelligible."[63] If the social relations of production of the various Kenyan communities (the Kikuyu included) were still semi-communal as recently as 1900, events could hardly have transformed them so fundamentally as to create a fully developed African capitalist class by the 1960s, or even the 1990s. If this were so, it would mean that a process that took centuries elsewhere had been accomplished in a matter of seventy years in Kenya, notwithstanding the fact that for most of this period, the white immigrant community, which dominated Kenya's politics, was opposed to such a development. Further, it is necessary to take into account the almost wholesale removal of the Kikuyu from the higher ranks of state power—power that had helped launch some of them into the realm of business before the Moi era.

It is, at any rate, debatable whether a revolutionary transformation of any society in such a short time is possible. The present stage, as far as the Kenyan African communities are concerned, may be compared with other earlier forms of capitalist development. For a description of what is going on we may look at such terms as: *transition from semicommunalist societies into capitalistic ones;* and *quasinational political elites that still have residues of localized and ethnic consciousness.* The Kenyan general elections of December 1992, in which opposition forces sought to end the fifteen-year rule of President Moi, confirm this. The Luo people, predictably, voted for Ford-Kenya, a party led by their long-standing leader, Mr. Oginga Odinga; the Kikuyu vote was split on traditional lines: the Kikuyu from Nyeri voted for the local leader, Mr. Mwai Kibaki, and his Democratic Party; the Kikuyu of Murang'a voted for Mr. Kenneth Matiba of Ford-Asili, who hailed from Murang'a, with the Kiambu fraction following the latter. The alliance of smaller tribes banded together behind President Moi. His "national" outlook was in question: he failed to win a single seat from the Kikuyu and Luo regions.[64]

In the meantime, the Kalenjin and their Masai allies were launching pogroms against other groups (mainly the Kikuyu) in the Rift Valley, leaving over one thousand dead.[65] All this flies in the face of existing conceptions of the Kenyan state as the cohesive instrument of a single social class.

The cohesion of the Kenyan Indian bourgeoisie is explained by their different historical background. They emerged from East African coastal merchant activities before colonial rule, led the movement into the interior, and up to the 1940s created the East African internal market. Having led the conversion of merchant into industrial capital from then onwards, their political isolation—in almost all phases—far from rendering them weak, exerted considerable pressure on them to survive in the new environment. It has rendered them a formidable and most dynamic force among the contending racial fractions of capital in Kenya and East Africa. In reality, the Kenyan case indicates that a technically capable segment of domestic capital exists among Kenyan Indians. Together with foreign capital and the African bourgeoisie-in-formation, this can deepen the Kenyan development process. It is the state that remains the most problematic aspect.

It must, however, be emphasized that the outcome in Kenya is not preordained, notwithstanding the dubious nature of the state: the combination of the above forces may conceivably succeed in reforming the Kenyan state apparatus. Meanwhile, presumably, a larger pool of Kenyan public technocrats and "detribalized" national visionaries is coming onstream.

Notes

1. In this category are neoliberal writers who follow the nineteenth century classical political economy that insists on the universality of competitive markets, capital accumulation, and individualist material incentives as the engine of development, at the periphery as well. This school of thought includes Bauer, *Economic Analysis*, 1954; Kindleberger, *Economic Development*, 1958; and Rostow, "The Take-off into Sustained Growth," 1958. For the Chicago School version of neoliberalism see Ohlin's article, "Retrospect," 1979. For modernization see Lerner, *Passing*, 1958, and his article "Modernisation," 1968.

2. Representatives of this school include Frank, *Latin America*, 1969; the Dos Santos article, "Crisis," 1981; Cockcroft et al., *Dependence*, 1972; and Amin, *Unequal Development*, 1976. For a good summary of dependency and other theoretical perspectives see Blomstrom and Hettne, *Transition*, 1984.

3. "Modified" dependency scholars include Cardoso and Faletto, *Latin America*, 1979; and Evans, *Dependent Development*, 1979. Lipietz, while sympathetic to the framework, also argued that real capitalist development at the periphery had taken place. See his *Mirages*, 1987.

4. Orthodox Marxism is understood here to mean the writings of Marx, Engels, and Lenin, which share the belief that capitalism was historically progressive in the European context and that imperialism performed a similar role at the periphery. Contemporary authors inspired by this tradition include Warren, *Imperialism*, 1982; and Kitching, *Perspective*, 1982.

5. Seers article, "Congruence," p. 1; and Lipietz article, "Marx or Rostow?" p. 49.

6. Amin article, "Agricultural," pp. 1–2. Other Africanist *dependentistas* include Onimode, *Nigeria*, 1982; Mamdani, *Uganda*, 1976; Mahmoud, *Sudanese*, 1984; and Coulson, *Tanzania*, 1982.

7. Sender and Smith, *Capitalism*, p. 34.

8. Sender and Smith, *Capitalism*, pp. 70–71.

9. These include Brett, *East Africa*, 1973; Leys, *Underdevelopment in Kenya*, 1975; Langdon's article, "Kenya," 1977; and Kaplinsky's, "Capitalist Accumulation," 1980.

10. Neoliberal writing on Kenya include Hazlewood, *Economy*, 1979; Holthham and Hazlewood, *Inequality*, 1976; and Miller, *Quest*, 1984.

11. For the orthodox Marxist position see Cowen's article, "Agrarian Accumulation," 1982; Leys's, "Capitalist Accumulation," 1978; and Swainson's, "National bourgeoisie," 1977.

12. One of the lively discussions on Kenyan development involved what became known as the Kenya debate, provoked by Colin Leys's reassessment and rejection of the dependency hypotheses—which he himself had applied to the Kenyan case. The principal background writings to the debate are Brett, *East Africa*; Leys, *Underdevelopment in Kenya*; Swainson, *Corporate Capitalism in Kenya*, 1980; Langdon's article, "State and Capitalism"; and Kaplinsky (ed.), *Multinational Corporation*, 1978. The debate itself comprised of the Leys articles,

"Capitalist Accumulation," 1978, his "What?" 1980, and "Ten Years On," 1991; Langdon's "Contributions to a Debate," presented to the conference on the African bourgeoisie, Dakar, 1980; Kaplinsky's, "Periphery," 1980; and Henley's "Straw Man," 1980. Critics of the debate were Beckman, "Critique of a Kenya Debate," 1980, and Kitching, 1985. For a recent critique see David Himbara, 1993.

13. An extensive literature on the subject now exists with different explanations of why African states are in crisis. A good summary of this literature is found in Beckman's article, "The Post-Colonial State," 1988.

14. See his article, "Korea and Dependency Theory," p. 30.

15. See his article, "The Search for Paradigms," p. 64.

16. Lipietz, *Mirages,* p. 4 and p. 68.

17. Leys article, "Ten Years On" (emphasis in original).

18. McDermitt, *British East Africa,* cited in Hill, *Permanent Way,* p. 24.

19. Robinson and Gallagher, *Victorians,* p. 310.

20. "Cairo was becoming more and more the pivot of their Mediterranean strategy. A foreign Power astride the Upper Nile would be in position either to blackmail or to lever them out of Egypt. . . . Thus the safety of the Nile had now become a supreme consideration." Robinson and Gallagher, *Victorians,* pp. 284–286.

21. "Governing East Africa and Uganda was not a profitable business as the British Treasury learned when it was called in to pay deficits ranging usually between one and two hundred thousand pounds a year, after taking over the Company's rights [i.e., Imperial British East Africa Company]. East Africa had cost the British taxpayers over sixty million dollars (in budget deficits and payments for the Uganda Railway). . . . But commerce measures the success of imperialism, and the total trade of British East Africa in 1923 was only 92 million dollars, as compared to $231 for British West Africa. . . . [U]nfortunate methods of exploitation in East Africa are probably accountable in part both for the smallness of the population and the relatively slower economic development." Moon, *Imperialism and World Politics,* pp. 128–131.

22. Van Zwanenberg, *Economic History,* p. 146

23. Van Zwanenberg, *Economic History,* pp. 146–147.

24. Kimambo article, "The Kamba 1850–1950," p. 29.

25. Leakey, *The Southern Kikuyu,* pp. 479–501. Leakey further indicates on page 503 the status of "money" as a medium of exchange among the Kikuyu: "The Kikuyu had no currency in the strict sense of that word, and for the most part, barter was carried out on the basis of exchanging goods of more or less equal value. The nearest approach to distinct currency among the Kikuyu was their conception of the goat or sheep under the general term of mburi [goat or sheep]. In assessing the . . . price of any object of value, the assessment was always made in terms of mburi, even though the payment might be made in other things to the value of the number of mburi assessed. Thus a piece of land might have been valued at 30 mburi, but paid for in cows, each cow or heifer being reckoned as 10 mburi."

26. Van Zwanenberg, *Economic History,* p. 145.

27. Muriuki, *The Kikuyu,* 1969, p. 103.

28. The literature on the Kikuyu in the precolonial period is more problematic than is generally admitted, especially on the issue of long-distance trade, as Kitching has indicated. Firstly, as he aptly asks, how does one measure *long* and *short* distances, historically speaking? "'Long distance' . . . is historically a very specific term, since in precolonial Kenya the distance which men might venture from their homesteads without fear of attack could in many cases be quite short: one or two miles in the case of those living in the boundaries between disputing ethnic groups. . . . Also of course in the nature of historical accounts in general and

oral research in particular the distinction between 'short' and 'long' distance is bound to be a shifting and fuzzy one." Kitching notes another controversy: "Leakey suggests that the Kikuyu trade with the Masai was actually monopolised by women, and the view is supported by Muriuki. . . . However, these general assertions are at odds with the one detailed study of a part of trade which we have (Marris and Somerset's account of the trade between Mahiga location of the present-day Nyeri district and the Rurko Masai). Leakey also notes that men monopolised trade with the Kamba. . . . [T]his confused state of the literature on the Kikuyu . . . clearly demands further research." Kitching, *Class in Kenya,* pp. 12–13.

29. Swainson article, "Bourgeoisie," p. 39. See also Swainson's subsequent presentation, "Comprador," a paper presented at the second biannual conference of the African Association of Political Science, Lagos, 4–8 April 1979.

30. Swainson, "Bourgeoisie," p. 44.

31. Swainson, "Bourgeoisie," p. 55. Kaplinsky drew his conclusions from the same source: "The empirical information is drawn from a detailed study of ownership patterns in all large-scale manufacturing activities and all tourist firms operating in 1976. The source material was drawn from annual returns of such companies to the Companies Registrar in Sheria House, Nairobi. As part of these annual returns, each company is required to name all current directors, and to list all other companies of which they are directors." See his "Periphery," p. 202. Leys's contribution relied on statistical abstracts from the Central Bureau of Statistics and concedes that "This chapter is based on a short visit to Kenya in the Summer of 1977." See his "Accumulation, Class Formation and Dependency," p. 190.

32. Kitching, *Class in Kenya,* pp. 451-452.

33. Kitching, *Class in Kenya,* p. 453.

34. Bauer, *Economic Analysis,* pp. 72–74.

35. Kennedy, *African Capitalism,* p. 32, and p. 26.

36. Chandaria article, "Entrepreneurship in Kenya," 1963.

37. Leys, *Underdevelopment in Kenya,* p. 39.

38. Murray article, "The Chandarias," 1978.

39. Coughlin article, "Glass Industry," 1989. This account is inaccurate in another sense. The Kenya Glass Works was established by members of the Patel community as shown in Chapter 2.

40. There are now many companies from India in Kenya including, for example, Raymond Woollen Mills and Pan-African Paper Mills and numerous other Indian-Kenyan joint investments. The use of the terms *Asian* and *Indian* capital without a clear differentiation between foreign investments and local Indian investments becomes all the more deceptive.

41. Swainson, *Corporate Capitalism,* pp. 16–18.

42. See this and numerous other 1950s documents on local Indian companies' protests against foreign competition in file MCI/6/462, KNA.

43. Berman, *Control & Crisis,* p. 272.

44. Berman, *Control & Crisis,* pp. 271–273.

45. The company is inaccurately cited as East African Industries in Berman's book.

46. Berman, *Control & Crisis,* p. 273.

47. Berman, *Control & Crisis,* pp. 14–15.

48. MCI internal memo, 31 January 1949, MCI/6/20, KNA.

49. Company profiles and applications for drawback rebates, 1952, in MCI/6/462, KNA.

50. "Some had struck into the interior along the Uganda road before the advent of the line, with the first Indian traders establishing themselves at

Machakos in 1895. The majority, however, came afterwards, setting up shops and bazaars at key points as the railway progressed, and steadily increasing in numbers ... applying for land to set up shops and do business with the tribes." Mungean, *British Rule,* pp. 62–63.

51. "The Indian currency system ... was lifted wholesale into East Africa. There was a certain logic about introducing rupees in East Africa. By the end of the nineteenth century Indian bankers dominated the Zanzibar ivory and caravan trade. Indians were the earliest financiers in the area. Then with the rapid expansion of trading activities, moving up along the line of rail, rupees became the currency of commerce at the turn of the century. It was the currency which was most readily available and acceptable to traders. Hence the British made the Indian silver rupee the standard coin in British territories in East Africa." Van Zwanenberg, *An Economic History,* p. 280.

52. Van Zwanenberg, *An Economic History,* p. 160.

53. Mangat, *Asians in East Africa,* p. 55. Norman Leys also stated that "then and for years later practically all the trade of Eastern Africa was in the hands of Indians. ... Indians built the railway to Uganda, and Indian armed police were attached to every important Government station. Indian traders and shopkeepers spread over the country, selling the calico of Lancashire and buying hides for export in return." Norman Leys, *Kenya,* p. 92.

54. Kitching article, "Politics, Method and Evidence in the 'Kenya Debate,'" pp. 131–132.

55. Kitching, "Politics" article.

56. Anyang' Nyong'o, "State and Society in Kenya," p. 241.

57. Wanyeki, *Weekly Review* letter, 1976.

58. This action "exposed GEMA's real intentions; the ostensible welfare association had become such a powerful political instrument that it was, not without justification, threatening to replace KANU in terms of national political supremacy. GEMA's leaders did not let-up in their anti-Moi manoeuvres and, a year later, they tried to oust Moi through KANU national elections that aborted." *Weekly Review,* 19 May 1988.

59. Republic of Kenya, *Njonjo,* p. vii.

60. *Weekly Review,* 20 July 1990.

61. World Bank, *Sub-Saharan Africa: From Crisis,* p. 61.

62. Excerpts of President Moi's speech on Kenyatta Day, relayed to the British Broadcasting Corporation. *Summary of World Broadcasts,* 22 October 1990.

63. Bloch, *The Historian's Craft,* pp. 27–28.

64. December 1992 general election results in the *Weekly Review,* 8 January 1993.

65. *Economist,* 24 April 1993.

2

Kenya's Indian Capitalists:
The Development Story

Immigrants from the Indian subcontinent played a determining role in the development of commerce and industry in East Africa. Beginning with coastal-based merchant activities before the colonial period, the commercial prominence they attained enabled them to remain the predominant force during the colonial period and after. This, in turn, provided them with a foundation for playing a similar role in industry, from the 1940s to the present.

Some of the determining factors that distinguished the Indians from businessmen in other Kenyan communities were their commercial skills, as evidenced by an ability to survive in remote areas on modest resources and by sheer determination and hard work; their vision of the potential mass market and the patience to transform it into an actual market; their general efficiency and competitive edge; and the role of family units and collective organizations in providing mechanisms to engender discipline and cohesion. Not even the domination of politics and agriculture, through legislative means, of the white settlers, and later Kenya Africans, could offset or reduce the critical importance of local Indian capitalists in retail and wholesale trade, finance, and manufacturing.

Three stages in which the above factors characterized the Kenyan and East African development process can be identified by tracing examples of commercial and industrial activities and the specific patterns of accumulation that followed. The initial phase was the entry into the hinterland of coastal-based Indian merchants and financiers, as well as new immigrants from the Indian subcontinent, beginning in the 1840s. This advance into the interior was accelerated by the intervention of the Imperial British East Africa Company (IBEAC) in 1888 and its establishment of a rudimentary infrastructure—trading routes and stations—and its treaty agreements with some African communities during the company's brief administration. In the aftermath of the IBEAC's collapse in 1895, formal colonial rule was proclaimed. Together with the railway built to link the coast and the hinterland, the embryonic state apparatus then in place provided both protection and physical infrastructures that enabled coastal merchants and new Indian immigrants to spread merchant activities throughout East Africa.

The next phase began with the Second World War, which effectively isolated East Africa from its traditional suppliers of goods, necessitating local improvisation of the manufacture of various products. More importantly, it exacerbated the British government's fiscal problems, precipitating a change in policy that looked to a more productive and protectionist Commonwealth vis-à-vis other economic zones. Thus, the wartime isolation of East Africa, and the accompanying reorientation of colonial policy, signalled the implementation of strategies aimed at stimulating productivity and self-sufficiency in British colonies, including Kenya. Among these strategies was a greater effort to coordinate East Africa as a single market. The effect of these changes was a spectacular pioneering of industrial activity on the part of some of the country's commercial bourgeoisie between the late 1940s and the early 1960s. It is during this phase that white settlers attempted but failed to establish themselves in the wholesale and retail distribution of their agricultural products. The period also marked a widespread attempt by Africans to enter commerce, but they had little success (see Chapter 3).

The third phase began immediately after independence in 1963, with localization-Africanization-Kenyanization-indigenization policies aimed at fostering an African capitalist class in commerce and industry. The outcome of this program was paradoxical: it temporarily precipitated a retreat by the domestic Indian commercial capitalists from the simpler forms of commerce and retail trading—but they went into more complex economic sectors not directly subject to Africanization, such as finance, construction, and manufacturing. The "Africanized" aspects of trade were, however, soon largely reclaimed by the Indian commercial bourgeoisie: the new owners, lacking experience, failed to secure a consistent support mechanism from the state. The Africanization program, in effect, rendered the economy more reliant on Kenyan Indian capitalists than before. The commercial and industrial strength they accumulated in terms of managerial, technical, and financial resources in response to Africanization was later reinforced by their acquisition of a number of large multinational subsidiary companies. MNCs (especially US MNCs) divested from Kenya in the wake of several events—the collapse of the East African Common Market (EACM) in 1977, the 1982 attempted coup, and the disintegration of a significant part of Kenya's infrastructural support systems in the 1970s up to the early 1990s. This was also the period in which some of the more notable surviving black businesses established after independence collapsed. A number of them were acquired by local Indian capitalists.

Rise of Indian Merchant Capital in East Africa

The rise of commerce and trade in East Africa is traceable initially to the coastal areas and to the determining role of the Indian community for several centuries. From the late eighteenth and early nineteenth century "there had been an increasing tendency [for them] to settle in East Africa and to break ties with Asia."[1] Hollingsworth estimates the Indian population in Zanzibar, Mombasa, and other coastal towns during the early nineteenth century at about six thousand.[2] It was from within this community that a merchant class evolved. They "quickly established themselves as the bankers and money-lenders."[3] Hill states that "Almost the entire trade of Zanzibar and the mainland, which was estimated to exceed £1,500,000 a year, passed through Indian hands."[4]

Tandberg remarks on the tenacity of the Indian trading community despite the unpredictable nature of the region's politics, writing: "When the Arabs ruled the East African coast the Indians were the traders and money lenders. When the Portuguese pushed the Arabs away the Indians remained. When the Arabs returned the Indians were still there."[5] Even when European participation in East African commerce increased towards the end of the nineteenth century, "the Indians' dominant position was still maintained. No imports could be distributed to native customers in the interior without [Indian] agency."[6]

Before the building of the railway, the expansion of commerce in East Africa by coastal Indian traders had been resisted by inland societies. The coastal merchants had to use Swahili and Arab traders, and some African groups acted as upcountry intermediaries. Godfrey Muriuki highlights the role played by the Kamba as the chief intermediaries for the coastal trade. They successfully denied the Kikuyu "access to the coastal trade. Equally, they erected many obstacles in order to dissuade Swahili from entering the region."[7]

There were exceptions to this coast-inland trading relationship when some Indians began to establish themselves directly in the hinterland. These included members of the Aga Khan community who had set up some trading posts by the early 1800s. "Pioneers of this community were among the first settlers in East Africa early in the 19th century. As early as 1815 the community settled at Bagamoyo."[8] However, it was not until the late 1890s that settlement by coastal traders became more widespread, when societies in the hinterland lost the capacity to withstand external encroachment. The forerunner in this operation was the British East African Association and its successor, the IBEAC, formed in 1888. The IBEAC's objectives were to levy taxes, to grant licenses, to construct roads and public works, to coin money, and "generally to exercise all the rights pertaining to sovereignty over acquired districts."[9]

The IBEAC experiment was short-lived. There were several reasons for this: poor finances,[10] a failure to attract British capital to the region,[11] and the company's composition. IBEAC was formed by "a curious amalgam of philanthropists, businessmen, and professional empire-builders which lacked the cohesion necessary for success in what was, from the first, an extremely dubious financial exercise."[12] Nevertheless, from the standpoint of the establishment of commerce and trade in Kenya, in a number of respects the company's pioneering undertakings were instrumental. First, they increased the geographical knowledge of the region through vital surveys and reports. These surveys paved the way for the installation, in succeeding years, of key infrastructures. In the process of undertaking these projects, the company set up forts, for example at Machakos and Kikuyu, in addition to constructing a road from the coast to Kibwezi in the interior. It was not by accident that towns such as Machakos attracted Indian coastal merchants, the most famous of whom included M.D. Puri and Adamjee Aliboy, long before the establishment of rail transport.[13]

Commercial Defeat of White Settlers

But by far the most influential factor in the opening up of East Africa for commerce and trade was the installation of railway and telegraph lines, linking the coast to the interior. The literature on the effect of the railway in this period is preoccupied with the European settlers' scramble for land.[14] But the railway also paved the way for coastal merchants and financiers, and augmented their numbers greatly by attracting immigrants from the Indian subcontinent. Joining the march into the interior were not only Indians who had been associated with the railway, and civil servants crossing over into private enterprise after completing their contracts, but new immigrant traders from India. These new Africans established themselves in almost every inland township. Even Nairobi, the future commercial, industrial, and administrative capital, with its "flourishing bazaar," was "more of an Indian town than a European township."[15]

By 1910, the initial rejection of the strategy of developing East Africa through the settlement of Indian immigrants, as opposed to white settlement, was beside the point. Before Commissioner Sir Charles Eliot embraced the strategy of developing Kenya through agriculture and white settlement in 1902—to "make the railway pay"—among the options considered was colonization by local and immigrant Indians. Lugard, for example, had stated that: "It is not as an imported coolie labour that I advocate the introduction of the Indian, but as a colonist and settler."[16] Sir Harry Johnston, special commissioner in Uganda 1899–1901, also saw the role of Indians as crucial. He described the whole of East Africa as a possible "America of the Hindu."[17] In fact, previous to Eliot's commissionership (1901–1905), successive secretaries of state had urged the protectorate commissioners to actively encourage Indian immigration into Kenya to stimulate development.[18] Lord Hailey noted that "from early days Indians played a considerable part in the development of East Africa. They controlled the greater part of trade with the whole coast, and the Imperial British East Africa Company contemplated Indian settlement on a very large scale."[19]

By the time Eliot's administration opted for white settlement, the leading role of the Indian community in almost all key commercial activities was firmly established. From import and export trade and banking to the general provision of local produce, and from construction and transport to the manufacturing sector, Indians were entrenched. The capacity already achieved by them is demonstrated by the legacy of such pioneers as Alidina Visram. An economic historian described him as follows:

> In the economic history of many countries such men emerge as leading characters, particularly in times of rapid growth—Arkwright, Carnegie, Ford—and entrepreneurial history is an important branch of the subject. In East Africa most entrepreneurs worked on a small scale, left no records, and are therefore forgotten; only a rare figure like Alidina Visram left his mark.[20]

The following official description of Visram's enterprises indicates the commanding position at least one member of the Indian community had already attained:

> A firm which employs more than 500 Indian clerks, besides carpenters, masons, and natives in great numbers deserves more than a passing mention. . . . Alidina Visram first opened his business at Bagamoyo in 1877, and afterwards started branches at Sadani, Dar-Es-Salaam, Kalima, Tinde and Ujiji. In 1896 he opened a branch in Zanzibar and in 1896 in Uganda. In 1899 branches were opened at Mombasa and other places of British East Africa. And branches continued to be opened in town after town till they spread through the great part of Uganda and the Nile District. At present the firm exports ivory, sheep-skins, hides, goat-skins, rubber, beewax, semsem, groundnuts, chilies and other products of East Africa, while for the use of the natives they import cotton goods, beads, enamelware, blankets, brass, copper and iron wire. . . . They also import goods for Europeans, such as cotton, silk, woollen goods, wines and spirits. In addition to this they have soda factories, factories colouring skins and making furniture, and factories at Kampala and Entebbe for manufacturing jaggery. . . . At Mombasa is their Visram Ginning and Oil Factory. . . . The firm are agents for Zanzibar Government's steamers, the British Dominions Marine Insurance Co. Ltd. . . . and are proprietors of the Victoria Nyanza Service between Kampala, Jinja and Kisumu.[21]

Another illustrative case is that of Esmailjee Jivanjee:

> There are few roads in Zanzibar and Mombasa where this enterprising firm is not represented. Mills, estate owners, land proprietors, general

imports and export merchants, and commission agents, Messrs. Esmailjee Jivanjee & Co. own extensive lands, estates, and buildings in East
Africa. The firm was founded in Zanzibar in 1819. His public and private
charities amounted to Rs500,000 including the building of a mosque and
a sanatorium . . . , a large garden. The establishment of public wells and
other buildings are too numerous to mention.[22]

In short, hardly any commercial transaction in imports and local
produce was carried out in East Africa without a local Indian agency
throughout the colonial period, much as in the period of the commercial
island-enclaves at the coast. Almost all goods from overseas still passed
through the agency of large Indian firms to Indian retailers.

European domination of politics and agriculture did not alter the
strategic position that Indian traders occupied in relation to the internal
market. MacGregor-Ross noted in 1927: "It has been, and still is, the
Indian who delivers goods and pushes trade into the interior of Kenya."[23]
Almost twenty years later, the East African Royal Commission came to
the same conclusion: "Indeed the remarkable tenacity and courage of the
Indian trader has been mainly responsible for stimulating the wants of the
indigenous peoples, even in the remotest areas, by opening to them a
shop-window on the world." The commission, in effect, dismissed white
settlers, attributing their failure to their approach and mentality:

> It is not an unwarranted generalisation to say that on the whole the
> European settler has tended to . . . regard the European economy as
> independent of all indigenous areas and was concerned above all to
> protect his own standard of living. . . . It is for this reason that much of
> the skilled work and commercial distribution was done by Indians.[24]

The white settlers, noted Huxley, "deplored the fact that all trade with
natives had fallen into Indian hands."[25] The historian Sorrenson concluded that the Indians "were just as essential as European settlers if the
protectorate was to be developed, and the railway was to pay."[26] This may
be an understatement, for white settlers actually came to depend on
Indians for almost all services. As far back as 1907 Winston Churchill—
later Sir Winston—had remarked:

> It is the Indian trader who, penetrating and maintaining himself in all
> sorts of places to which no white man could go or in which he could make
> a living has more than any one else developed the early beginnings of
> trade and opened up the first slender means of communication. . . . It is
> the Indian banker who supplies perhaps the larger part of the capital yet
> available for business and enterprise and to whom the white settlers have
> not hesitated to refer for financial aid.[27]

Hollingsworth did point out that white settlers came to depend on Indian
merchants and financiers. In effect, "the entire country had grown up on

the Indian trader," he wrote. "Without him the whole economy would have collapsed like a burst balloon."[28] Mangat concurred that Indian merchants planted "the first seeds of economic progress."[29]

The agricultural sector was dependent on many other economic sectors, all of which, as Huxley puts it, had fallen into Indian hands. The following letter from the president of the Kenya Farmers' Association (KFA) to Mr. E.A. Vasey—later Sir Ernest, but at that time an elected member of the Legislative Council and an emerging political figure—reveals the efforts of white settlers to retail their own agricultural products in the 1940s:

> The Kenya Farmers' Association, with the support of a great proportion of its members, is more or less committed to a policy designed to attract the trade in primary products away from the Indian. As you know we are considering an attack on the retail trade by opening a chain of co-operative stores. Under these circumstances it is impossible for a director of the KFA, who is also a member of the Legislative Council to subscribe to a policy of Indian development in the Highlands. . . . [The] Indian question is extremely inflammable and if rashly handled it could wreck the electors' union quicker than anything else. I suggest that you should be wise to confine your policy fairly closely to the lines [sic].[30]

The many responses from Vasey to such representations are summed up in the following, written in 1952 when he was in the cabinet as finance minister:

> Does anyone really believe that . . . they can drive the Government to the demands [sic] of European Elected Members and lose the confidence of the representatives of other races? Something which cannot be done, for the Government in a multi-racial country, must pay fair attention to the claims of all other communities.[31]

By this time, the struggle for commercial superiority had long been won, on the basis of the Indian position in commerce and their sheer hard work, as an anonymous white newcomer-industrialist assessing the East African scene observed in 1949:

> One has to acknowledge that in their own business they are workers in every sense of the word. . . . [If] we compare Indian shop hours with those recognised by the European shopkeeper, we begin to see both the problem and the answer. . . . [At] six o'clock at night I can usually find an Indian still right on his job—but not the European.[32]

Talk of an attack on the retail trade by white farmers "opening a chain of co-operative stores" was as absurd as talk of the Africanization of commerce and industry by legislative fiat some twenty years later.

The highwater mark in the defeat of the white settlers was, perhaps, the rise of the Ministry of Commerce and Industry (MCI) from 1947 to 1949 and the corresponding decline of the Ministry of Agriculture and Natural Resources. Before the 1940s, commercial and industrial interests were not represented in any organized form. Towards the end of the Second World War, however, the importance of the commercial and industrial sectors began to be taken more seriously, leading to the appointment in 1944 of an "economic and development secretary." In explaining this appointment to the regional chamber of commerce organization, Governor Sir Henry Moore stated that, as secretary, the person responsible would have "access to the Governor and I trust that the commercial community generally will regard him as their main channel of communication with the Government."[33] Commercial capitalists and the emerging industrial bourgeoisie were not satisfied with this. An editorial in the *East African Standard,* reflecting their views a year later, said there was "no one in authority to whom local manufacturers could go for guidance or the redress of their problems."[34] The associated chambers of commerce passed a unanimous resolution demanding that early provision be made by the government "for the representation of commerce and industry."[35] This pressure led to the appointment in 1945 of Mr. A. Hope-Jones as the governor's "economic and commercial adviser."[36] But this did not arrest demands for the appointment of a member for commerce and industry with the same status on the executive council as, for example, agriculture. The *East African Standard* objected to the appointment of an adviser, editorializing: "Mr. Hope-Jones as an advisor has neither the status nor the responsibility for initiating any direct policy on the part of Government."[37] Finally, the sector was given ministerial standing in 1947–1948.

The main loser in the creation of the MCI was the white settler–influenced Ministry of Agriculture and Natural Resources, which lost roughly half of its responsibilities to the new ministry. Portfolios shifted from agriculture to the new department included trade and commerce, economic cooperation agreements, liaison with the chambers of commerce, trade missions, trade relations, export marketing, industrial licensing and research, industrial development (including rural and secondary industries), distribution controls, import and export trade, banks and banking, price control, and more.[38] White settlers and the Ministry of Agriculture appear to have faced defeat after defeat in this period.

When the Athi River township and its surrounding area was redesignated from ranching to being an industrial area, the Ministry of Agriculture refused to go along with the decision, prompting MCI to state that "if the Member for Agriculture and Natural Resources persists in his objections to the site, the company might be driven to another territory." The company—East African Portland Cement—subsequently was allowed to set up at Athi River: so were many other local Indian companies in the sand and construction business.[39]

White settlers remained a source of irritation up to the end of the colonial period, as can be illustrated by the case of the East African Match Company, a settler-operated enterprise that collapsed and was placed under receivership in 1957. When a group of local Indian capitalists purchased the plant, they could not operate it from its location in the White Highlands, where nonwhites could not own land. MCI established the guilty party in this affair with the following words:

> Mr. Khimasia, a paternal brother of the Chandarias of Kenya Aluminium and Industrial Works Ltd. . . . purchased the equipment of the E.A. Match Co. Ltd., and offered to purchase the buildings on the existing site subject to being permitted to operate the factory there. An application was made to the Land Control Board and was rejected.[40]

The plant was eventually shifted to Mombasa where, in the 1990s, it remained a viable enterprise—a Comcraft-affiliate—no longer limited to making matches but now manufacturing batteries.[41]

As for the Ministry of Commerce and Industry, by the mid-1950s, it occupied a powerful position in the Kenyan administrative apparatus. In its 1956 survey of Kenya, the *Financial Times* of London wrote of "an active Ministry of Commerce and Industry pursuing the policy of using Government resources to promote expansion of private enterprise, particularly in the industrial field." The result was that Kenya, by this time, had an "expanding and malleable policy designed to promote both industrial and commercial strength."[42]

Conversion: Merchant Capital to Indian Industrialism

Before the Second World War, Kenya's manufacturing sector was still in its infancy. Enterprises processed local crops—sisal, coffee, sugar, wheat, and maize.[43] Similarly, the role of the state in coordinating and promoting both the commercial and the industrial sectors was rudimentary. A more consistent policy came with the war, resulting from the disruption of supplies of manufactured goods to Kenya. Shipping priorities were modified to accommodate war conditions and the requirements in Britain. This development led to the creation of more defined supranational agencies, both national and East African, to provide conductive policies for capital accumulation. The aim was to make the sterling zone self-sufficient relative to the dollar zone (see Chapter 4). More importantly, the isolation of Kenya and East Africa from foreign supplies led to the improvisation of products locally. Some enterprising commercial groups used the disruption to move into the manufacturing sector. The commerce minister described the role of Indian capitalists in the emerging manufacturing sector to Governor Evelyn Baring in a confidential document as "outstanding."

> The Asian community is playing quite a considerable part in this development and Asians have, in many instances, shown themselves to be enterprising industrialists. You, yourself, recently opened the new rolling mill of the Kenya Aluminium and Industrial Works Ltd. at Mombasa, which is an outstanding Asian achievement.[44]

Two years later, the governor was to open another major industrial undertaking by a Kenyan family, the House of Manji, with these remarks:

> This is an example of effort and enterprise by a man born and brought up in Kenya. Mr. Manji was born in Nyeri—his life has been spent here—it is here that he has gained his experience, and it is this country which will benefit from his initiative. . . . Asians have played a very important part in the development of Kenya since its earliest days. They have been notable for their enterprise in trade and commerce. . . . [This] is another example of a local Asian industrial enterprise.[45]

Evidently, because of their predominance in commerce and their knowledge of the East African market, Indian commercial capitalists were in a position to exploit new opportunities during this period. From the late 1940s to the early 1990s, they continued to lead in establishing manufacturing firms. At the same time, they continued to constitute the predominant segment of domestic commercial capitalists, notwithstanding the so-called Africanization of commerce and industry after 1964. Indu Chandaria's 1962 study of fifty-eight manufacturing enterprises with over fifty employees found that 67.2 percent of these companies were owned by local Indians, 24.1 percent by Europeans, 5.2 percent by interracial partnerships, and 3.4 percent by international firms.[46]

The results of my own survey of one hundred manufacturing enterprises in 1989 and 1990 are shown in figures 2.1 to 2.11. These enterprises constitute one-sixth of the approximately six hundred manufacturing firms belonging to KAM, which includes most "formal sector" manufacturing.[47] The survey being more qualitative than quantitative, the original sample of two hundred companies was not constructed on a random basis (see the Preface) and consequently the following figures cannot be taken as representative of all companies in KAM. Limitation to KAM membership already excludes "informal sector" manufacturing and, no doubt, some in the "formal sector." However, detailed information was obtained directly from one hundred firms with over fifty employees and the sample included those that were well known to be leading companies in their sectors. Within the category of medium- and large-scale manufacturers, there is no reason to believe that the overall patterns of ownership displayed would be different for the total KAM membership.

With this caveat, I give below a summary of the overall patterns. Figure 2.1 shows that almost two-thirds (63 percent) of the manufacturing firms sampled in 1989 and 1990 had been established since 1970; almost four-fifths had been established since 1960. Figure 2.2 shows that 71 percent of manufacturing companies established before independence (i.e., before 1964) belonged to Kenyan Indians. In the 1960s (Figure 2.3) the proportion established by Kenyan Indians increased to 79 percent; in the 1970s (Figure 2.4) it fell back to 70 percent; in the 1980s (Figure 2.5) it rose sharply to 85 percent. For the years 1964–1990 as a whole (Figure 2.6) the share of new manufacturing companies owned by Kenyan Indians was 78 percent; while from 1977 (when the East African Common Market collapsed) to 1990 (Figure 2.7) the proportion rises to 84 percent. Figures 2.8 and 2.9 show the overall result in the various periods of growth by 1990, with 75 percent of all manufacturing companies, and 73 percent of manufacturing companies with over one hundred workers, owned by Kenyan Indian capitalists. Figure 2.10 shows Kenyan Indian capitalists owning 86 percent of manufacturing companies with a capital of over Kenyan Shs100 million. For good measure, Figure 2.11 shows the ownership of companies in the sample which were in financial or mismanagement difficulties (i.e.,

Figure 2.1   Period Firms Were Established

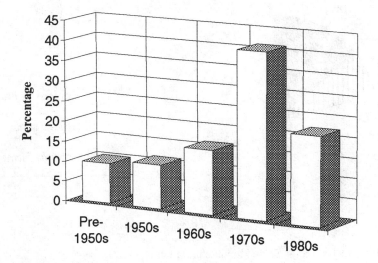

Sample of 100 Large-Scale Manufacturing Firms

Figure 2.2 Firms Established Before Independence (1963)

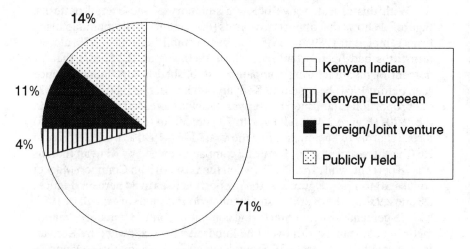

Sample of 100 Large-Scale Manufacturing Firms

Figure 2.3 Firms Established in the 1960s

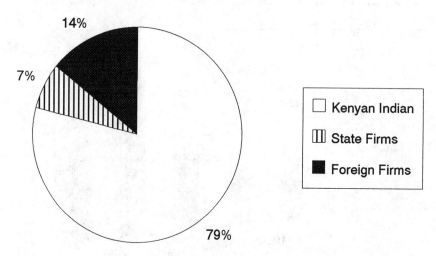

Sample of 100 Large-Scale Manufacturing Firms

Figure 2.4   Firms Established in the 1970s

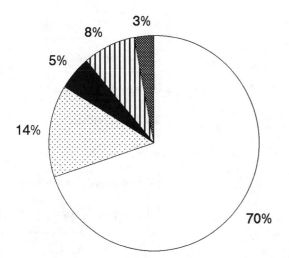
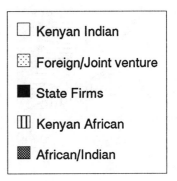

Sample of 100 Large-Scale Manufacturing Firms

Figure 2.5   Firms Established in the 1980s

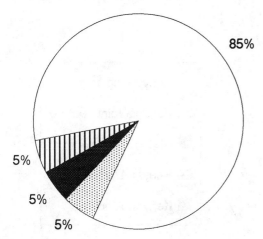
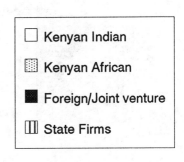

Sample of 100 Large-Scale Manufacturing Firms

Figure 2.6   Firms Established in 1964–1990

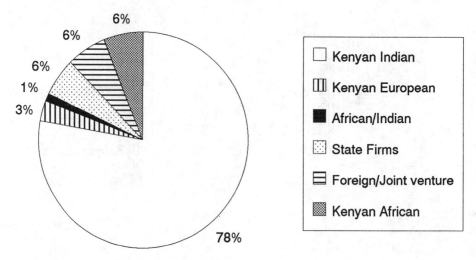

Sample of 100 Large-Scale Manufacturing Firms

Figure 2.7   Firms Established After the Demise of the East African Community

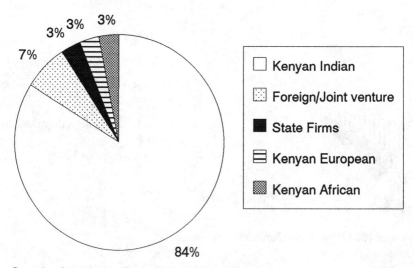

Sample of 100 Large-Scale Manufacturing Firms

Figure 2.8 Ownership by Race or Type

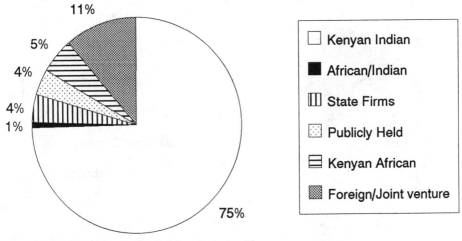

Sample of 100 Large-Scale Manufacturing Firms

Figure 2.9 Ownership of Firms with over One Hundred Workers

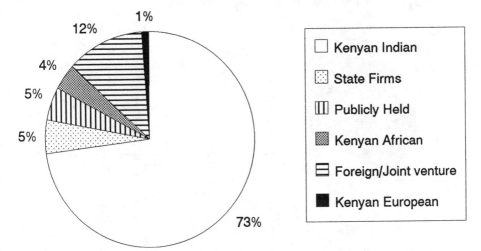

Sample of 100 Large-Scale Manufacturing Firms

Figure 2.10   Ownership of Firms Valued over KShs100 Million

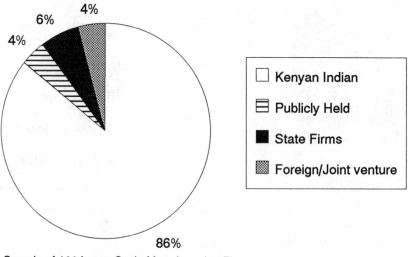

Sample of 100 Large-Scale Manufacturing Firms

Figure 2.11   Firms Under Receivership in 1989–1990

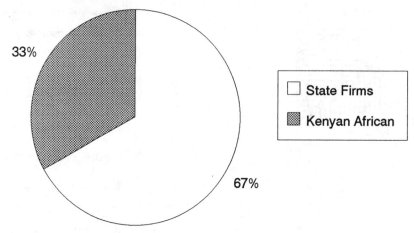

Sample of 100 Large-Scale Manufacturing Firms

under receivership) in 1989 and 1990. No Kenyan Indian-owned company was in this category. While the role of local Indians in commerce and industry has continued to increase, the performance of private African companies and state parastatals has ranged from mediocre to total failure.

Pioneer Industries: Patterns of Accumulation

The following section gives some industrial case histories, detailing patterns of accumulation followed by local Indian industrial groups, to illustrate the role they have played in spearheading industrial development in Kenya and East Africa. Also described are the roles played by "collective" organizations of capital, most of which were led by East African Indian capitalists.

Comcraft

Among the examples of industrial groups that began in petty trade are a group of companies that currently form the Comcraft Group. According to R.P. Chandaria, who with D.P. Chandaria oversaw the later consolidation of their business empire, the family had a history of pioneering. "From early on, our family has never been satisfied with the status quo," he told me. "We always had the urge to create something new."[48] From hawking, retail, and wholesale trades, the family graduated into manufacturing when they formed the Kenya Aluminium and Industrial Works Ltd. (Kaluworks) in 1929. Kaluworks pioneered the manufacturing of articles made from aluminium and mild steel, such as cooking pans and pots, hurricane lanterns, and wire nails. Other industrial activities by the group included, in the 1940s, wheat and maize milling and food processing. Pure Food Products, a food processing company started in the 1940s, was later sold during a streamlining program in the early 1950s. This operation is still in existence and remains one of the largest companies in this subsector under the name of True Foods and Kabazi Canners.[49]

In the post–Second World War period, with the more defined policy mechanisms and the greater participation of the state in creating an enabling environment for industrialization, Kaluworks undertook its own restructuring programs to take advantage of the changes. In fact, pioneering companies such as Kaluworks influenced the way the state implemented its programs of protection and the provision of key infrastructures. For example, Kaluworks requested that the Kenyan state not charge duties on its raw materials, to make the company more competitive. This was among the first instances of relations between emerging local industrial capital and the state. Kalworks stated:

We have risked a great deal of our capital and are prepared to risk still more in a new enterprise which we venture to suggest is of a great potential value not only to Kenya, but also to the East African territories. ... [W]hat we now request is the removal of an import tax on such an essential raw material.[50]

Most often the state (through the Committee on Drawbacks, which is discussed in more detail in Part II) responded favorably to such requests. In this case:

The Committee, having considered the Company's letter of the 10th November, 1953 . . . considered that there was a case for making a recommendation for the full refund of duty on aluminium ingots. . . . So far as is known, this company is the only user of aluminium ingots in East Africa.[51]

With these favorable conditions, a more integrated Kaluworks could mass-produce its cooking pans and lanterns and also process aluminum ingots to provide itself with aluminum circles for these items. It was the first company in East Africa to establish an aluminum rolling mill—in 1952. Kaluworks was now producing plain and corrugated sheets, strategic products that stimulated other industries in the construction, retail, and wholesale trades.

The pioneering role of the group was soon reflected in export markets, long before there was a Kenyan state administrative and legal mechanism to assist such transactions. When Kaluworks began to export, the government admitted that there were "no legal means by which the Commissioner of Customs and Excise can grant a drawback of duty."[52] This export drive by the company prompted the state to create such a system. The company was "granted a 100% refund of duty on imported aluminium circles used exclusively in the production of aluminium hollowware for the export."[53]

If the role of Kaluworks and associated companies (together known as Comcraft) was crucial in Kenya's industrial development during the colonial period, its postindependence record—in areas such as job creation for example—is even more remarkable. The Comcraft Group employs directly more than three thousand people.[54] Indirect employment created by the group in such areas as construction and retail and wholesale trades is also considerable. Moreover, Comcraft companies such as Mabati Rolling Mills, East African Match Ltd. (battery manufacturing division), and Kaluworks (the rolling division) are located outside major towns, in accordance with the government's program of rural industrialization that seeks to create jobs in rural areas. The group paid nearly KShs600 million in duties and taxes to the exchequer for fiscal year 1989. By comparison, sixty Kenyan state-owned companies paid in all KShs50 million.[55]

The Madhvani Group

One of the most dynamic pioneers of many manufacturing industries in East Africa is the Madhvani Group. A 1972 report appropriately described the group as "the largest industrial and commercial enterprise in Africa."[56] Before the expulsion of Ugandan Indians by the Ugandan dictator Idi Amin in 1972, the group consisted of sixty-six commercial and industrial enterprises operating throughout East Africa. The group's products included sugar, steel, metal containers, textiles, beer, tea, glass, oil, soap, confectionery, and chain-link fencing. There were more than twenty thousand East Africans on this combine's payroll.[57]

From petty merchant activities, founder Muljibhai Madhvani moved in 1908 onto what became a 40-acre coffee farm in tsetse-ridden bushland near Jinja in Uganda. When the world price for coffee plummeted at the end of the First World War, Madhvani branched into sugar. The first sugar industrial complex in Uganda, including plantations and factories, was established in the early 1920s. Sugar manufacturing by the group was not limited to Uganda, however. An application by the group to erect a sugar refinery at their Ramisi sugar estate in Kenya was granted in 1954.[58]

By the 1960s, not even the MNCs' subsidiaries setting up in the East African market could successfully compete with some of the group's companies, which now diversified into many economic activities. For example, in an effort to establish itself in the manufacture of edible oils, a sector controlled by the Madhvani Group and other local Indian companies, East Africa Industries, a subsidiary of Uniliver (in which the Kenyan and British governments had shares through the Industrial Development Corporation [IDC] and the Colonial Development Corporation [CDC] respectively) requested a governmental refund of customs duties. A Kenyan official commented:

> Three firms in Uganda engaged in the milling of oil seeds and the production of cooking fats and edible oils have cornered the market by purchasing the bulk of the cottonseed available and by refusing to release bulk supplies of semi-refined oil on the market. The largest of these firms is Muljibhai Madhvani and Company, which is in direct competition with East Africa Industries as regards the manufacture of cooking fats, margarine and vegetable ghee. . . . It is competition from Uganda manufacturers that East Africa Industries is unable to face and not competition from overseas. . . . What they [East Africa Industries] are asking for is Government assistance to defeat the Muljibhai Madhvani attempts at monopoly. . . . [T]hey are in fact asking the Kenya Government to refund duty so that they can compete successfully with another manufacturer in another East African territory, who had by his own acumen obtained a virtual monopoly of local edible oil production through control of the milling industry. . . . [I]t must be remembered that Muljibhai Madhvani and Co., are also investing in industry in Kenya and I find it difficult to

raise strong feelings over this firm's actions in Uganda.[59]

The application by EAI for a customs drawback was subsequently rejected on the grounds that "It was not the Committee's practice to recommend drawbacks to meet local competition between local industries in East Africa. For these reasons the committee does not recommend the grant of a customs drawback."[60]

The Madhvani Group—like Kaluworks—was encouraged by the Kenyan state to invest in manufacturing enterprises. As already noted, the IDC participated with the group in the Steel Corporation of East Africa Ltd., a steel rolling mill at Dondora, Nairobi. Through the 1960s up to 1972, the group's industrial capacity continued to expand in all three East African countries, in sugar-related areas, the steel sector, textile industries, glass, food and beverages, and soap manufacturing.[61]

After the rise of Idi Amin and the devastation of most of Uganda's industrial plants, and with the nationalization of private sector companies in Tanzania, the Madhvani Group lost most of its enterprises in those countries, but it retained those based in Kenya. There was also a split in the family, a development that resulted in a division of the group's assets in Kenya. Surviving plants include the steel mill at Dondora, which became more integrated by the 1989 acquisition of Steel Billet Casting Ltd. (renamed Emco Billets Ltd.). The company is now in a position to supply its sister companies and other producers of steel products with steel billets; the company also exports steel billets into the preferential trading area (PTA).[62]

Kenya Glass Works

Glass manufacturing in East Africa was pioneered by members of the Patel community that included A.B. Patel, I.S. Patel, B.S. Patel, M.B. Patel, and S. Bansal. The Patels were to be found in almost all fields of specialization from the late 1890s onward. By the 1940s, some members of the community were beginning to enter manufacturing, pioneering a number of industrial projects. A government report noted that the Patels had

> supplied their virile energy to the creation of substantial industrial organizations. The Kenya Glass Works Ltd, and the Absorbent Cotton Industries Ltd (both first of their kind in East Africa) and the Kenya Casement Company Ltd, are outstanding examples in that line, in addition to the old established Fundisha Salt Works at Malindi. The locally floated and flourishing Insurance Company Ltd is their creation.[63]

Created in the late 1940s, the Kenya Glass Works commenced production of bottles and glassware in 1952. Along with Kaluworks and Elephant Soap Factory, Kenya Glass Works was among the first domestic capitalist groups to seek state protection:

> We have plans ready at hand . . . [to] place our bottles completely on the
> line with imported bottles as far as quality is concerned, and will increase
> our output at the same time by about 50% which will decrease the cost
> of production. . . . We can consider such installation only if we have
> sufficient protection by the Government from overseas competition.[64]

The state encouraged these industrial pioneers. In 1954 the firm
received the following state response:

> The Government has viewed the development of this industry sympa-
> thetically; it has sponsored the addition of this manufacture to the
> Schedule of the East African Industrial Ordinance, and has imposed a
> suspended duty of the 20% *ad valorem* on certain types of imported
> glassware to afford protection to the locally produced articles.[65]

The state helped local companies in other ways. Britain adopted a protectionist stance vis-à-vis other trading blocks, in particular the dollar zone.
In the case of imports of machinery and plants, for example, a directive
from the British state had instructed the governor in 1941:

> As you are aware a large proportion of the commodities imported from
> the United States are now subject to control. . . . Goods shipped from the
> United States without an import licence should in no circumstances be
> allowed into the Dependency concerned and dollars in no circumstances
> released.[66]

There is evidence that sections of the Kenyan bureaucracy were not
adhering to this regulation. When the Ministry of Education, Labour and
Land (MELL) reminded the commerce minister of this policy, with regard
to the source of machinery imported by Kenya Glass Works, the minister
responded: "Undue influence will not be given to the fact that the company has obtained part of its equipment from the USA."[67] On another
occasion the commerce ministry told the firm that the government was
"interested in ensuring that industry will develop on the best lines to the
advantage of East Africa." Noting that glass manufacture was comparatively new to the region, an official letter conceded that the best technical
advice and guidance "may not be available locally" and to remedy the
situation the government arranged for "the services of an American glass
expert to pay a brief visit to Kenya and to report on the industry and give
advice on techniques and future development plans."[68] In this atmosphere,
Kenya Glass Works became successful. A progress report by the East
African Industrial Council in 1954 notes the assertiveness of the company
in seeking new markets and a broader range of products. This report states
that the samples of the company's bottles were being made "for Pepsi Cola

and Canada Dry. . . . If approved the firm will then try to sell the bottles to any licensed bottler of Pepsi Cola and Canada Dry. . . . Bottles have been sent to Usumbura, Ruanda-Urundi, and it is hoped to do business there."[69] By early 1961, when the company was sold to the Madhvani Group, it had not only captured the East African local market but was exporting extensively to neighboring countries, not only Rwanda-Urundi but also Belgian Congo.

The Kenya Glass Works, still in production in the 1990s, has recently lost some beer markets to Central Glass, an ultramodern plant commissioned by Kenya Breweries in 1982 that began to produce in 1987.[70]

The House of Manji Group

The conducive industrial environment of the late 1940s and 1950s also helped the House of Manji. Now it is one of the most influential industrial groups in Kenya. Like most Kenyan Indian enterprises, the House of Manji began in trade. The Manji family were general merchants as early as 1905, trading around Nyeri, Karatina, and Murang'a. Medatally Manji, founder of the house, was born in Nyeri but he grew up in neighboring Karatina. His father had finally settled there as a merchant. The younger Manji moved to Nairobi during the Second World War, seeking business opportunities. He bought a bakery and provision store on Ngara Road.[71] Because of wartime conditions, it was no longer possible freely to import products and Manji sought to produce some items himself. Before the end of the war, Ngara Bakery was producing vermicelli and other pasta products for the Muslim community. Traditionally, Muslims eat vermicelli during the month of Ramadan.

Manji's entry into mass production of these products was unusual. When the British Army sought to feed some sixty thousand Italian prisoners brought to Kenya from Ethiopia, Ngara Bakery was—in Manji's words—"the only large bakery in Nairobi that could improvise spaghetti and macaroni, and so they approached me. But I could only produce a couple of hundred pounds each day, an amount that obviously could not feed sixty thousand people."[72] It turned out that the army had dismantled and brought with them a large macaroni plant from their campaign in Ethiopia and they had installed it at Nyeri with the idea of getting Italian prisoners to use it and feed themselves. But, Mr. Manji told me, "once the plant was installed, the Italian prisoners refused to work it, as they considered this to be an equivalent to working for their conquerors."[73] As one of the largest bakeries around Nairobi, the Ngara Bakery was asked to buy the plant and produce the pasta. The plant was bought for Shs25,000. It was the beginning of large-scale production of pasta products in East Africa.

Enterprising Manji embarked on still bigger projects. In 1946, he went to Britain for six months to study automated breadmaking. The result was the creation in 1949 of the Whitehouse Bakery with a capacity of twenty-three thousand loaves of bread per day.[74] House of Manji, a yet more ambitious venture, was established in 1954. In 1953, founder Manji explained the vision behind the project: "I intend to produce English biscuits in the English manner and when we go into production next year . . . I hope these biscuits will compare favourably with anything produced by the famous English firms who were making biscuits before East Africa was thought of."[75] The opening of the biscuit factory was a major event in Kenya. Governor Sir Evelyn Baring was guest of honor.[76] In 1955, House of Manji went into the export trade outside East Africa, creating for its biscuits and pasta products markets in Zambia, Mozambique, Rwanda-Urundi, and Belgian Congo. By the mid-1970s the company was also exporting to the Middle East and Nigeria, and by the end of the 1980s was selling as far afield as India.[77]

The House of Manji is also active in finance, through its associated companies such as House of Manji Management Property Ltd., House of Manji Investment Ltd., Consolidated Finance Ltd., and Mua Park Investments Ltd., backing real estate and housing development.[78] The group directly employs four hundred people in the manufacturing sector, and provides indirect employment to hundreds of others in retail and wholesale trades, packaging and printing, transportation, and wheat and maize farming.

Other Industries

There are other examples of pioneer industries. The Mehta Group has had industrial projects all over East Africa since the 1930s, producing sugar, steel, and plastic products. The Nalin Group operates such companies as Gnanjivan Screws & Fasteners, Gnanjivan Wire Galvanising Mills, Nalin Nails, and the Special Steel Mills (since the 1940s).[79] Others include the Chandaria Group (not related to the Comcraft Group) in paper/packaging industries, since the 1950s; Elephant Soap Factory, since the 1930s; and Sunflag Textile Mills, since the 1950s. In banking there is Lalit Pandit's East African Building Society (EABS), started in 1959. By 1989, EABS held KShs2 billion in assets.[80] Lalit Pandit's enterprising spirit is nicely illustrated by correspondence dated 1955 between the governor's secretary and the Asian minister without portfolio, A.P. Patel. "The Governor," wrote the secretary, "has asked me to enquire whether you know anything about Lalit Pandit. He certainly seems an enterprising young man and the Governor remembers meeting him at Tanga Airport." Patel's reply was: "Mr. Pandit is a young man of 19 years and is certainly a charming promising young man. However, his sole desire in meeting the Governor is to canvas a life insurance policy of the Governor."[81]

All these industrialists and financiers share a common beginning—in commerce and trade. It bears repetition that the experience of these companies between the Second World War and independence questions the conceptions of the colonial state that depict it as an instrument of British capital (as in Berman) or an agent for local white settlers (as in Swainson). This topic is addressed fully in Part II.

Collective Organizations of Capital

It is important briefly to discuss the *collective* role of pioneer commercial and industrial entrepreneurs in Kenyan development. Among the leading organizations of capital were the Association of Chambers of Commerce of Eastern Africa (ACCEA, formed in 1920), which included both the Indian and the European chambers of commerce and industry; and the Federation of Indian Chambers of Commerce of Eastern Africa (FICCEA), which incorporated all the Indian chambers of commerce and industry. The latter had existed in some form since 1902. Among the concerns of the ACCEA, especially during the 1950s, was coordination of the region's economies and the adoption of single company laws under "the orbit of the East African High Commission."[82] Executives of both organizations corresponded with governors. They even sought direct influence with United Kingdom secretaries of state. For example, the Ugandan industrialist R.J. Mehta, president of the ACCEA in the mid-1950s, wrote to Mr. Lennox-Boyd, the secretary of state for the colonies, in the following terms:

> I was very happy to meet you again and find you in restored health. Feeling that the question of unified legislation on commercial matters is of greatest importance, I have thought it fit to address to you this personal letter. . . . Ever since its inception in 1920, my Association has endeavoured to express the vital need for the closest possible integration of the [East African] Territories. . . . My Assocation, representing organised commercial, industrial and agricultural interests in Uganda, Kenya and Tanganyika, begs, therefore, to bring the situation to your notice.[83]

The FICCEA was equally assertive in articulating the interests of commercial and industrial entrepreneurs.[84]

As more manufacturing enterprises were formed in the late 1950s, the Association for the Promotion of Industries in East Africa (APIEA) was incorporated in 1958 under the chair of the Ugandan industrialist Madhvani.[85] One of the association's early concerns was to increase local industry's share of the domestic market by attempting to replace the crown agents as suppliers of the Kenya government's requirements of manufactured products. It also called for the establishment of inter-territorial common standards and the formation of an export promotion council (which was formed in the mid-1950s). A major confrontation between capital and the state came through the APIEA on the eve of independence. The Kenyan government, due to fiscal constraints, sought to eliminate the drawback program. The APIEA was adamant in its opposition, saying that if the drawbacks "are not renewed the effect on many of our industries could be catastrophic, and could not only be injurious to industry itself but could have a great effect upon the number of unemployed."[86] The uproar saw the rebate restored by the colonial secretary in London.[87] The APIEA, evidently, was an effective pressure group. With its dynamic mix of local and foreign capital (the former constituting the overwhelming majority of its membership) it was able to affect policy up to 1963. Subsequently, its counterparts in the state were equally effective. Together with the commerce ministry and its board of industrial development, the APIEA and individual capitalists such as Mehta, Chandaria, Madhvani, and many others, oversaw an industrial revolution in East Africa.

Impact of Africanization on Kenyan Indian Capitalists

An entirely different environment emerged after independence in 1963. In place of the supportive policies noted above, a ferocious and protracted struggle ensued between a state now controlled by an African political elite, and the commercial and industrial bourgeoisie. The main point of contention was and remains the desire to empower a black Kenyan business class to play leading roles in commerce and industry. However, the legislative measures introduced, targeting Indians in retail and whole-sale trade to achieve this goal, largely produced the reverse effect. Many if not most black Kenyans who acquired businesses through legislative means did not last, as they possessed neither sufficient business skill nor the financial resources to survive in the market place. Further, nonblack entrepreneurs forced out of their businesses were either lost to Kenya as they emigrated to other countries, or moved into more complex sectors of the economy, such as manufacturing, finance and banking, insurance, tourism, and construction. When the would-be African traders floundered, Indians, former traders turned industrialists, gradually returned to reclaim the trading sector, this time as part of a strategy of integration with their new more sophisticated activities. In this way, another peak in industrialization in Kenya occurred, rendering Kenyan Indian capitalists even more important than before.

The main legislative means used to create space for Africans in commerce was the Trade Licensing Act of 1967, which was designed to limit the trading activities of noncitizens. The act stated that "No person who is not a citizen of Kenya shall conduct a business (a) in any place which is not a general businesses area; or (b) in any specified goods."[88]

"General business areas" were designated only in large towns—central Nairobi, Mombasa, and a few others. This meant that noncitizens were excluded from trading in the rural areas and the noncentral areas of major towns. As a result, hundreds of *dukawallahs* (or small-scale Indian merchants) were given notice to wind up their businesses to make way for African traders. In practice the term *citizen* was often equated with "African," and not only noncitizens but nonblack citizens were given quit notices. For example, leading ministers such as Mr. Mwai Kibaki could say that shops left by Indian traders must "be reserved for the exclusive use of Africans. . . . The owners of the business premises affected are expected to let them out to citizens and particularly to Africans who in the past have been discriminated against."[89] The climate in which the Africanization program was attempted was obviously hostile. When reporting the progress of Africanization, Mr. A. N. Gakunja, the provincial trade licensing officer, stated:

> I will be a happy man if I can get rid of the city's 500 noncitizen businesses. . . . The total asked to quit their premises or refused licenses so far is in the region of 350. But the exercise is not yet over. . . . Government Road and Bazaar St. do not appear to be geared to the same speed as the overall operation. I will be happy if I can find 15 Africans to take up business in these two areas.[90]

Apart from its overtly racist tone, this statement confirms that there was actually not a large enough pool of African traders to replace all the local Indian businessmen, especially in the more sophisticated segment of the retail sector. In fact, the Africanization drive not only undermined local Indian businesses but African communities as well. A crisis in Kitale township exemplified this dilemma in 1969. With local Indian traders denied trading licenses, and with no Africans to take their places, the Kitale town council was threatened by a loss of local businesses, and in turn a loss in its tax base. The town subsequently passed a unanimous resolution asking the commerce minister to exempt the town from the Trade Licensing Act:

> There is a feeling of depression in the Town. . . . The Council are worried that if shops are forced to close there will be no one, particularly among the Africans, who will be able to buy their businesses. If the shops remain closed the loss in the rates revenue to the Council will be disastrous.[91]

The alternatives facing local Indians in the 1960s and 1970s were in effect either to leave Kenya or move from trade into another sector. As was stated by the commerce minister: "The government expects that the majority of the affected noncitizens will either leave Kenya or move into other sectors where their contribution is required such as the manufacturing industries."[92] However, the Africanization of commerce and industry was flawed from the beginning, as indicated below. The limited number of Kenyan Africans who did acquire businesses saw their enterprises collapse. Most often, they sold them back to their former owners. This episode was described by Mr. Sam Waruhiu, chairman of Barclays Bank and former chairman of the trading appeals tribunal, the office that was responsible for enforcing the regulations for the Africanization of commerce and industry in the 1970s:

> When the window was opened for African businessmen through the Trade Licensing Act, and various schemes such as the ICDC at independence they had no experience. . . . The experiment was not only a major failure from the perspective of African businesses, it backfired in another respect. The Act forced the Indians into the more challenging sections of the economy—the manufacturing especially. After their largely successful movement into this sector, they came back, ironically, with a much larger base and reclaimed the retail and wholesale sector. The reason was simple and historical. The Asian businessmen were already established at the coast before the colonial rule, and they followed the railway to consolidate their position, despite the fact that they held no political power. At independence, they took advantage of their position in the economy. This is the single most important reason why the programme of assisting Africans' move into retail trade by inducing Asians' withdrawal completely backfired. . . . The mistakes made by us include the role played by our institutions such as the ICDC whose objectives included provision of capital and technical know-how. Instead of assisting Africans, the ICDC became an entrepreneur itself thereby taking away the critical input the budding African businessmen needed most—capital. Like all parastatals, it could not manage to do this well enough either. It is fair to conclude that the ICDC became a "white elephant" with its participation in sometimes trivial and small companies, including supermarkets; the whole policy was misguided.[93]

Manufacturing firms owned by local Indians were also, initially, not immune to the threats of African takeover, despite the fact that the Africanization of even the smaller retail outlets was faring very badly. Following the extension of the Trade Licensing Act in 1974, a number of manufacturing firms were issued with quit notices. In 1975, the Flora Garment Factory (valued at KShs400,000 in 1975 with eighty employees), Capital Knitwear (KShs2 million and one hundred employees), Pactco Industries Ltd. (KShs4 million and fifty employees), and Karania Packers (KShs4 million and sixty employees) were issued quit notices. A report indicated that black Kenyans that had been "allocated" these companies. The Kenya Association of Manufacturers (renamed from the APIEA after the latter was restructured) said these companies

> have received quit notices [and have been asked to] wind up their businesses. . . . According to the Provincial Commissioner of Nairobi, who is the Chairman of the Provincial Business Allocation Committee,

Nairobi Area, Karania Packers business is allocated to Hon. Mrs. Eddah
Gachukia. Flora Garment Factory business is allocated to Messrs.
Nderitu Drapers of Karatina.[94]

Disintegration of the Africanization Program

The Kenyan state soon realized that attempting to dislodge defenseless
dukawallah merchants was one thing; taking on large manufacturing
industries was quite another. Due to the scale of the managerial skills and
capital involved in the latter, and more importantly to the effective
intervention of their collective organizations such as the KAM, industrialists successfully deflected takeovers of their businesses. They used three
main means—legal arguments, the international implications of racial
harassment, and reminders of Kenya's stated objectives of encouraging
local and international private investment. The following representation
from KAM is characteristic of their opposition based on citing international implications:

> On August 16 last year, Legal Notice No. 229 was published bringing
> industries under the Trading Licensing Act....New industrialists coming
> to Kenya seek the advice of other manufacturers....When they are told
> of the new Amendment, they are frightened to enter into any financial
> commitment, realising that they might be given a "quit notice" by a Trade
> Licensing Officer under the new Amendment at any time. Similarly, the
> existing manufacturers see this amendment as a potential threat to their
> investments, and will refrain from investing further capital.[95]

The following protest emphasized the stated private investment strategy
of development by the Kenyan state:

> We find it rather difficult to believe that the Kenya Government invites
> foreign and local investors alike, to participate in local manufacturing
> industries whilst at the time industries are taken over contrary to
> Government's stated policy.[96]

Individual companies protested on purely legal grounds:

> I was visited by two representatives from Messrs. Century Distributors
> who attempted to apply a considerable amount of pressure on my
> company to persuade us to give them our distribution....Since we are
> operating in accordance with the Law, ... we must protest this kind of
> interference.[97]

The following example indicates how a multinational firm repulsed attempts to appoint distributors not based on expertise:

> The main reasons why the existing type of Distributors continue in their
> present form is because they are mostly hardware merchants whose

scope of business includes paints for retail. . . . Paint is not a pure consumer product that can be sold over a shop counter like sugar, milk, tea, etc., which require no technical expertise.[98]

Another protest comes from a joint venture between local capital and capital from India that manufactured automobile spare parts:

We have been given to understand that the new distribution policy affects only manufacturers of essential commodities, i.e., food stuffs, cooking oils and cereals. . . . If this is so we are in complete agreement with the new policy. However, if this is not so, a company like ours which is manufacturing motor vehicle components will find it almost impossible to operate.[99]

There is, in effect, further evidence to illustrate the fact that the Kenyan state was merely paying lip service to its Africanization policies, having long recognized that it neither possessed the power nor the will to force foreign and domestic large-scale Kenyan Indian manufacturers to appoint African distributors. For example, in 1967, perturbed by the "exceedingly disappointing" rate of progress in the appointment of African distributors by manufacturers, the Kenya government stated that "strong warning is given that actions designed to frustrate Government's efforts should be avoided as much as possible, as such actions could have serious consequences."[100] More than half a decade later, in August 1973, the manufacturing sector was reminded that the government

has indicated to you its determination that the distribution of locally manufactured products should be passed on to Africans as quickly as possible. As you are already aware we are taking appropriate steps to see that the program gets underway. . . . [You are] fully aware of the urgency which Government attaches to this matter.[101]

In November of the same year, it was stated that in conformity with Africanization, it has been decided that "immediate steps be taken by all concerned to ensure that distribution of all locally manufactured goods is in the hands of Kenya citizens. . . . The Government is desirous that this exercise gets underway without too long delays. . . . You must furnish us with a progress report by not later than 31th [sic] December, 1973."[102]

A circular letter issued in the following year directed that "the distribution and retailing of locally manufactured goods should be handled by Kenya Citizens before 30th April, 1974" and that "we would like to know immediately the agents you have appointed." On this occasion, the course of action that the state was to take, if manufacturers failed to comply, was indicated: "Failure to submit the list of agents will result in your wholesaling retailing licenses withdrawn until this directive is complied with."[103] Yet again in 1976, manufacturers were informed that unless they followed government directives, additional legislation to force them to do so would soon follow:

> You are no doubt aware of His Excellency's directive that was issued two
> years ago to the effect that locally manufactured products be distributed
> by *Wananchi* [i.e., citizens]. You are also aware of the effort that this
> Ministry has been making towards this end and the fact that very few
> manufacturers have complied with this directive.... [It has] become clear
> that there is a need for some Legislation with which a manufacturer
> should comply.[104]

It is worth emphasizing that the Kenyan state was very aware of the limits
of its power vis-à-vis the manufacturers. Its rhetoric was essentially intended for public consumption. In the just quoted circular letter, for
instance, the manufacturers were reassured that "by revocation of Legal
Notice No. 229 of 1974 manufacturing as such ceased to be under the
Trade Licensing Act and therefore a manufacturer cannot be issued with
a quit notice."

Meanwhile, the state continued to engage in a make-believe exercise
that gave the impression that the Africanization of commerce and industry
was still being implemented. For example, in 1980, the state issued yet
another "threat" to Kenyan-based manufacturers:

> As you are well aware, the Government has decided that the distribution
> of essential commodities will in future be done through citizen distribu-
> tors only. In the exercise of appointing their distributors ... manufactur-
> ers are expected to work in close liaison and consultation with this
> Ministry.[105]

In the following year, however, the government appeared finally to accept
defeat gracefully, appealing to manufacturers in the following terms: "The
slow tempo with which Kenyanization of trade and commerce has been
implemented has, to a large extent, proved to be disappointing.... I wish
to appeal to the entire business community to support Government
measures in earnest."[106]

The effective defeat of the Africanization of the manufacturing industry through state intervention, combined with the law that forced local
Indian traders into other sectors, accelerated another round of locally
propelled industrial development. The number of local Indian companies
entering the manufacturing sector after the 1960s and the 1970s (at the
height of Africanization attempts) is striking. As indicated in figures 2.1
to 2.11, out of one hundred manufacturing companies studied, 41 percent
of firms were incorporated in the 1970s; this compares with 10 percent
established before 1950, 11 percent in the 1950s, 16 percent in the 1960s,
and 22 percent in the 1980s. More revealing is the fact that of manufacturing enterprises established in the 1960s, local Indians were responsible for
founding 79 percent of them. This compares with 70 percent of enterprises
established by Kenya Indians in the 1970s and 85 percent in the 1980s.
These manufacturing companies were in textiles, pharmaceutical and
chemical industries, plastics, steel and equipment manufacturers, and

specialized engineering firms. The owners of all these companies are either descendants of coast-based merchants and financiers whose presence in East Africa dated back several centuries, or of railway immigrant workers and petty accumulators who came to Kenya from the 1890s onward. Current (third or fourth) generations of these families transformed their grandparents' financial and commercial activities into large commercial firms or moved into manufacturing before or after independence. In the latter phase, the incentive was mostly defensive, as the manufacturing sector was seen as a more secure investment in the aftermath of the Trading Licensing Act.

The Latest Trend in Patterns of Accumulation

With the breakup of the East African Common Market and joint common services, as well as the decline of the civil service and physical infrastructures in Kenya (see Chapter 5), foreign interest in investment in the country declined sharply. The last major foreign investment in Kenya was in 1977, with the establishment of General Motors Kenya Ltd. In fact, since the mid-1980s foreign companies have been divesting and selling their subsidiaries to local industrialists. The most remarkable divestments, in 1986, involved Firestone (EA) Ltd., Eveready Batteries Ltd., Marshalls Ltd., the Commercial Bank of Africa, and Twentieth Century Fox Cinema. Due to the size of these companies—in terms of their managerial requirements, capital, and the international sophistication of their credit transactions and technical agreements and arrangements—they were all acquired by local Indian entrepreneurs[107]—the only group capable of taking over large foreign industries. As can be seen below, the state parastatals were collapsing in the late 1970s and 1980s, and African companies faced the same fate. Local Indians, however, continued to create new enterprises, indicating that they were either more committed to Kenya than foreign capital, or that they were less free to invest elsewhere. Mr. P.K. Shah commented:

> Despite the Trade Licensing Act and the associated issues, we had confidence in Kenya; this is proved by industries created by our community since independence. Then came the attempted coup of 1982 which blew this confidence. But even after this regrettable event, we have no choice but to keep investing as this is our home. In our case we have moved into almost all sectors of commerce and industry, including retail trade, transportation and farming wheat in the Narok area. Our largest industrial investment after the attempted coup is our Eldoret Steel Mill.[108]

Irrespective of the motive, the one hundred company sample studied confirmed the predominant role of the Indian community in establishing

manufacturing industries in Kenya, despite the evidently poor investment climate during the 1970s and 1980s. Of companies established in
Kenya after the collapse of the East African Common Market in 1977,
83.9 percent belonged to local Indians. Some of the industrial projects
started in this period represented some of the largest and most sophisticated enterprises in Kenya, particularly in the steel sector—e.g.,
Mabati Rolling Mills (established in 1988 at Mariakani), Standard
Rolling Mills (established at Kaloleni in 1989), and Kaluworks Rolling
Mills (at Mariakani in 1988). The most expensive of these ventures was
Mabati Rolling Mills, which cost the Comcraft Group KShs1 billion.
Other groups, such as the East African Foundry Works (which was
supplying large quantities of pumps to the World Bank and other aid
agencies for their projects across sub-Saharan Africa), Specialised
Engineering, and Marshall Fowler, were now manufacturing fairly
complex industrial goods and components—e.g., lathe machines,
pumps and industrial plants, tea and coffee processing machinery, and
ventilating fans and conveyors for both local and export markets. Both
Specialised Engineering and Marshall Fowler exported products not
only to African countries but also to China and Australia. Steel Structures Ltd. and others were manufacturing industrial and milling plants,
concrete mixers, and plough and block-making machines. Orbitsports
Ltd. was exporting sports balls to Germany, France, and Britain. Vic-
toria Furniture Ltd. and other firms manufactured office and industrial
furniture for domestic and export markets. In the pharmaceutical field,
Cosmos Ltd. emerged as a leader in local and export markets. Companies such as Ken-Knit Ltd. (textiles with a subsidiary in steel and
wheat-farming), Orbit Chemicals Ltd. (detergents and chemicals), and
Doshi Ltd. (steel tubes), moved into the manufacturing sector from
wholesale or retail sectors—as did most of the firms listed above. Mr.
Mohan Galot, an industrialist, promoter, and coffee farmer, with an
industrial park in Athi River, was also making a mark during the late
1980s and early 1990s. His business empire included textiles, liquor, and
glass manufacturing. By 1993, some Kenyan industrialists were operating industrial parks that specialized in exports. The most successful of
these was associated with industrialist Naushad Merali, whose Sameer
Industrial Park was the first "export processing zone" to come on-
stream in Kenya.[109]

Collective Organizations of Capital After 1963

In the more hostile environment of the post-1963 years, the sectoral
organizations were adversely affected. Their role ultimately became
insignificant. All the chambers of commerce were integrated in 1965
into a single Kenya National Chamber of Commerce and Industry

(KNCCI). Far from becoming an effective business lobby group, after it was "Africanized" the KNCCI became a running spectacle.

> Its executives fought publicly over who should head the chamber and even when there should be elections at all. The image presented to the public is not of business people in a unity of purpose but of people driven by hunger for power. These are politicians in business garb.[110]

In effect, the character and role of the KNCCI mirrors that of the Kenyan state itself. Besides mismanagement and corruption[111] KNCCI's demands for Africanization of commerce and industry alienated Kenyan Indian capitalists. In abortive chamber elections in 1987, for example, the Macharia regime accused Macharia's electoral competitor, Nicholas Gor (a director in the Chandaria Group of Industries), of being backed by local Indians, as if that, if true, was sinister. Advice that the chamber "should avoid squabbles and groupings which are harmful for an organisation whose objective is to represent the interests of the entire business community," does not appear to have had any effect.[112]

The APIEA was greatly affected after 1963 by events that began with tensions and policy modifications within the three East African community member countries. In Tanzania, changes in the marketing structure sought to limit inter–East African trade in favor of self-reliance. By 1967, Tanzania had formed its own local products council in the aftermath of the Arusha Declaration, and Tanzania's representative resigned from the APIEA. Changes in Kenya included the introduction of exchange control regulations leading to the breakup of the common East African currency, while Uganda instituted local taxes on motor vehicles visiting from Kenya. These contradictions resulted in 1969 in the disintegration of APIEA. The Kenyan chapter was renamed the Kenya Association of Manufacturers (KAM), its goals being "to promote and protect the interests of industrialists and manufacturers in Kenya . . . and to advise the Kenya Government of any measures considered by the Association to be necessary from time to time for the establishment and support of industries in Kenya."[113] KAM remains effective, but in a much more defensive role, given the changed environment. With an executive commitee of seventeen—chief executives of local private and public companies, MNCs, and parastatals— KAM is probably the most informed and best organized body concerned with industry in the country. Its annual publication of a business index and periodic reports are far more reliable than anything produced by government departments.[114] KAM's membership of about six hundred industries is divided according to goods manufactured into twenty sectors. The main difficulty for KAM is that its counterpart organs of the state, such as the commerce and finance ministries, became extremely inefficient. Consultation on industrial and other economic policy matters has become a one-sided and largely unrewarding affair.

The Swainson Interpretation: Further Comment

The account of Kenyan commercial and industrial development in this chapter is fundamentally different from that of Nicola Swainson, the main author of reference on the development of corporate capitalism in Kenya. This is especially true in regard to the role of Kenyan Indian capitalists who in this thesis are presented as having spearheaded the process and who Swainson does not consider important.

According to Swainson, "very few Asian merchants had ventured into manufacturing" before 1945. A number of these merchants became "in-volved in a whole range of activities" that included "small-scale grain milling, sugar refining, oil refining and the manufacture of aluminium hollow-ware" from the late 1940s to independence. In Swainson's view, however, their role was destined to remain marginal, due to one factor: they lacked political power. A "few isolated incidents confirmed settler supremacy" in the 1950s, before being supplanted by African supremacy after independence.[115] Thus Swainson's account of the failure by "Asian capital" to become a significant force in the industrialization process of the 1950s differs from that of Berman. For the former, the European settlers' political hegemony blocked their role; for Berman, the industrial policy pursued by the British and the Kenyan states sought to protect British metropolitan capital—thereby forestalling merchant and indus-trial capital associated with "Asians." In Swainson's view, the political weakness of "Asian" capitalists in the colonial and postcolonial periods precluded the possibility that they would fulfill their "potential as a domestic industrial class," with the exception of "a few large conglomer-ates," such as Chandarias (Comcraft Group), Khimasias (Thika Cloth Mills), and the Madhvani Group.[116]

Swainson's analysis of the Kenyan bourgeoisie is criticized in previous chapters. Here it will suffice to note that her treatment of "Asian capital" is objectionable on several grounds. A highly instrumentalist conception of the state leads her mistakenly to fuse political and economic supremacy. Since the European settlers, and later Africans, controlled the state and politics—Swainson maintains—Asians could not conceivably succeed as a domestic industrial class. In other words, political forces in the control of the state are bound to succeed in the economic sphere. For Swainson, therefore, the principal economic actors, and thus the main objects of her analysis, are those groups that controlled the state. It is primarily due to this perspective that Swainson is almost dismissive of the Kenyan Indian bourgeoisie, whom in her book of three hundred pages she reviews briefly as "Asian capital" at the end of Chapter 3.

The Kenyan realities hardly correspond to such deterministic propo-sitions, however. As I demonstrate, the domination of the Kenyan state and politics by the Kenya Europeans and Africans rarely sustained them in the economic arena. There is no evidence to support the notion that the white settlers were effective in commerce and industry, or even in agriculture, notwithstanding the fact that they possessed political power. Their disintegration soon after independence, and the near extinction of the Kikuyu business elite after their loss of the state in the post-Kenyatta phase, is indicative of this. Conversely, the political isolation of the Indians proved to be a source of strength. It forced them to acquire the commercial and industrial skills that enabled them to survive in the market place (as opposed to relying on state handouts in the form of contracts and financial subsidies). Further, they had to develop their own protective social networks to withstand political and social pressures in the new environment. They could not rely on the state to do this. It is remarkable that Swainson acknowledges their entry into a "wide range of manufacturing activities" during the colonial period. She also refers to the "few" conglomerates that continued to operate in the Kenyan market after independence. Swainson refuses to recognize the centrality of the facts she herself reports, and so she prejudges the Kenyan Indians to be destined to remain unimportant. A more objective, openminded view, less driven by abstract theory, would have led her to a more balanced and accurate analysis.

An Industrial Revolution

In summary, I have shown that a combination of factors led to the evolution of a conducive environment permitting an industrial revolution in Kenya. First, the interruption of shipping arrangements by the Second World War curtailed Kenya-bound goods leading to import-substitution industrialization. For this process to take place, a second factor was needed: a state apparatus to both facilitate and regulate the program and to formulate and implement policy. A number of ministries and departments, especially commerce and industry, played this role skillfully. The commerce minister throughout the 1950s, Mr. A. Hope-Jones (along with Sir Ernest Vasey in finance), appears to have developed a "nationalist vision" for Kenya, to the extent that imperial concerns were at times secondary. The board of industrial development was effective, co-opting leading industrialists to help formulate policies conducive to industrialization. The role of the East African High Commission (with its related services, especially railways and harbors), and the vision that called for a unified common market, were part of the drama. The third and most decisive factor in this combination was the presence of a large pool of commercial capitalists, whose presence in the region pre-dated colonial rule—a community whose strength colonialism augmented. From within their ranks emerged an industrial bourgeoisie that took advantage of the policies introduced in the postwar period. In the 1940s and 1950s came the fourth factor: the entry of foreign capital into East Africa. Together, this and local capital created the sectoral organizations of capital such as the APIEA that influenced commercial and industrial policies. All these factors weakened the influence of the white settlers, whose more narrow interests attempted to frustrate efforts to industrialize.

The post-1963 period brought a different orientation, with industrialization taking place by default as commercial capitalists escaped from a threatened retail trade into manufacturing. Thus, the minimum of political stability that was maintained in Kenya, during Africanization, including (especially) a degree of toleration, if not affection, for local Indian capitalists, unwittingly turned into an advantage for Kenya's industrialization process. As to collective associations of capital, the KAM remained effective, albeit defensively. But this was not true of the KNCCI, which ceased to serve the interests of the Kenyan industrial bourgeoisie, or of the more sophisticated segments of commercial capitalists. KNCCI, in fact, became the mouthpiece of African petty accumulators.

Notes

1. Colony of Kenya, "Mombasa Surveys," OP(EST)/1/465, KNA. This voluminous survey is representative of annual and occasional surveys undertaken by the government on many aspects of Kenyan life conducted by various departments at the central, provincial, and district levels during the colonial period. The survey cited throughout this chapter is the 1958 Mombasa Social Survey conducted by a research unit (comprising G.E. Bennett, F. Burke, Surendra Metha, G.M. Wilson, and Edward Rodwell) to look into Mombasa urban conditions, especially race and labor relations.
2. Hollingsworth, Asians of East Africa, p. 28.
3. Hollingsworth, Asians of East Africa, p. 12.
4. Hill, Permanent Way, p. 255.
5. Tandberg article, "Duka-Wallah," p. 48.
6. Hollingsworth, Asians of East Africa, p. 28.
7. Muriuki, "Kikuyu Reaction," p. 107.
8. Colony of Kenya, "Mombasa Surveys," KNA.
9. Hill, Permanent Way, p. 11.
10. McDermitt, British East Africa, p. 39.
11. Mungeam, British Rule in Kenya, pp. 9–10.
12. Mungeam, British Rule in Kenya, pp. 9–10.
13. Macgoya, Story of Kenya, 1986, p. 16.
14. The many books with this bias include Elispeth Huxley's two volumes of White Man's Country, 1935.
15. Sorrenson, Origins, p. 34.
16. Cited Gregory, India and East Africa, p. 45.
17. Cited in Mangat, Asians in East Africa, p. 63.
18. See Gregory, India and East Africa, pp. 67–68.
19. Lord Hailey, An African Survey, p. 335.
20. Ehrlich article, "Economic and Social Developments Before Indepen-

dence," p. 323. Elsewhere, Ehrlich called Visram "perhaps the greatest single figure in the economic history of East Africa." See *Uganda Journal,* March 1956, p. 21.

21. Foreign and Colonial, *British East Africa,* pp. 120–122.
22. Foreign and Colonial, *British East Africa,* p. 420.
23. McGregor-Ross, *Kenya From Within,* pp. 415–416.
24. East African Royal Commission 1953–1955, pp. 65–194.
25. Huxley, *White Man's Country,* Vol. 1, p. 204.
26. Sorrenson, *Origins,* p. 23.
27. Quoted in Chandaria, "Development of Entrepreneurship," p. 33.
28. Hollingsworth, *Asians of East Africa,* p. 52.
29. Mangat, *Asians in East Africa,* p. 96.
30. Hill, Director of the Kenya Farmers' Association, to Vasey, 8 March 1945, *Vasey Papers,* KNA.
31. Vasey to Hill, 22 February 1952, *Vasey Papers,* KNA.
32. Interview with Mr. X, a newcomer industrialist, *East African Standard,* 8 June 1949, as found in MCI/6/20, KNA.
33. Extract from the speech made by Sir Henry to the Association of Chambers of Commerce and Industry of Eastern Africa, 2 October 1944. MCI/4/5, KNA.
34. *East African Standard,* 23 August 1945.
35. Cited in the *East African Standard,* 23 August 1945. For the association's letter to the chief secretary, dated 21 August MCI/4/5, KNA.
36. Legislative Council debate, 26 November 1945.
37. *East African Standard,* 21 November 1947.
38. See Secretariat, Confidential. MCI/4/5, KNA. See also Colony of Kenya, Circular No. 24, 25 March 1948, MCI/2/3, KNA.
39. MCI minutes of 3 December 1953. MCI/9/678, KNA.
40. G.P. Henderson, MCI, 26 October 1957. MCI/6/554, KNA.
41. For the views of the domestic Indian bourgeoisie and the Federation of Indian Chambers of Commerce and Industry on this issue, see file MCI/6/722, KNA. The source for the contemporary East African Match was derived from a 1990 questionnaire with the company and an interview with Mr. Manu Chandaria, head of Comcraft, in 1990.
42. *Financial Times,* "Colonial Survey—I: Progress in Kenya," London, 25 January 1956.
43. Colony of Kenya, "Industrial Development in East Africa," 1952, MCI/6/1275, KNA.
44. A. Hope-Jones to the governor, 19 February 1952, MCI/6/726, KNA.
45. Sir Evelyn Baring at the opening of the House of Manji biscuit factory in Nairobi, 27 September 1954, GH/4/735, KNA.
46. Chandaria, "Development of Entrepreneurship," p. 28a.
47. See sample of the questionnaire used in the Appendix. A discussion on the method used to select the firms surveyed can be found in the Preface. For the official analysis of the manufacturing sector, see Republic of Kenya, *Economic Survey 1989.* The data used in this survey is said to have been obtained "from the Business Expectations Enquiry" (p. 118). Such aspects as value of sales, value of stock, and capital formation by individual companies are either "provisional" or "estimates . . . awaiting final figures from the 1982 Census of Industrial Production." Evidently, no primary industrial census has been attempted in Kenya since 1974, a fact conceded by the Central Bureau of Statistics, the Ministry of Planning and National Development, and the government in *Development Plan 1989–1993.*
48. Interview with R.P. Chandaria, Nairobi, 1989.

49. Interview and questionnaire from True Foods and Kabazi Canners, 1989; see also file MCI/6/20, KNA, for a discussion on the role of the Chandaria family in establishing True Foods (then known as Pure Food).

50. R.P. Chandaria, director, to MCI, 10 November 1953, MCI/6/694, KNA.

51. Minutes of the ad hoc Committee on Drawbacks of Customs Duty, 17 November 1953, MCI/6/694, KNA.

52. Minutes of the Committee on Drawbacks, 5 December 1955, MCI/6/694, KNA.

53. Minutes of the Committee on Drawbacks, 5 December 1955, MCI/6/694, KNA.

54. Data from questionnaires to Galsheet, Mabati Rolling Mills, Kaluworks, Insteel, and other companies in the group. Also from interviews with Manu Chandaria and Dilip Chandaria and company reports, 1989.

55. The Comcraft Group data are from company reports, questionnaires, and interviews with the head of the group, Manu Chandaria, and Dilip Chandaria. For data on state companies, see Industrial and Commercial Development Corporation, *Annual Report, 1989.* The role of the Comcraft Group in Kenya is by no means limited to industry. The group's Chandaria Supplementary Foundation is involved in health and education activities, and in effect is one of the best organized and funded NGOs in Kenya (it was included in the survey of Kenyan NGOs by the Ford Foundation in 1988). In one of its largest projects, the foundation donated litter bins city-wide to Nairobi and Mombasa.

56. *East African Trade and Industry* report, "Madhvani Group," 1972.

57. *East African Trade* report.

58. L.N. Madhvani to MCI, 1954, MCI/9/678, KNA.

59. P. C. Harris, assistant secretary, MCI, 1960. MCI/6/697, KNA.

60. Minutes of the ad hoc committee, 16 August 1960, MCI/6/696, KNA.

61. *East African Trade* report, 1972.

62. Interview and questionnaire, Mr. Muthui Kariuki, Kenya Breweries Ltd. and Central Glass Ltd., 1989.

63. Colony and Protectorate, "Mombasa Survey," OP(EST)/1/465, KNA.

64. Manager, Kenya Glass Works Ltd., to MCI, 22 April 1954, MCI/9/554, KNA.

65. G.P. Henderson for the secretary for commerce and industry to the manager, Kenya Glass Works Ltd., 9 July 1954, MCI/9/554, KNA.

66. Secretary of state, Colonial Office, Circular 217, to the governor, August 27, 1941.

67. For this and other correspondence between MCI and MELL, see the period between 24 March 1952 to 1954, MCI/9/554, KNA.

68. G.P. Henderson, MCI, to the manager, the Kenya Glass Works, 9 July 1954.

69. East African Industrial Council (EAIC), *Progress Reports,* 7 February 1954, MCI/9/554, KNA.

70. EAIC, *Progress Reports,* 1954.

71. Medatally Manji has an excellent photographic history of the House of Manji, documenting key stages in the company's development—including the early days of the Ngara Bakery and Provision Store.

72. Interview with M. Manji, 1989.

73. Interview with M. Manji, 1989.

74. *East African Standard,* "House of Manji: How It All Started," 11 September 1980.

75. *Sunday Times,* Nairobi, 27 September 1953.

76. Baring's speech of 27 September 1954 is in GH/4/735, KNA.

77. Pictorial report in the London *Sunday Times Magazine,* "Biscuit Baron," February 16, 1986.

78. The group is also in Tanzania (Tanzania Food Corporation Ltd.). Source: Interview with Medatally Manji.

79. Interview with Mahendra Nagda, group planning/development manager, 1989.

80. From an interview with Lalit Pandit, chairman, East African Building Society, 1990, and the company's *Annual Review,* 1989.

81. File CS/1/16/35, KNA.

82. Association of Chambers of Commerce and Industry of Eastern Africa, resolution 13, Kisumu, February 1957, CS/1/16/35, KNA.

83. R.J. Mehta to Lennox-Boyd, 10 October 1957, CS/1/16/35, KNA.

84. For cases in which the Federation of Indian Chambers of Commerce (FICCI) intervened on behalf of its members see Board of Commerce and Industry, MCI/6/697, KNA. In the case of the noted match factory located in the white highlands, FICCI made several representations to the commerce minister and to the governor with little success. The issue resurfaced at the FICCI's 1959 annual meeting, with the governor in attendance. The chamber's president, K. P. Shah, castigated the government: "The Kenya Government through its Minister of Commerce and Industry is shouting from the housetops that it wants capital from outside to help develop industry in this country. But I regret to say that it is acting exactly in the opposite direction. Some Indian industrialists who purchased a match factory in the highlands area at Kinangop were not allowed to operate at the site which was built for that purpose, and made to remove the machinery. I ask the Government, is this policy going to help the industrialisation in the country?" MCI/6/722, KNA.

85. Earlier, in 1956, the Federation of Kenyan Employers (FKE) was established to "encourage the principal of the development and maintenance of good relations between employers and employees; to encourage the observance by employers of fair conditions of employment; to promote the interests of the members in relation to the foregoing stated objects. . . . " Quotation from the constitution of the FKE.

86. E. Hollister, director of APIEA, in a delegation to the acting governor, Mr. Griffith-Jones cited in *East African Standard,* "Firms Alarmed at Threat to End Duty Rebate," 25 October 1961.

87. *East African Standard,* "Kenya Firms Win Battle over Customs Duty Rebates," 18 November 1961.

88. Laws of Kenya, *Trade Licensing Act 1980* p. 5.

89. Mwai Kibaki, minister for commerce and industry, cited in the *Daily Nation,* 1 January 1969.

90. *Daily Nation,* 10 January 1969.

91. Mr. A. Sirali, chairman of the Kitale Town Council, cited in the *East African Standard,* 23 January 1968. See also Muller: "Kitale used to be a flourishing centre of a . . . farming area. As a result of Africanisation policies, it has changed into an insignificant rural town." From "The National Policy of Kenyanisation of Trade: Its Impact on a Town in Kenya," p. 301.

92. Mwai Kibaki, cited in the *Daily Nation,* 1 January 1969.

93. Interview, 1989.

94. KAM report, "Quit Notices," 1975.

95. J.B. Wanjui, chairman of KAM, to J.G. Kiano, the commerce minister, 25 February 1975. KAM files.

96. T.W. Tyrrell, KAM's executive officer, to the minister, 30 May 1975. KAM files.

97. A. Bennett, managing director of Chesebrough-Pond's Kenya Ltd. to E.T. Mwamunga, the commerce minister, 6 September 1977. KAM files.

98. J. Allan, managing director of Crown Paints & Building Products Ltd. to the permanent secretary, 27 October 1980. KAM files.

99. Harshad V. Patel, managing director of Auto Spring Manufacturers Ltd., to the permanent secretary, 12 November 1980. KAM files.

100. MCI press release, "Africanization of Commerce and Industry," 5 April 1967.

101. C.N. Kebuchi, MCI, to KAM, 3 August 1973, MCI/CONF 73/02 (246).

102. G.M. Matheka, permanent secretary, MCI, to all manufacturers, 29 November 1973, MCI/CONF 73/01 (143).

103. L.M. Kabetu, permanent secretary, MCI, to all manufacturers, 6 May 1974, MCI/CONF 73/02 (79).

104. L.M. Kabetu, permanent secretary, to KAM, 6 April 1976, MCI/A 93/9/01 (84).

105. J.G. Shamalla, permanent secretary, MCI, to KAM, 3 October 1980, TS.45/04/ (46).

106. E.T. Mwamunga, commerce ministry press release, 1981.

107. *Weekly Review* report, "Magnate Merali Increases Empire," 15 July 1988. See also *Financial Review,* "Who Is Buying the Town?" and "The House Alibhai Rebuilt," 5 December 1988.

108. Interview, P. K. Shah, sales director, Nairobi, Ken-Knit Ltd., and Eldoret Steel Mill Ltd., 1989.

109. Republic of Kenya, *Kenya: Export Processing Zones,* p. 7.

110. *Sunday Nation,* 28 June 1987.

111. For reports of misappropriation of funds by KNCCI see *Daily Nation,* 25 April 1983, *Standard,* 24 April 1985, *Sunday Times,* 7 September 1986, *Kenya Times,* 3 November 1989, and *Industrial Review,* September 1989.

112. *Industrial Review,* September 1989.

113. Kenya Association of Manufacturers report, "KAM Organization Structure."

114. For the territory covered by KAM reports see the Preface.

115. Swainson, *Corporate Capitalism,* pp. 125–126.

116. Swainson, *Corporate Capitalism,* p. 130.

3

African Entrepreneurs: Capitalists-in-Formation?

It is established in this chapter that Kenyan African businessmen do not yet constitute a significant force in Kenya's commercial or industrial activity. By the early 1990s, they still played a negligible role in Kenya's commercial and industrial sectors.

A number of explanations have been advanced to explain this poor performance, the most prevalent being that Africans were incapacitated by discriminatory barriers erected by the colonial state to prevent competition with immigrant communities. This view, however, does not take into account the fact that the most successful commercial and industrial entrepreneurs did not emerge from within the white settler community—which was state protected—but from the local Indian commercial community, as illustrated in the previous chapter. The success of the Indians had little to do with favorable treatment by the state, and everything to do with their experience, accumulated over a number of centuries, in East African coastal merchant activity. The protected white farmers discovered this truth when they failed successfully to compete with the Indians, even in the distribution trade of their own agricultural products, let alone in other commercial niches.

But to return to the Africans: contrary to the obstruction myth, various schemes to help Africans with finance and training were established, ironically as a state response to the widespread African business failures of the 1940s and 1950s. These schemes were largely unsuccessful in engendering a business culture that would lead to sizable and durable commercial and industrial activities by Africans during colonial rule.

The experience of African businesses in the postcolonial period does not significantly differ from the colonial phase: in effect, the period witnessed a replay of earlier failures. And not only were the post-1964 policies even less successful in reversing this, they introduced a contradiction into Kenya's development process. Whereas local nonblack and foreign capital was identified as the principal agency for the implementation of the industrialization plan, the Africanization of commerce and industry was perceived as a primary goal. Evidently, the latter policy placed the pro-Africanization forces and the forces that were to spearhead the industrialization drive on a collision course, although this need not have been the case if a more competent state had been at hand to mediate creatively between the various segments of capital and racial groups.

The First Widespread African Attempts to Enter Business

The civil service appears to have been the initial avenue for Africans to enter business, as both Leys and Kitching indicate. Leys points to African government employees who were able to accumulate some capital "in the course of wielding executive power on behalf of the colonial administration."[1] Kitching similarly found that Africans were able to begin petty trading in colonial times. Starting in the 1910s and expanding after 1925 with the establishment of Local Native Councils (LNCs), there was, said Kitching, "a considerable degree of overlap" between the LNC administrators and "the first group of African entrepreneurs."[2] Scope for further expansion using the public service avenue into business was limited, however, since African movement into higher administrative grades (and therefore into having access to larger state funding) was not a real option until independence. Thus, particularly in the early colonial period, this route of entry into business by Africans was very limited.

The Second World War marked the emergence of the independent market-place pattern of entry into business for Africans. They not only began to engage in a wider variety of businesses involving trading, transportation, and service industries (such as small eating-houses and general provision shops), but also set up some more complex enterprises, including limited liability companies and public companies. The main source of investment was the relatively large amounts of money from the earnings and gratuities of former soldiers who had participated in the war. The pooling of some of these earnings resulted in a boom in trade. Many companies were formed. It was reported, for example, that while trading by Africans was inconsequential prior to the Second World War, there was one shop per 360 head of population in some areas by 1946. A provincial commissioner reported:

> In the districts of Kiambu, Fort Hall, Nyeri and Machakos, there is a steady pressure from a large number of Africans for facilities to engage in trade. This pressure comes from all sections, including, queerly enough, existing traders, and refusal to allow more shops is merely construed as a device of the Administration to restrict trade to the African's detriment.[3]

In regard to the formation of limited liability and shareholding enterprises, the registrar of companies stated in 1950 that "The first companies incorporated by Africans were registered at the end of 1945," and that "1945, 1946 and 1947 were boom years, and to a lesser extent 1948, but there was a very great falling off in 1949 which has continued during the present year."[4] By 1949, seventeen African public companies with a nominal capital of Shs4,270,000, were incorporated. Africans had further established fifty-three private companies, with a nominal capital of Shs2,706,000.[5]

However, no sooner were most of these companies formed than they disintegrated. The problems seem to have been a lack of basic understanding of business goals, lack of experience in management, and lack of control of company finances. A 1945 report by the registrar of companies had already cautioned that African managers and promoters of companies were

> defrauding shareholders of the funds of companies which they are running. . . . [I]n such cases action has to be initiated by the shareholders themselves and, of course, the majority of Africans concerned have no knowledge of the provisions of the law and are, therefore, completely defenceless. . . . Some tightening up of the legislation on this score appears to be necessary.[6]

Five years later, the performance of African companies had worsened. A 1950 assessment by the registrar reported:

> I have looked into the files of all these Companies and do not think there is a single one whose affairs I can honestly describe as satisfactory. Generally speaking, the Companies are either not functioning at all, or functioning at a substantial loss, and in either case the capital assets of the Company are steadily being dissipated in management expenses and salaries. . . .
>
> Having only recently arrived in the country, I cannot express any opinion from personal experience, but from examining the files, it seems quite clear that none of the Africans forming companies have any idea of the duties or responsibilities they are incurring. It must also be appreciated that even where Africans attempt honestly and consistently to operate Companies, there are practical difficulties which do not exist in the case of other communities. For example, calling of a general meeting is exceedingly difficult when the members of a Company are almost all illiterate and have no postal addresses. Again, the fact that these members have no understanding whatever of the way in which a company should be run makes it impossible for them to produce any constructive criticism at such meetings as are held. . . .
>
> I cannot help feeling that legislation is necessary to control the formation of Companies by Africans. I fully realise the political dangers in that the cry of discrimination would at once be raised, but the fact remains that the Companies already incorporated by Africans during the last five years have collected from a vast number of African individuals a sum certainly in excess of 1 1/4 million shillings, of which by far the

greater part is now hopelessly lost.[7]

Government officials in other areas and departments arrived at the same conclusions and expressed similar concerns. A district officer in Nyeri responded that African aspirants at business lacked

> understanding of economic factors and business methods. . . . Capital without the ability to use it properly can achieve no improvement—it can merely lead to disaster on a grander scale. . . . This has been illustrated "the hard way" by the fate of Askari gratuities which were pooled to capitalize a large variety of enterprises in the immediate post war years.[8]

A brief review of two African companies of this era will serve to illustrate the nature of these enterprises as well as the predicament of the state. Luo Thrift & Trading Corporation Ltd. was formed in 1946 as a limited liability company. Between 1946 and 1950 the company grew at an astonishingly fast rate, expanding into numerous activities. These included a shop at Maseno (valued at Shs44,817), Ramogi House at Kisumu (Shs63,725), a printing press in Nairobi (Shs27,922) a lorry (Shs4,000), and miscellaneous activities (Shs12,400). The company had 1,100 African shareholders and a paid-up capital of Shs300,000.[9] The vision behind the formation of the company and its rapid expansion was described by Mr. Oginga Odinga, the managing director and future party leader, at the opening of Ramogi House in 1950:

> The Luo Thrift & Trading Corporation . . . had very humble beginnings. It started as a thrift association. . . . Our aims then and even thoughts were not only dim but could be said to be utterly confused. However, we groped our way until 1946 when a second idea flushed into our minds. A new shaft of light led us to the point of establishing a limited liability company. . . . The first large project of the Company was the establishment of the Ramogi Press in Nairobi. . . . As we were novices in this commercial venture we needed to publish and circulate such information as would infuse into our members strong love for our enterprise. . . . It may be of interest to you to know that the Press in question has been transferred from Nairobi to our town here—Kisumu. Meanwhile another and even bigger project was already budding. . . . I refer to the Maseno Store. This was erected [in] early 1948 when the Ramogi Press had been on for only [a] few months. . . . I come now to the subject of our today's assembly: the Ramogi House. The idea of a hotel was first mooted in 1948 by the Directors and was wholly approved by the members. . . . An attempt [was made] with a strong backing of Mr. Atkins [district commissioner, Central Nyanza] to obtain a loan from the Local Native Council but without a success. . . . Our funds were thinning out faster than we expected and in our hour of need we turned to the Diamond Jubilee Trust Ltd.[10]

With this impulsive approach to commercial undertakings, it was only a matter of time before the company went bankrupt. In fact, the same year that the company launched its largest project, Ramogi House, an official filed the following assessment of its performance with MCI:

> In September [1950] I was advised by the District Commissioner, Kisumu, that the corporation was in a parlous financial state and might shortly go into liquidation as it is heavily in debt to Asians. . . . Trading losses published in the prospectus so far are: August 1947 to December 1948—shs.38,126; 1949: shs.41,468; seven months of 1950: shs.9,877. . . . Ramogi House is now to be let to an Indian . . . to be run, I understand, as the Cosmopolitan Hotel. . . . It is all extremely shaky.[11]

In the second case a sum of six million shillings was raised from would-be shareholders by two Kikuyu businessmen, Mr. H.M. Kanja and Mr. Koigi, in order to form a company and take over the operations of a company under receivership: the Karatina Dried Vegetable Factory. The two African directors of the company-in-formation approached Mr. Stephen of Stephen, Gillett & Co. Ltd., for assistance with the technicalities of forming a company. Mr. Stephen reported to them that his concerns were mainly the lack of experience of the directors, the scale of the project, and the fate of its capital. On the question of experience, the African directors were advised:

> The management of a business having a capital of £300,000 needs, I am sure you and your colleagues realise, a great deal of experience and I, personally, do not feel that without the assistance of European directors it would be fair to encourage you to start this company. You know, as all the Africans in the Nyeri/Karatina district who have been to see me in the last six months must know, that I always give you frank advice. Do not, then, be in a hurry to form this company . . . [before you] gain experience of business in a hard world of competition with Europeans and Indians. . . .The majority of Africans who are going into business at this moment have seen, during the war particularly, something of the world, and have the desire to "advance"; these Africans, however, except in rare cases, have no business training or experience, and as I have warned you and your friends before, I have grave fears that you may find competition with the Indian or European very difficult for the first few years. Both the European and Indian when they are young go into business as assistants in some office or factory and start learning the simple things before they go on to learn the management of businesses. The Africans, however, who are starting companies and shops have, as a rule, no previous experience, and they will, I am afraid, learn about business the hardest way of all, which is by risking their money in trade, and in many cases losing it. . . .[12]

On the issue of sources of money and what was to be done with it, Mr. Stephen emphasized that:

> If you have started collecting money for the company you must, in my opinion, tell everyone that the company is not going to be formed for

some time, and give them the chance to have their money back; it would be unfair to do anything else.[13]

The government agreed, saying "such a company would be premature."[14]

The State's Role in Fostering African Capitalism, Pre-1963

Most published scholars in the field believe that the colonial state and immigrant minorities blocked African capital accumulation and participation in commerce and industry. For example, in explaining the poor performance of African businessmen after independence, Peter Marris and Anthony Somerset maintained that "the colonial administration was indifferent or restrictive, directing openings for trade towards immigrant communities. The isolation of African businessmen can be seen as a consequence of policies which ignored the opportunity to train and finance them."[15] And E.A. Brett in his analysis of the colonial phase held that their failure "stemmed directly from the limits imposed on the free operations of the market system by the State."[16] Nicola Swainson also writes of "the extensive restrictions placed in the way of indigenous capitalism."[17]

The truth is that as early as the mid-1940s, following the *Stirton Report on Rural Industries* (more on this below), the colonial state was establishing a remarkable network of infrastructural support aimed at engendering a business culture among Africans. Its reasons included such factors as the need to prevent rural-urban migration, to decentralize commerce and industry from the major centers of Nairobi and Mombasa, to provide Africans with useful skills—the "civilizing" mission—and to create employment. Perhaps the most compelling reason for facilitating African businesses was simply that African businesses which emerged on their own accord, especially after the Second World War, required a state response: they were not only unsuccessful but involved considerable malpractice. Many investors lost their money. Moreover, some sections of the state bureaucracy genuinely wanted to help Africans, a factor that cannot be dismissed however paternalist this may have been.[18] A voluminous body of records and minutes of commissions and advisory committees indicates that during the 1940s and 1950s almost all levels of the Kenyan state, including the Executive Council, became involved in the debate about African businesses, particularly in the aftermath of the failure of many of them. The Executive Council minuted in 1950:

> Council took note ... that the formation of companies by Africans was on the increase and that in many cases share certificates were issued and the Companies went bankrupt. .... This was leading to considerable hardship amongst African subscribers. Council advised that the matter

should be investigated by the Member for African Affairs and the Secretary of Commerce and Industry.[19]

The response of the various segments of the state bureaucracy varied, with two main views becoming predominant. One side wished to restrict licenses; the other sought a laissez-faire response. The latter view seems to have been adopted, with modifications. A provincial commissioner reported:

> The more we endeavour to keep down the number of shops by refusing licences on the grounds of redundancy, the more we will harden African opinion against us. . . . [T]he only way to deal with the problem is to allow the local authorities more latitude, and if certain Africans burn their fingers as they will, it will in the long run be a salutary lesson, and a lesson they must learn. Until they do . . . the African will not regard limitation as being in his interest. The African at the moment will not believe the hard economic facts of life, and the only way he will learn is by hard knocks. It is however necessary to limit the ill effects of the lesson as much as possible. . . . The District Commissioner should continually impress on the local authorities concerned that 500:1 is a reasonable ratio and that if they go much above that they will merely ruin existing traders.[20]

That officials gradually adopted the view that government had to intervene on behalf of African businesses by providing them with some form of guidance, as opposed to discouraging them altogether, is illustrated in various documents. The Nyeri district officer, for instance, reported:

> The Kikuyu traders have chosen their vocation and if they fail, as I believe very many of them will, for there are far too many for the District, it will be due to economic laws and their own shortcomings. But they will not easily be convinced of this, and will put the blame on Government and the other races of the Colony. . . . In spite of innumerable failures the enthusiasm for trade has in no way abated. . . . The question now arises as to whether the Government, in its capacity as trustee for the emergent communities, should attempt to temper the wind of normal economics to give Africans some protection and assistance while they gain experience and understanding of economics and commerce. We can already see the results of a policy of laisser faire. Much African capital and endeavour will be wasted. . . .[21]

In the view of this official, if the state did not assist Africans to enter business on proper lines, the main agencies of economic development would remain in non-African hands and capital would continue "to be subscribed by small African investors in African enterprises only to be lost on account of incapable management or deliberately fraudulent intent on the part of the promoters."[22]

Once it became official policy to assist African businesses, the state designed and initiated a number of schemes for that purpose, beginning, interestingly enough, in the early 1940s, with "quit notices" to some Indian traders. The practice was a forerunner of that which was to be repeated after independence. A report, classified as secret, by the Nairobi district commissioner's office in 1944, stated:

> There are 28 Indian lessees of stalls in the Nairobi Municipal Market. In addition Indians rent 15 stalls as stores. Their premises were built as stalls ... but were let as stores before the war since they were lying unused.... The Town Clerk is therefore serving notices on a number of these store lessees to quit within a reasonable period. Court action will be taken if they do not comply. These premises will be made available for African occupation.[23]

Kenyan literature on the subject for this period focuses primarily on restrictions on African credit, and African protests against these restrictions, rather than the aim of state policy, which was to channel credit into the hands of a new African entrepreneurial class capable of using it productively. To check loss of monies and high indebtedness among African businesses, the Credit to Africans (Control) Ordinance was amended (31 August 1948), not only to limit the credit given to an African by a non-African to Shs200, but to enable more competent traders to borrow larger sums of money "where application for such credit is made in writing and approved by an Attesting Officer."[24] Next was the drive to create mechanisms through which aspiring African businessmen could acquire more knowledge in such subjects as bookkeeping, marketing, and other matters deemed necessary by state agencies. MCI's Department of Trade and Supplies began to sponsor African traders to attend the Jeanes School, where they could acquire basic business skills. The full cost of subsistence and tuition for all candidates attending the school was underwritten by the department up to 1959.[25] A working party on assistance to African traders was set up by the Board of Industrial Development in the early 1950s. The objective of the working party, which was made up of state officials and leading businessmen, was to devise means through which the government could provide African traders with specialized financing and management assistance. The East African Royal Commission of 1953–1955 also recommended financial aid through special programs, although it cautioned that it was "clearly dangerous to offer Africans terms so easy that their education in the hard facts of economics is delayed, and even hindered."[26]

A number of specialized schemes along these lines had been implemented throughout the 1940s and they continued up to 1963. One of these schemes was formulated in the 1945 *Stirton Report*. "Rural industries" included brick and tile manufacturing, handicrafts, tannery industries, and the manufacturing of curios for export and the tourist trade. This scheme was implemented from 1946 until the early 1960s, although its commercial implications met resistance from white settlers who saw it as a threat to their own industries. The East African Tanners' Association, for example, protested that "an established tanning industry" already existed in Kenya and that to involve the African was "unnecessary waste of time and money."[27] A government official responded: "I do not anticipate that the introduction of such a village craft will in any way affect the established Kenya tanning industry."[28]

By the mid-1950s, the working party was advocating an increase in credit to what it called "more progressive" African businessmen. It was felt that the substantial number who were graduating from the Jeanes schools at Kabete and Maseno could perform better than previously. Consequently, the Credit to Africans (Control) Ordinance of 1948 was amended, in 1957, raising the credit ceiling tenfold, from Shs200 to Shs2,000, and in selected cases more than this.[29]

Perhaps the most ambitious program was Loans to African Industrialists, Artisans and Businessmen, a scheme that became operational in 1956. The program was designed to provide working capital and credit for other requirements to more able Africans in the commercial and industrial sectors (but not agriculture). The loan ceiling was raised to Shs10,000: applications in excess of that amount had to be processed by the commerce ministry instead of local boards or loan committees. The stated policy objective was that

> Africans should be trained and possibly be given financial assistance so as to operate their own commercial projects or small industrial concerns. This work, which has already begun, will continue over [a] considerable number of years and will be progressive in its effect.[30]

The applicant had to be an African who had "established himself in a trade, business or industry" and who had "indicated through his own efforts that he has the necessary ability to operate his business with a reasonable measure of success," or had "a suitable qualification granted by a recognised technical school."[31] The security for loans included "a simple agreement" at the discretion of the local board or loan committee. This scheme was operative up to 1965/66, when the ICDC took over responsibility for financing small businesses.[32]

Among other projects attempted by state officials as the 1960s drew closer was the creation of African chambers of commerce. The Kiambu African Chamber of Commerce was one of the first. Ministry officials maintained that "we regard it as most important that these African chambers should be established on a proper basis. . . . We have in mind establishing some kind of model draft . . . which could be used for other districts." In 1959 the local district commissioner wrote to the registrar of societies to say that the Kiambu African Chamber of Commerce was close to becoming a reality.

> I enclose a copy of the proposed constitution [he wrote] . . . , signed by
> the inaugural President and Secretary, Mr. D.W. Waruhiu and Mr. James
> Njenga Karume respectively. I recommend the Chamber for registration
> as a Society and shall be grateful if you will approve the registration as
> soon as possible.[33]

However, such projects did not engender a notably successful class of
African commercial or industrial entrepreneurs by the end of colonial
rule. In the mid-1950s reports such as the following were still common:

> Though the African in Kenya, particularly the Kikuyu, has shown that
> he is anxious to participate in trade and industry, . . . his initial attempts
> in this direction have not been successful, mainly because of his lack of
> experience in business matters and his limited education. The conception
> of the Limited Liability Company with all its attendant duties and
> responsibilities, is one which has not been grasped readily. . . . We found
> . . . that the African tends to be an individualist who resents any form of
> organisation in his commercial activities, and this tendency will have to
> be overcome before there can be a really profitable partnership with him
> in such activities. I think that the Kikuyu are likely to realise the advan-
> tages . . . more quickly than others.[34]

The Loans to African Industrialists, Artisans and Businessmen Scheme
had its troubles too. The commerce ministry's permanant secretary stated
in 1959:

> We seem to be faced with too many traders and a marked reluctance to
> repay loans. . . . [A] great deal of work will be required before we can
> adjust the attitude of mind which is clearly holding up the implementa-
> tion of the scheme. . . . Mr. Parkin and myself believe that there is
> considerable need for it to enable the better African traders to compete
> . . . with the Asians.[35]

There was also concern about management and marketing problems
facing African companies. In an interdepartmental letter, an MCI official
stated:

> I have been visited on the 13th May, 1959, by the Secretary and two
> Directors of the Akamba Handcraft Industries Ltd. . . . They had received
> letters from America and with proper guidance they will no doubt be
> able to establish a successful trade. On the other hand without proper
> guidance they might well antagonise the American buyers who could not
> be aware of the circumstances. I shall be grateful if you feel that you could
> give the company any assistance or advice in resolving their problems.[36]

His correspondent replied that "although it is not possible to take any
active part in their affairs I will do my best to put them on the right track."[37]
The schemes summarized above and the positive tone in some of the

correspondence call into question the conventional wisdom on the attitude of the colonial state with regard to Kenyan African businessmen.

Problems of Entrepreneurship Among Africans: Postcolonial Era

The assumption that black Kenyans had been excluded by the colonial state from participating in private enterprise was widely shared by the postindependence African leadership and government bureaucracy. *Development Plan 1964–1970,* for example, stated that "many of the economic opportunities which existed in Kenya have not been available to Africans." To reverse this, the government "will promote vigorously increased African participation in every sphere of the nation's economy."[38] And the Kenyan National Assembly heard many speeches similar to the following in the early 1960s: "During the days of the colonial regime the foreigners tried to protect some of their big businessmen.... We must have a sort of monopoly so as to get our people into business."[39] This view was still influential in government circles during the 1980s. In a paper presented at the Industrial Strategy Conference in 1986, an official with the Ministry of Planning and National Development stated that "indigenous (Africans) were virtually excluded" from commerce and industry.[40]

One of the main agencies responsible for facilitating African businesses, the ICDC, administered four main programs. The Small Industrial Loans Scheme assisted small African businesses in simple production; the Commercial Loans Scheme financed African traders to expand their activities; the Property Loans Scheme was to help Africans purchase or construct commercial premises; while the Small Loans to Purchase Shareholdings Scheme was to enable Africans to purchase shares in larger companies.[41] Another scheme, established in 1967, was Kenya Industrial Estates (KIE), which initially was a subsidiary of the ICDC but became autonomous in 1978. KIE's main purpose was to provide industrial sheds, machinery, and equipment to African manufacturers.[42] Another ICDC subsidiary, the Kenya National Trading Corporation (KNTC), was created in 1965 for the localization-Africanization-Kenyanization-indigenization of the distributive trade. The KNTC aimed to achieve this goal through a monopoly in the marketing of some essential commodities, starting with salt and sugar. The list of commodities was expected to be enlarged eventually to include most locally manufactured products. The main goal of the KNTC was, in effect, to nurture African independent businessmen by appointing them its agents throughout Kenya. Part of its agenda was also to participate in the takeover of noncitizen businesses that were to be handed over to Africans.

The Industrial Development Bank (IDB) was created to supplement the efforts of the ICDC in providing loans for industrial projects. Two pieces of legislation were passed to enforce and assist ICDC and its subsidiaries to achieve these goals: the Trade Licensing Act, 1967, and the Import, Export and Essential Supplies Act, 1967. The former excluded non-Africans from trading in noncentral areas while the latter enforced the monopoly position of KNTC in the wholesale and retail trade of key commodities, mainly sugar and salt.

However, as indicated in Chapter 2, the Africanization of commerce and industry almost never got off the ground, not just because the agencies responsible for implementation of such policies barely functioned (see Chapter 5) but because of problems of entrepreneurship among Kenyan Africans. Among these problems was the issue of creditworthiness, an issue that was continually being raised by Kenyan Indian capitalists and foreign investors. The state was attempting to force them to appoint Africans as the distributors of manufactured products, and while there is evidence that Kenyan manufacturers were not opposed to such involvement, they questioned the Africans' ability to handle it—especially with regard to the issue of credit. In fact, KAM asked the Kenyan government to help them with a remedy for this by cosponsoring a Credit Guarantee Scheme for African traders. The KAM letter proposed guaranteeing credit:

> on a "say 50% of cred: given" basis. The need for such a scheme is brought out by lack of cash, on the part of most African traders, thus reducing their ability to carry large enough stocks to ensure full distribution. . . . The inability to establish credit worthiness or to control cash flows is no reflect on upon African traders but due to lack of experience, which must in some way be countered.[43]

The government most often ignored such suggestions or did not grasp their implications. It also seemed unaware of the conflict between the desire for rapid industrialization and the desire for Africanization. For example, six years after the above quoted letter, the commerce minister told KAM:

> The Government is very desirous to expand the manufacturing sector of our economy and wishes to maintain the closest co-operation with all manufacturers for the rapid growth of our economy. The Government directive to appoint citizens as distributors of locally manufactured products is aimed at promoting Africanization of the economy without in any way affecting adversely the growth of industries in this country.[44]

For Africans who did acquire distributorships, what followed was more or less a repeat of the problems of the 1940s and 1950s. Mr. S.J. Fabian, the managing director of Firestone (EA) Ltd., describing in an interview his firm's experience with African distributors, said:

> The experiment of African distributors of Firestone tires in the early 1970s was disastrous. They assumed that goods delivered to them were

their profits before sale and payment for these goods to us the manufacturers. Firestone had to resort to "COD," that is, Cash On Delivery, or bankers' guaranteed checks, which most of them could not understand or afford. This led to the collapse of many of these African "businessmen" who were now forced to sell their businesses at half their value, often to their previous owners. Credibility which is imperative in business remains the main shortcoming for African businessmen. Regrettably this can be said of most government ministries and companies as well.[45]

Mr. Fabian's views can be collaborated by studying the fate of state corporations responsible for facilitating African business. Most of these agencies were adversely affected by the extremely high rate of loan defaults by their African clients (not to mention their own incompetence, as shown in Chapter 5). As early as 1972, for example, the International Labour Office (ILO) had found that KNTC had run up losses of KShs16 million. The high rate of defaults and bankruptcy among its African clients led the corporation to abandon credit trading in favor of cash-on-delivery arrangements (as was practiced by Firestone), while the corporation was also failing to supply surviving retailers.[46] The government's reaction to the lack of business skills and loan defaults of African businesses in the early phase of independence was denial. Some MPs began to blame the failure of African retailers on government for issuing too many trading licenses to too many traders, asserting, for example, that there were "too many traders competing among themselves."[47] In 1964, the commerce minister, Dr. J.G. Kiano, claimed that the high rate of defaults was due to a lack of field officers in the ICDC—a lack he said he would remedy by increasing its staff "to supervise the use of loans." He further promised that "as a matter of fact . . . there will be no defaulters at all under the supervision of the ICDC."[48]

However, by 1969 it was increasingly evident that more fundamental causes were at work. The types of management problem that began to result in the collapse of many new African companies led a new commerce minister, Mr. Mwai Kibaki, to lament in the National Assembly:

> The management available from our people has been really inadequate. It has been inadequate and there is no point for any hon. Member in this House pretending otherwise. . . . [T]he truth is that the managerial cadre, the people who have been dealing with the responsibilities, have not really performed to the satisfaction either of their shareholders, or anyone in the Government. This is continuing to be with us. Above all, there should be more integrity than there has been right up to now.[49]

More objective ministers and MPs had already recognized what was at play. For example, the minister for labor, Mr. E.N. Mwendwa, warned in 1968 that "unless there are long-term plans to train Africans to fill management jobs, they will be seriously embarrassed and may even be forced out of business in the not-too-distant future."[50] As far back as 1964, one

MP had anticipated the problems that would arise from lack of business experience, and from the faulty assumptions on which new programs to assist Africans were being initiated. He told the assembly: "Giving loans in itself is not sufficient. I would say that the Ministry or Government should take some drastic steps to enable our people to understand business methods."[51] Another MP, perplexed by the evictions of non-Africans from their businesses, coupled with lack of skills on the part of their African replacements, and the confrontational manner in which this was sometimes done, said:

> Instead of sending people away from this country, he [the Minister] should keep them here, so that the African small traders can be taught, be given directions as to handle their business and keep their cash books properly.[52]

In fact, most African Kenyans who entered business via the marketplace route did not make much headway under the government programs. The list of initially promising African commercial and manufacturing firms that collapsed due to either management or financial difficulties includes J.K. Industries Ltd., Unisack Ltd., Madhupaper International, and the Chui Soap Factory; and in the banking sector, Continental Bank Ltd. and Rural and Urban Credit Finance Ltd. Perhaps the most spectacular of all the failed projects was that of the Continental Credit Finance Company. Established in 1979 by Philip Wahome, the company's early success was shown by the fact that it founded a subsidiary in 1982 (Continental Bank of Kenya), becoming the first commercial bank in Kenya started by a black Kenyan. By 1983 the company had not only undergone further expansion but had created several other subsidiaries, all of which was valued at over KShs757 million, with loans exceeding the magic half-a-billion shillings. By the sheer magnitude of the failure of these operations "the city's financial district had been severely jolted."[53]

When Continental Group was placed under receivership, along with most other African companies in banking and manufacturing, nearly all of which collapsed in 1985–1987, it was found that these companies shared one problem: mismanagement. In the case of Continental Credit Finance and its burgeoning subsidiaries, it was reported that "too much money apparently led to a chaotic 'each for himself greed-syndrome' as directors competed against each other for grabbing the biggest slices of loans."[54] A chapter in the story of African credit companies was closed in January 1990 when the Kenyan government took over five ailing African financial enterprises (the Business Finance Company, the Estate Finance Company of Kenya, Home Savings and Mortgages, the Estate Building Society, and the Citizen Building Society) to form a new state bank (Consolidated Bank) with expatriate management.[55] Twelve additional such banks, often termed *political banks*—they thrive on political connections rather than business acumen—were closed by the Kenya government in April 1993 under pressure from the donor community to end corruption (see Part II).

Clearly, the underlying source of the problems in these companies cannot have been the deeds of the state or the immigrant communities, as is often claimed. It had more to do with the fundamental issues of a continued lack of entrepreneurship, involving such aspects as vision, management, and the ability to conceive and execute investment plans. In their 1971 study, Marris and Somerset, who speculate that it was the colonial state that hindered African business, nevertheless found plenty to criticize in the characteristics of African entrepreneurship. They wrote:

> The lack of higher learning, which provides his incentive, also isolates him [i.e., the African businessman]. He does not have the sophistication or social contacts to handle confidently his relationships within the economic system of which he is part. He is suspicious and hostile towards the Asian suppliers on whom he depends, and shy of banks. . . . This insecurity drives him back upon a mistrustful, self-reliant style of management, where he attempts to keep all aspects of the business under the control of himself and his partners—whom he may not trust either. . . . In these circumstances he appeals for further training, more capital, more restrictions on Asian competition, without seeing the underlying sources of frustration in his style of management.[56]

A local observer writing in 1965 placed an even stronger emphasis on the impact of traditional values on African businesses:

> [African] entrepreneurs are expected to share their incomes with other members of the extended family. They are expected to come to aid in case of financial hardships and to employ relatives regardless of whether they are efficient. These considerations lead to a withdrawal of a substantial amount of capital from an enterprise and its eventual failure. Bonds of the family and the tribe [block] the formation of partnerships and limited liability companies.[57]

Local observers were endorsing these judgements in the mid-1970s:

> Most African businessmen started off with limited horizons and limited resources. They could move into Nairobi's River Road, formerly dominated by Asian shopkeepers who were being given quit notices. It took, so they thought, little skill to run a shop and the ICDC or some banks advanced money. . . . But shop-keeping is not as easy as it looks. Within a short period of time a good many of the African businessmen who had taken over from the Asian shopkeepers had lost most of their capital and turned thriving shops into bars and lodging rooms instead. Others were inviting back previous owners as partners. And some were trying to blame their failures on competition which they claimed was being generated by Asians still operating in the retail or wholesale [trade]. Compounding their problems was their general reluctance to employ competent personnel to man their businesses. Instead they relied on

relatives and close friends, with all too predictable consequences. With this kind of experience, it is unlikely that they will have the vision or courage to venture beyond the small business area into a more competitive field where skills and stamina count.[58]

In my interviews with bankers and African and local Indian business-men, I was told time and again that a continued lack of entrepreneur-ship and persisting cultural values were the main drawbacks for Africans, as summed up in the following sampling of interviews. An African executive in an international bank candidly told me:

> African businessmen tend to act and behave like "chiefs" running things themselves, or their close relatives, a problem that makes them reluctant to employ qualified personnel. It is not rare to find an African businessman whose position in his company is all things— managing director, chairman, production manager, public relations manager, the marketing director, and chief accountant. This problem is further complicated by the fact that professional consultancy is nonexistent, and therefore there is no cost control and no cash-flow projection. Such a business person merely sees money in the bank, his buildings, or machinery, but is completely unaware of the viability of his project, a serious shortcoming that soon results in bankruptcy. They also tend to engage in too many businesses at the same time, a practice that automatically reduces concentration. It is not rare to find an African businessman that is all things at the same time—a *matatu*— owner, a farmer, a trader and a transporter.[59]

According to the same executive, "traditional values" that also under-mine African commercial and industrial undertakings include fascina-tion with unproductive investments, especially in land:

> Almost all African businessmen still have a sentimental value for land. Rather than plough profits back into their businesses, they transfer them to purchasing land that has little economic value. Bank overdrafts provided for capital purposes are, in such cases, trans-ferred to farms, often resulting into quarrels with their bankers, thereby undermining their future source of credit and expansion.[60]

An independent African businessman confirmed these views, contend-ing that African businessmen were still learning:

> This has taken a longer time than anticipated. The main problem is lack of concentration in a single commercial endeavour which an entrepreneur knows best and can therefore master instead of spread-ing him thin in a variety of unrelated activities. Additional problems are related to cultural hangovers, for example fascination with rural homes even when one no longer resides in a rural setting. Dual homes "eat" money. But the most damaging problem is the inability by [the] African businessman to delegate responsibilities to those who know best, and the insistence on doing everything for himself. It is, therefore,

a fact that African businessmen do not fully grasp the concept of money and how to transform it into capital. This problem results in their reaching a ceiling prematurely. Money for most of them is just notes, with little understanding of such complexities as interests, percentages, credit technicalities, etc. The result is an extraordinary rate of failure among African businesses. It is the younger, educated generation that will replace the current breed of African businessmen that might learn from their parents' mistakes and participate in business on an equal footing with Indians.[61]

A local Indian industrialist agreed, noting unrealistic expectations for quick results in business by both the state and African businessmen themselves:

Business, like any other field, evolves and goes through a period of growth. It is not just a matter of taking an executive chair or legislation. The African business failures through the 1970s must be understood in the evolutionary context. Indian businessmen have a longer historical participation, and some of their family members had a chance to go overseas and expand their business horizons. But it is the same evolutionary process from which their success comes.[62]

With the failure of mainstream African businesses, the Kenyan state was forced to turn to the informal sector. This was a strategy for creating African capitalists it had long resisted. The turning point was reached in 1986 when it was stated in *Sessional Paper No. 1 on Economic Management for Renewed Growth* that:

The informal sector suffers from a negative public image, yet it possesses many positive characteristics and has a vital role to play. . . . [Informal sector] activities require very little capital to create jobs, rely primarily on family savings, often provide their own skill training at no cost to the Government, and are a prime training ground for future African entrepreneurs. . . . They fulfil key functions in support of agriculture and other local production by marketing inputs such as fertilizer, making and selling small tools, maintaining vehicles and equipment, marketing produce, and providing local inhabitants with a wide range of inexpensive basic consumer goods and services for everyday life. Small local firms can be especially efficient at producing bulky or heavy items such as building materials, especially bricks and tiles, and furniture, thus saving on transport costs.[63]

The *Development Plan 1989–1993* confessed to an "omission," stating:

Since the attainment of independence, Government has given strong support to the industrial and commercial sectors of the economy. . . . Apart from structural problems that have since emerged. . ., a serious omission has been the neglect in exploiting the full potential of the small-scale and Jua Kali [informal] sector enterprises. This potential can no longer be ignored.[64]

The 1992 *Economic Survey* further acknowledged the potential of the informal sector, but falsely claimed that government policy all along had "enhanced its growth."[65] As to the potential, the survey explained that the success of *jua kali*

> results from the multiplicity of the informal sector activities, the use of simple and inexpensive technologies which do not require specialised skills, its higher labour intensity and ease of entry. These factors permit the informal sector to generate more jobs rapidly with very little capital investment.[66]

It is ironic that this strategy had already been formulated in the mid-1940s and was implemented throughout the 1950s. A 1945 report on rural industries argued in strikingly similar terms:

> It is quite obvious that anything requiring large capital and the importation of expensive machinery are not within Africans' means just yet, and that the smaller war time industries at present tiding over a period of want must have a doubtful future. It is essential, therefore, to commence at rock-bottom and to look to the future in the industrious African who is catering for the peoples' needs. The man with his own workshop, the man who can train apprentices in the shop where time is important, the man who will employ other craftsmen, the man who will utilise power when the stage of his business needs it, and the man who can keep pace with progress of the times. The production of building materials, building construction, black-smithing and repairing, tailoring, spinning, weaving, bicycle repairing, lorry and car repairing, cart making, soap making, furniture making, pottery and other crafts in a small way may not be regarded as fully fledged industries, but ... these form the only basis ... upon which can be built a standard of industry that will cater to African markets, and ultimately absorb large numbers of persons in employment not directly concerned with the land. *Hence the reason for the suggested concentration of activity on minor works already established, in preference to frantic efforts to introduce something that is likely to fade out with the first signs of failing enthusiasm.*[67]

In 1972 the ILO had suggested in its report that instead of harassing the informal sector government should promote it.[68] With UNDP and UNIDO, the ILO became a keen advocate of informal, *jua kali* capitalism. A main reason for this support was the fact that the *jua kali* sector proved to be the most dynamic entrepreneurial training ground for Africans, notwithstanding its postindependence neglect by the state until the noted 1986 shift in policy due to the failure of Africanization.

If the considerable technical skills accumulated by *jua kali* entrepreneurs had escaped the attention of the state, this was not the case with the large-scale firms. They began to subcontract to small businesses in an attempt to cut production costs. Studies done by the Kenya Management Assistance Programme (K-Map) suggest that some sophistication had been acquired by *jua kali* operators, noting the extent to which subcontracting had evolved. The industrial subsectors in which this was taking place on a relatively large scale included furniture, the garment industry, and construction. The large firms provided design and quality control mechanisms. In 1990 Morara reported:

> Already, there are firms in Kenya experimenting on sub-contracting through supplier development programmes. A case in point is the manufacturing of car seats and upholstery through sub-contracting . . . to small stitching firms . . . and even individuals; they retain quality and design control. Even in the construction industry . . . sub-contracting seems to have taken root in this country.[69]

In Part II of this book there is a brief review of the impact of the support provided by the UNDP, ILO, and UNIDO to *jua kali* entrepreneurs, especially attempts to link them to medium- and large-scale firms in the formal sector through a centralized exchange network.

Routes for Entry to Business—MNCs and Civil Service

In the following pages we consider the two other paths of accumulation for Africans, namely, directorships in foreign companies and employment in the Kenyan civil service. The MNC route was highlighted by Swainson, who identified two subgroups in this pattern of accumulation. On the one hand, some Africans who became directors in foreign companies acquired substantial shares in them; on the other hand, African directors acquired technical know-how that enabled them to establish their own companies and even to compete with their former employers. Using shareholding as evidence of accumulation has been questioned by Kitching (among others). Kitching aptly remarked that "evidence on shareholding is itself a very partial guide to crucial issues of control and accumulation. In any case what is required in assessing possible or likely trajectories of indigenous Kenyan capitalists is evidence of a dynamic process."[70] There is even more of a problem in citing the cases of the companies formed by Africans on the basis of technical know-how obtained from MNCs. Two companies, Chui Soap Factory and Tiger Shoes Company, were used by Swainson to illustrate manufacturing enterprises founded by former African directors who began to compete with their former MNC employers. Writing in 1987, she asserted that

> the Tiger Shoes Company and the Chui Soap Factory were both set up in direct competition with powerful multinationals (Bata Shoe Company and Uniliver, respectively). It was during this period, also, that financial institutions and commercial banks were extending special loan schemes to African industrialists.[71]

The challenge posed to Bata by Tiger Shoes Company was grossly overstated. Bata's annual sales are over KShs1 billion, compared with Tiger Shoes' sales of KShs24–25 million.[72] And while Tiger Shoes did enjoy rapid expansion up to 1976, it then began to experience financial and management difficulties. From the late 1970s, the company was on the verge of collapse and was frequently under receivership in the 1980s.[73]

In the case of Chui Soap Factory (which actually collapsed in the late 1970s), it is difficult to envisage it competing with Uniliver's East Africa Industries, a company with an annual turnover of over KShs3 billion, a direct workforce of 1,700, and a nationwide network of two thousand wholesalers and twenty thousand retailers.[74]

By far the most important launching pad for African businessmen during the postindependence period was the civil service, which gave senior government officials and politicians access to loans and influence. But here, too, a rapid rise was to be followed by disintegration of the enterprises created. The experience of GEMA illustrates this pattern. During its peak years, in the mid-1970s, GEMA was described by Swainson as

> representing the dominant fraction of the Kenyan bourgeoisie. It is developing into the main arm of Kenyan industrial capital. This associa- tion is not only used to consolidate the political position of this bourgeois class but more important, spearheads the move of indigenous capital into production.[75]

Writing in 1978, Leys also saw the emergence of "mass investment companies, of which the prototype is Gema Holdings Corporation."[76] Both Swainson and Leys overstated GEMA's potential through their disregard of its overdependence on the state. GEMA's leadership in- cluded Mr. Njenga Karume, the only non–civil service businessman in- volved in beer and cigarette distribution continuously since the 1950s. With his friend Kenyatta in power, Karume also served as a nominated member of Parliament. Other GEMA leaders were Kikuyu ministers and heads of key state corporations. These included Duncan Ndegwa (the first African head of the civil service before becoming governor of the Central Bank of Kenya in the mid-1960s); Kihika Kimani (chairman of KANU's Nakuru branch); Mr. E. Matu Wamae (executive director of the Industrial and Commercial Development Corporation); Mr. M. Gecau, (chairman of the East African Power and Lighting Company); the minister of fi- nance, Mr. Mwai Kibaki; and the commerce minister, Dr. Julius Kiano.[77] Others in GEMA included John Muchuki (executive chairman of the Kenya Commercial Bank) and President Kenyatta's daughter, Margaret Kenyatta (who was mayor of Nairobi and women's treasurer of GEMA's Nairobi branch).[78] In effect, through its control of state machinery and political power, GEMA came close to eclipsing the ruling party, KANU.

It increasingly became the vehicle for ensuring the domination of national affairs by the Kikuyu ethnic group. The *Weekly Review,* looking back in 1989 on GEMA, said it

> became the vehicle for advancing the more chauvinistic and parochial tribalist elements among the Kikuyu with the two other groups, the Embu and the Meru being a little more than hangers-on. . . . One of GEMA's principal objectives was clearly to ensure that the presidency would never leave the "House of Mumbi" (Kikuyu hands). . . . [T]he change-the-constitution conspiracy of 1976 saw GEMA take the lead in calling for an amendment of the constitution to bar an incumbent vice president from automatically succeeding the president.[79]

With this contentious backdrop involving excessive concentration of tribal political and economic power over national affairs, it was only too predictable what a new leadership in Kenya would do, especially one that had been subjected to considerable political harassment at the hands of GEMA, as Moi had been. On becoming president in 1978, Moi convened a leaders conference, resolving that all tribal organizations, including GEMA, should disband. After this, high-profile names in GEMA could not survive, either in the political or the economic realm. A fierce struggle ensued among the directors for control of GEMA's properties: mainly, two farms totalling 75,000 acres (valued at KShs35 million) and supporting seven thousand livestock (KShs7.3 million), and 75 percent of Clayworks Ltd. (a brick factory worth KShs21.3 million).[80] The highly publicized conflict recalled the character of African businesses in the 1940s reviewed above. GEMA's directors were accused of using their positions to acquire personal wealth at the expense of the 3,555 members of the Ndumberi Farmers Company and the 7,000 members of the Embakasi Ranching Company, among others.[81] An internal committee set up to investigate the financial situation of GEMA revealed that it had incurred debts of over KShs10 million.[82] In an episode that indicated how quickly things changed after Kenyatta, the formerly dominant Kikuyu circle that had monopolized the key positions in government and state corporations were forced, as leaders of GEMA, to make appearances in court.[83] Karume eventually took control of what remained of GEMA Holdings (renamed Agricultural and Industrial Holdings Ltd.), with President Moi's help. The president declared Karume's main rival in GEMA, Kihika Kimani, as unfit to participate in public life and Kihika lost all his positions in the group, including his directorships.[84] A local magazine later said: "President Daniel arap Moi intervened in the former GEMA Holdings leadership wrangle and declared that Mr. Kihaka Kimani was not yet fit to re-emerge on the national political scene."[85]

As a route to becoming successful in business for themselves, it would appear that the MNCs and civil service had not been very productive for

Africans. Notable success was found only among those Africans who either remained chief executives of MNCs and large local public companies, or who were in partnerships with local Indian or local white businessmen. Those who remained chief executives of MNCs included such distinguished and able African managers as Mr. J.W. Wanjui (a former director of the ICDC in the 1960s) who has been executive chairman of East Africa Industries since the 1970s. Another, Mr. B.M. Gecaga (a former civil servant in the colonial period in the department of the registrar general) has also been the chairman of British American Tobacco (BAT) for almost two decades. Executives of large public companies include the chairmen of such companies as Kenya Breweries Ltd. (along with KBL's subsidiary, Central Glass Ltd.), and the Unga Group Ltd. In 1989–1990, KBL was under the chairmanship of Mr. Jeremiah Gitau Kiereini (the first African district commissioner of Embu, in 1962). Kiereini was permanant secretary in the Ministry of Defence during the crucial years of 1970–1971 when Kenya was expanding its military infrastructure; and chief secretary to the government in 1979–1984, an influential position that meant he was also secretary to the cabinet, as well as permanent secretary to President Moi. Established by settlers in 1922, KBL is, perhaps, the single largest corporation in Kenya, estimated to be worth KShs190 billion, with a workforce of 4,700 (excluding transporters, stockists, and wholesalers) and a technical management that includes ten expatriates. KBL is probably the largest taxpayer in the country: it augmented the Kenyan national revenues in the fiscal year 1988/89 by KShs3.6 billion, or KShs300 million a month.[86]

The Unga Group Ltd., another settler-established company, was under the chairmanship of Duncan Ndengwa, who reportedly controls 50 percent of the company's shares with another African. Besides milling activities, the Unga Group has continued to expand. New industrial projects include Elianto Ltd. and Ufuta Ltd. (both in edible oil), which were established in the 1980s with Italian expertise and management.[87]

Examples of African partnerships with local nonblack businessmen include the highly successful Mareba Enterprises Ltd., a manufacturer of tiles established in 1972 by the joint efforts of an African politician, Mr. Moody Awori (assistant minister for tourism), and Mr. Horacias da Gama Rosa, a local Goan. The company is managed by Mr. Gerard Vaz, a local Goan.[88] Another successful local partnership was that of Mr. Kenneth Matiba and Mr. Stephen G. Smith, a local European, in Alliance Hotels, a group formed in 1970.[89] Matiba is another African with a civil service background. In the early 1960s he was a higher education officer; and later he was permanent secretary in a number of ministries (including commerce and industry). After moving into the management of KBL, he entered politics in the late 1970s.

The difference between these success stories and the record of most

African private companies has been the full-time commitment and professional management of the nonpolitical participants. This has ensured continuity and concentration, and business survival has become much less dependent on political survival. In the case of Alliance Hotels, for example, the nonpolitical partner manages the group's business while Matiba is in politics. It is worth noting that the experience of local whites resembles that of Africans: both groups have performed relatively better in public companies, rather than private companies. An example of a public company with local white management is Car and General (a manufacturer of rubber products and assembler of a number of products, such as refrigerators), under the chairmanship of Mr. F.J. Addly.[90] Another is Timsales (incorporating Amalgamated Saw Mills and Sokoro Sawmill). This company, a market leader in timber products, is managed by Mr. G.B. Jennings.[91]

A Period of Learning?

In summary, it is evident that entrepreneurship in the early 1990s among Kenyan Africans was still very limited in scope. The state support system that set out to nurture African businessmen in the 1940s and 1950s did not appear to have succeeded. Various schemes had to be introduced in the aftermath of widespread African business failures in the 1940s. These involved both training and financing, endeavors in which local non-African entrepreneurs participated. The postcolonial era witnessed a replay of these 1940s failures on a larger scale. Policies based on the belief that other social forces had blocked African success were even less successful in producing African entrepreneurs—and at the same time they undermined previous mediation between racial segments of capital and sectoral interests.

As we see in Chapter 5, part of the problem had to do with the fact that the Kenyan state apparatus was itself unravelling in the frenzied process of Africanization of the civil service. It was in this period that the "public service" pattern of African entry into business was established: public servants responsible for policy formulation and implementation tried to become businessmen themselves. This overlapping of state personnel and African businesses rarely led to success in business—but it did largely succeed in undermining the civil service.

Possibly the period from the late 1940s to the 1990s was a period of learning—a period for the acquisition of entrepreneurial skills by Africans, laying a foundation for future African capitalism. It is a fact that there are African Kenyans who have acquired enormous wealth in the process. However, the existence of such people does not establish as a fact that a productive class of capitalists has been formed; that must be established on the basis of appropriate evidence.

Notes

1. Leys, *Underdevelopment in Kenya,* pp. 50–51.
2. Kitching, *Class,* p. 189.
3. Provincial commissioner, "Trading Licences," 15 November 1946. See also circulars from the secretariat, reports, and correspondence between commissioners and the registrar of cooperatives. MCI/6/782, KNA.
4. Registrar of companies, 12 October 1950, MCI/6/789, KNA.
5. Registrar, "African Companies," 23 June 1949, MCI/6/788, KNA.
6. Registrar, "African Companies," 23 June 1949, MCI/6/788, KNA.
7. Registrar, "African Companies," 12 October 1950, MCI/6/789, KNA.
8. D.J. Penwill, district officer, cited in "The African in Business: Memorandum for Meeting of Provincial Commissioners," February 1950, MCI/6/782, KNA.
9. Report of chief native commissioner, 6 November 1950, MCI/6/783, KNA.
10. Speech at the opening in Kisumu. MCI/6/783, KNA.
11. Chief native commissioner, 6 November 1950, MCI/6/783, KNA.
12. A "Mr. Stephen" of Messrs. Stephen, Gillitt, & Co. to Mr. H.M. Kanja, 25 November 1946, MCI/6/782, KNA.
13. Ibid.
14. A. Hope-Jones, 27 November 1945, MCI/6/782, KNA.
15. Marris and Somerset, *African Businessmen,* p. 228.
16. Brett, *Colonialism and Underdevelopment in East Africa,* p. 294.
17. Swainson, "Indigenous Capitalism," p. 140.
18. A glimpse of attitudes towards Africans is given in a 1945 report by Mr. Stirton, who was inquiring into the feasibility of setting up rural industries. Stirton wrote: "Many were the people with whom the writer came into contact. Administrators, educationalists, missionaries and others too numerous to mention. All were approached because of their interest or direct contact with the African. Many were encouraging, many were not, some were with hope, some were hope-less, and expression of opinion are merely recorded to show that the organisation does not yet exist through which a flying start can be made in tackling rural industries. *An administrator:* "About time something was done about rural industries." *Another administrator:* "What are rural industries anyway?" *A school-master:* "Good, a lot can be done in rural industries." *Another school-master:* "I am sorry, all I can offer is sympathy." *And another:* "I am pessimistic, there may be hope in building, perhaps, birth control and basic English." *An agriculturalist:* "Rural industries can do nothing to relieve pressure on the land." *Another agriculturalist:* "There is not only a crying need but a great desire by Africans for rural industries; but don't ask us to help; let us get on with agriculture." *A lady missionary:* "You need not look to the women for help in rural industries—African women already have far too much to do in their own homes." *A missionary school-master:* "Rural industries are a necessity and technical courses should run parallel with and be considered as important as academic training." *Another missionary:* "The African is so darned lazy that nothing short of compulsion will make him do something for himself." *And another:* "Let Government arrange to get goods at wholesale prices for the African and he will show that he can look after himself and compete on equal terms with the European and the Asian." *A technical missionary:* "You don't know anything about African psychology otherwise you would know that an African will not buy anything made by an African." (This statement from one who

has given the greater part of his life to Africans, whose ex-pupils are earning livelihoods as artisans in native reserves, and who lives near the market where thousands of Africans meet each week to buy and sell each other's goods.) *An African:* "The African is capable of very great work but he does not get encouragement." *A lady who voluntarily expressed an opinion:* "But surely the idea is to get the native to buy British goods." *Stirton Report on Rural Industries*, 15 June 1945, MCI/6/1833, KNA.

19. Colony of Kenya, Executive Council minute 552, 29 October 1950, MCI/6/675, KNA.

20. Provincial commissioner, Central Province, to chief secretary, 15 November 1946, MCI/6/782, KNA.

21. D.J. Penwill, cited in MCI/6/782, KNA.

22. Ibid.

23. District commissioner to the chief secretary, 29 December 1944, MCI/6/782, KNA.

24. Board of Commerce, working party, 22 May 1955, MCI/6/821, KNA.

25. G.D. Parkin, director, 28 May 1959, MCI/6/1275, KNA.

26. Cited by the working party on credit to Africans, Treasury/4/4797, KNA.

27. J.P. Gaynord, secretary, to the director of veterinary services, 27 November 1956, OP/1/759, KNA.

28. K.D.S. MacOwan, director, to the tanners' association, 6 December 1956, OP/3/759, KNA.

28. Department of Trade to MCI, 28 February 1957, MCI/6/782, KNA.

30. Department of Local Government to all local authorities, 15 August 1955, MLG/3/144.

31. MCI "Manual of Instructions," MCI/6/1275, KNA.

32. See *Report of Controller/Auditor General, 1965/1966*, p. v.

33. A.J.F. Simmance, Kiambu, 22 April 1959, MCI/6/738, KNA.

34. V.A. Maddison, "Scheme of Assistance to African Industrialists, Artisans and Businessmen," 11 September 1956, MCI/6/782, KNA.

35. V.A. Maddison, 29 June 1959, minutes on C/TRDS/Central/Vol D/, MCI/6/1275, KNA.

36. G.P. Henderson to J.D. Lewin at Trade and Supplies, 18 May 1959, MCI/6/782, KNA.

37. Lewin to Henderson, 20 May 1959, MCI/6/782, KNA.

38. Government of Kenya, *Development Plan 1964–1970*, 1964, p. 41.

39. Balala, MP, "African Businesses," p. 2723.

40. Mwaura, "Kenya's Industrialisation Strategy," 1986.

41. ICDC, *Role and Activities*, 1989.

42. KIE, *Indigenous Entrepreneurship*, 1989.

43. KAM to MCI, 16 October 1968. KAM files.

44. J.G. Kiano, minister, to KAM, 13 June 1974, MCI/CONF 75/01(154).

45. Interview in 1989.

46. ILO commented that the government's participation in wholesale trade through the KNTC "should in principle facilitate regular supplies of commodities to retailers. However, this does not seem to happen at present." See ILO, *Employment, Incomes and Equality*, p. 207.

47. Mbeo-Onyango, in National Assembly official report, p. 51.

48. National Assembly official report, p. 2716.

49. National Assembly official report, p. 3199.

50. Cited in the *Daily Nation*, 23 July 1968.

51. Wariithi, in official report, p. 2717.

52. Oduya, official report, p. 2725.

53. Reported in *Finance*, a Kenyan monthly magazine, September 1988.

54. *Finance,* September 1988.

55. *Daily Nation*, "Cunningham: Long Career in Banking," 11 January 1990.

56. Marris and Somerset, *African Businessmen*, pp. 226–227.

57. Kamau, "Problems of African Business Enterprise," p. 5.

58. *Weekly Review,* 13 October 1975.

59. Interview with J.B. Kariuki, senior manager, Barclays Bank of Kenya, 1989.

60. Ibid.

61. Interview with Kyale Mwendwa, chairman, Academic Services, 1989.

62. Interview with Arun Devani, chairman, Synresins Ltd., 1989.

63. Republic of Kenya sessional paper, pp. 54–55.

64. Republic of Kenya, p. 164.

65. Republic of Kenya, p. 50.

66. Page 50.

67. J.S. Stirton, "Rural Industries," 1945. See also Secretariat circular letter 4 and correspondence, 25 January 1945, MCI/6/1833, KNA. (Emphasis added.)

68. ILO, *Employment,* p. 5.

69. Morara, "Linking industry," 1990.

70. Kitching, "Politics, Method and Evidence," p. 127.

71. Swainson, "Indigenous Capitalism," p. 158.

72. *East Africa Report on Trade and Industry*, January 1988.

73. *East Africa Report,* 1988.

74. Interview, J.B. Wanjui, executive chairman, East Africa Industries, 1990.

75. Swainson, "National Bourgeoisie," pp. 50–51.

76. Leys, "Accumulation," p. 183.

77. *Weekly Review,* 19 May 1975.

78. *Weekly Review,* 16 August 1976.

79. *Weekly Review,* 24 March 1989.

80. GEMA Holdings annual general meeting reports, cited in the *Daily Nation,* 10 October 1980.

81. *Daily Nation,* 9 January 1979. See also the *Daily Nation,* "Members Urge Sub-division and Allocation of Land," 17 December 1984.

82. *Daily Nation,* 22 November 1981.

83. *Standard,* 2 February 1979.

84. In 1969 Kihika Kimani had founded a large land company, Ngwataniro Farmers Company, which had provided him with an impressive political base in the Nakuru area. In the process of the dismantling of the Nakuru anti-Moi political machinery, Kihika was also ousted from his offices as chairman and director of this company. *Weekly Review,* 24 June 1988.

85. *Weekly Review,* 1 January 1982.

86. Interview and questionnaire, Mr. John Kariuki, public relations officer, KBL, 1989. Also annual reports for 1988 and 1989.

87. Questionnaire and Unga Group annual report, 1989.

88. Interview and questionnaire with Mr. Vaz, general manager of Mareba Enterprises, 1989.

89. *Daily Nation,* 30 December 1989 (advertising feature by the group).

90. Interview and questionnaire with Mr. C.C. Campbell Clause, company secretary, 1989.

91. Interview and questionnaire with Mr. Jennings, managing director, 1989.

Part II

The State and Capitalism

4

Before Independence

In the early stages of formal colonial rule, up to the mid-1940s there was almost no mechanism specifically related to commerce, and the still embryonic industrial sector, within the Kenyan state apparatus. During the later phase, which began with the Second World War and ended with independence in 1963, an accelerated augmentation of state machinery took place, leading to new and more coordinated programs that aimed to foster commercial and industrial development in both Kenya and East Africa as a whole. The institutional framework established in this period included a ministerial system in which the Ministry of Commerce and Industry was given a prominent role, in addition to specialized departments to provide professional guidance and technical support systems. Also created, or strengthened (for those already in existence), were a number of locally administered state corporations and some supranational agencies that incorporated Kenya, Uganda, and Tanganyika under the auspices of the East African High Commission. These provided vital economic infrastructures, in particular, those of the East African Railways and Harbours Corporation, around which most development programs revolved. By the end of the colonial period, a fairly complex and ambitious administrative regime to foster commercial and industrial development was in place.

An Unforeseen Development

Before World War II, the role of the Kenyan state in promoting and coordinating both commercial and industrial development was remarkably rudimentary. Kenya essentially drifted along, in the absence of both institutions and policy, as the minister for finance through the 1950s, Sir Ernest Vasey, noted:

103

> Kenya's real history of economic development . . . seems to have been, for many of those early years, a development through accident rather than by design. And, by that, I mean that the channels . . . of our social and economic development were not consciously planned, but evolved from the circumstances of the day. That development really began when the British Government decided to build a railway to Uganda . . . [that] happened to pass through Kenya.[1]

A more focused policy came with the Second World War. Referring to changes brought about by the circumstances of 1939–1945, the Kenyan government itself acknowledged that "the rate of development has been far greater than contemplated or indeed could have been foreseen."[2]

The changes were not anticipated because they were generated by a series of external events, beginning with the disruption of the supply of manufactured goods to Kenya as shipping priorities were modified to accommodate war conditions and the requirements in Europe. This development led to the improvisation of products by some enterprising commercial groups who took advantage of the situation to move into manufacturing, as shown in Chapter 2. More important—and linked with this—were the policies introduced by the United Kingdom to counter Britain's industrial decline. The UK had suffered massive destruction of its physical assets during the war and had a deficit in its balance of payments. The policies, which were essentially protectionist, meant that, on the one hand, countries of the sterling area were encouraged to become self-sufficient in raw materials, food, and manufactured goods; on the other hand, goods produced within the sterling zone had to be exported as much as possible to hard currency areas, especially the United States, to earn foreign exchange. A Kenya government document, describing the changes caused by the war and the fiscal problems they entailed, noted what this meant to countries of the British Commonwealth. It stated:

> Before the 1939–1945 war, there was little industry in Kenya apart from the processing of certain agricultural produce. . . . During the war it was necessary to improvise to make up for deficiencies caused by shipping difficulties. . . . This improvisation laid the foundation for a number of industries. There was further stimulation arising from the Commonwealth policy of seeking new sources of supply within the "Sterling Area." The process of industrial development has continued.[3]

In the more economically backward regions of the Commonwealth, such as Kenya and the rest of East Africa, productivity could not be raised before an enabling institutional framework had been created and before policies had been formulated. The existing state apparatus was too primitive to undertake these assignments. The priority then became the building of key state institutions. Not until this exercise was underway could East Africa absorb the relatively large development funds that became available, nor set in motion a productive agenda. It was in this context that the UK wrote off the original grant (and the capital repayments and interest) of the Kenya-Uganda railway, under the Colonial Development Act of 1940.[4]

A developmentalist framework was adopted fairly quickly, beginning with the enhancement of the principal state structures. New ones were created where necessary. This program was followed by a proliferation of supplementary policy instruments.[5] Among the key administrative units created in Kenya in this period were the Ministry of Commerce and Industry (1947–1948) and its multitude of subordinate regulatory bodies and advisory committees. Almost all of these were aimed at encouraging both local and foreign capital to enter more challenging sectors of the economy, particularly manufacturing.

In 1948, trade and industry were given ministerial representation in the Legislative Assembly and administrative apparatus was created to deal with commercial and industrial concerns. The responsibilities of the new ministry included fostering secondary industries, the provision of industrial licenses (in conjunction with the East African Industrial Board), undertaking trade missions, monitoring and assisting banks and banking, and improving import and export trade. The Board of Industrial Development was charged with "advising the Minister of Commerce and Industry on all matters referred to it concerning the development and encouragement of industry in the Colony."[6] This new board thus replaced the Board for Commerce and Industry that had been the main advisory body on "policy concerning the encouragement and development of industries . . . in the colony."[7] The board was made up of ministry officials, East Africa supranational representatives, and local entrepreneurs.[8] Kenyan Indian leaders such as D.P. Chandaria, director of Kaluworks, and B.S. Mohandria, president of the Nairobi chapter of the Federation of Indian Chambers of Commerce of Eastern Africa, were among the early members.[9]

A Special Assistance to Industry scheme was also set up, under the Ministry of Finance, revolving around the new Industrial Management Board (that was to be replaced by the Industrial Development Corporation [IDC] in 1954). These state agencies were to assist in financing large industrial enterprises.[10] A 1962 report by the corporation stated:

> Some Pounds 400,000.00 have been made available either by equity or loans in enterprises such as hotels, the canning industry, the fishing corporation, the packaging industry and tea production, etc. The corporation's work has been invaluable . . . assisting the creation of a large number of viable projects.[11]

The Steel Corporation of East Africa Ltd., a rolling mill at Dondora, Nairobi, is an example of a large industrial project, started by a local

industrialist, in which the IDC participated. The Madhvani Group, the
initiator of the enterprise, controlled 59.9 percent of the equity; 10.1
percent was held by Italian Steelworks and Manufacturers, 20 percent by
the Colonial Development Corporation, and 10 percent by IDC.[12]

Perhaps most important in facilitating capital accumulation in this
period was a series of fiscal policies. For example, a suspended duty of 20
percent ad valorem was imposed through the 1950s on various imported
products to protect domestic manufacturing industries. Products to which
this tariff applied included glass, soap, and aluminum articles manufactured in East Africa.[13] To facilitate industrial development, secondary
industries were also refunded 100 percent of the duties they paid on
imported raw materials. The drawback system, as it was known, allowed
manufacturers to reduce their production costs to help them be more
competitive. A government report listed the criteria for granting assistance to industry via either of these fiscal policies:

> (a) whether the existence of the industry will result in an increase of
> exports from the colony or a saving of imports into the colony; (b)
> whether the industry will be a large employer of labour; (c) whether the
> industry will cause development of ancillary industries; (d) whether the
> industry has available or will attract sufficient capital for development.[14]

Besides such continuing means of supporting local industrialization, periodically measures were taken in response to specific needs. For example,
in seeking to make the glass industry more durable, a subsector dominated
by local Indian companies (as shown in Chapter 2), the Kenya government
offered to help secure technical assistance for manufacturers.[15] The facts
do not support the thesis that Kenyan industrial policies during the 1950s
were "pushed by pressure from British capital," and that the system of
licensing "forestalled" the involvement of local Indians in industrial undertakings.[16]

These programs effectively encouraged commercial capitalists to
enter manufacturing. Their spectacular industrial activity quickly led to a
shortage of industrial space in the major industrial towns—Nairobi and
Mombasa. This in turn led to the rezoning of major agricultural lands into
industrial usage in such areas as Athi River, Thika, Kisumu, Nakuru,
Eldoret, and Kitale. These industrial areas were served by rail, road, and
drainage systems. The desire of domestic commercial capitalists and
financiers to enter the manufacturing industry, with its resulting competition for industrial plots, had apparently been underestimated:

> Private capital has been attracted in large amounts and in the vicinity of
> Nairobi alone, nearly 500 industrial plots have been sold . . . and since
> 1947 new factories have been going up in the Nairobi area at about the
> rate of 50–100 a year, the rate of progress accelerating as we move down

to the present time.... The same applies, on a smaller scale, in Mombasa. ... The position in Kisumu, Nakuru, Eldoret and Kitale is that industrial plots... have recently been marked out. There is every reason to believe that in the next two years there will be development on a considerable scale at these centres.[17]

It has been contended that "the overall objectives of government policy on industrialisation remained hazy until the mid-1950s, while senior officials' understanding was rudimentary and often confused."[18] In light of the above, this needs qualification. Indeed, the policies of the Ministry of Commerce and Industry were already so successful, and its experience in facilitating the entry of entrepreneurs into manufacturing so remarkable, that Kenya received inquiries from other colonies about the means and strategies employed. In response to official inquiries from Northern Rhodesia, an enthusiastic Kenyan civil servant responded:

> We have not, in fact, quoted special reduced rates for these plots and initially the valuation put on them . . . was criticised as being high. . . . However, the demand has always far exceeded the supply. . . . At the present time we are seeking ways of making more land available in order to satisfy outstanding applications. . . . One of our difficulties is . . . [that] we are hindered by the general difficulty of obtaining prompt delivery of adequate supplies of electricity. . . . I hope, however, that by 1953 we shall be in a more satisfactory position.[19]

By the mid-1950s, the *Economist Intelligence Unit* reported that there has "been a great wave of industrial development in Kenya," predicting that in the next decade "industrial development will increase rather than diminish."[20] Surveys by the *Financial Times* of London in 1956 showed that rapid industrial development continued. The paper reported:

> Industrial investment . . . has been on a significant scale. Starting with the processing of agricultural products, such as sisal, tobacco, hides and skins, and canning . . . Kenya now possesses a wide variety of secondary industries. . . . In 1953, 189 new companies were registered, with a nominal capital of Pounds 3,711,520. In 1954 there were 243 new registrations, with a nominal capital of Pounds 9,824,170.[21]

Rise of the East African Supranational State

Another crucial indicator of the expansion of the Kenyan state apparatus related to commerce and industry was the East African High Commission and the common services administered by it. These services underwent a drastic transformation in the late 1940s and 1950s. Concerted efforts toward a common market were compelled by the realization that the larger East African market afforded better chances of developmental success. The combined populations of Kenya, Tanganyika, and Uganda represented a significant volume of purchasing power. In 1952 the population of the three countries was estimated at 76,000 Europeans, 254,800 Indians, 47,100 Arabs, 11,400 "other non-Africans," and 19,178,000 Africans. The Africans represented most of the potential increase in consumer demand: their patterns of consumer demand were changing rapidly. A far higher proportion of Africans wore shoes, smoked cigarettes, drank tea and European beer, used matches, consumed sugar and wheat flour, purchased European style clothing, and rode bicycles. This had "a very significant effect on the local market," and it was predicted that demands "for better types of housing, greater recreational facilities and improved farming methods will see further major changes in the market in the very near future."[22]

Coordination of East African economic development began to be facilitated by both policy changes and specific development schemes. The East African Governors' Conference, which in the 1940s became the East African High Commission, was an embryonic East African government. Livingstone and Ord aptly noted: "The High Commission operated to great extent as supranational organisation, that is to say, as an independent institution rather than a meeting place at which the separate territorial interests could be discussed and harmonised."[23] The responsibilities of the High Commission included the administration of common services such as the East African Customs and Excise and the East African Income Tax Department. These and other regulatory bodies were responsible for harmonizing tariff policies aimed at streamlining the common market and preventing the duplication of industrial projects to allow development of economies of scale. For example, the large, modern Nyanza Textile Mills at Jinja in Uganda were given protection in the East African common market. A key policy instrument for these tasks was the East African Industrial Council, whose primary role was to consider and advise the high commission on "questions of policy relating to industrial development in East Africa."[24] More importantly, the industrial council was a licensing authority, used by the commission to coordinate industrial location.

Complementing the industrial council was the East African Statistical Department. Founded in the same period, the department compiled industrial statistics and kept records on factories, showing the numbers of persons employed, activities carried out, details of production, and the consumption of raw materials. This allowed, for the first time, more consistent industrial planning in Kenya and East Africa.

There also were efforts to coordinate East African energy development. East African governments began to search for electrical energy to meet the demands brought about by rapid social and economic transformation. This was not very successful in its initial stages. Coal deposits discovered in Tanganyika were not economically viable due to their remoteness from railway systems and industrial centers. Energy problems were subsequently overcome by the building of hydroelectric projects around East Africa. The largest of these was the Owen Falls hydroelectric scheme in Uganda. In addition to supplying Ugandan consumers, Owen Falls adequately provided electrical power to Nairobi and other Kenyan towns. In Kenya itself, a new hydroelectric scheme at Lower Tana became operational in 1956. The same year, construction of another project at Seven Falls on the Tana River got under way.[25]

By the 1950s, the East African supranational state agencies included EAR&H, East African Posts and Telecommunications (EAPT), East African Airways Corporation (EAAC), the East African Income Tax Department, and the East African Customs and Excise. This rapid expansion caused staffing problems, consistently exceeding the availability of both local and expatriate personnel. The shortage was aggravated by the security emergency in Kenya, as indicated by the case of the railways in 1954:

> The most serious handicap suffered by the railways at the present time is undoubtedly the shortage of manpower. Very large numbers of Kikuyu, Embu and Meru have been lost by arrest, detention, or desertion. . . . No fewer than 600 have been lost in the Nairobi area alone, of whom a high proportion were men in the essential artisan class. . . . [T]he loss of 40 Europeans now serving with the Emergency Forces is being more acutely felt.[26]

Even so, economic growth was maintained during the 1950s. Major expansion programs of East African economic infrastructures continued—for EAR&H in particular. Its Western Uganda extension reached Kasese in 1956 and port services at Mombasa and Dar-es-Salaam were modernized and expanded. The enlarged services, and the introduction of increased charges at the ports for shipping dues, cargo, handling, and other services, improved the EAR&H revenue base by over 40 percent in 1956.[27] The role of EAR&H was remarkable in the area of infrastructural support for domestic and foreign capital, rendering it by far the principal basis of industrial development in East Africa.

Key Role of Railways

The corporation, begun as Uganda Railway, amalgamated with Tanganyika Railway after the First World War to become EAR&H. Prior to the Second World War, rail systems were relatively well equipped and had capacity well above the requirements of the existing volume of traffic. However, the commercial, industrial, and agricultural development after the war changed this. By 1950, it was reported that:

Further capital investment was essential if the capacity of the system was to be expanded to relieve the strain which was already evident and to cope with the additional traffic expected as a result of the development of the economies of the territories.[28]

Among modifications made in a restructured EAR&H to stimulate development was what was termed the "differential tariff" that made possible

a number of specific measures introduced to afford rating assistance to particular industries and individual development projects. . . . [For example] it appeared virtually impossible for the glass industry of East Africa to maintain its position in local markets and develop an export industry sufficient to ensure production at an economic level. . . . The case for assistance was accepted and export rates were introduced. . . .[29]

EAR&H was also a key player in administration of development. Jointly with the Ministry of Commerce and Industry, the Board of Industrial Development, and the Ministry of Local Government, EAR&H developed and allocated industrial plots in major centers such as Nairobi and Mombasa.[30]

The Eve of Independence

Other state corporations that were undertaking expansion programs in response to the improved economic performance included EAPT, EAAC, the East African Income Tax Department, and the East African Customs and Excise; and implementing a plan for regional self-sufficiency was the Committee for Economic Co-ordination.[31]

The Kenyan and East African administrative apparatus had thus become quite elaborate on the eve of independence. From official minutes, correspondence, reports, commissions, and media reports of the period, it is evident that the bureaucracy was fairly efficient and quite responsive to the commercial and industrial community. There was a clear vision of the advantages of a large market, and the need to maintain a number of supranational economic departments and economic infrastructures. Sir Ernest Vasey, minister of finance in the 1950s, stated:

It should be realised that the existence of an East African market, completely free from territorial restrictions, with its potential of over twenty million consumers, is a factor in the decision of industrialists to establish in East Africa. . . . [T]he break-up of the Customs Union could damage the whole [region]. . . . The benefit is really East Africa's as a whole.[32]

State records of this period disclose a strong administrative culture that carefully observed a specific division of responsibilities and established codes of conduct and regulations. The Kenyan state apparatus of this period was, by any criteria, a bourgeois state, as was indicated by its institutions and its commitment to the development of a national capitalist economy. The creation of the Ministry of Commerce and Industry by dividing in half the Ministry of Agriculture and Natural Resources, with its ties to white farmers, indicates a firm (and no doubt difficult) state response to the changing patterns of development, and to the sectoral constituencies of Kenya and East Africa. The sophistication of the Kenyan civil service in the 1950s was acknowledged in the report of a postindependence commission:

> The Civil Service... became complex, the departments being arranged with 12 fully fledged Ministries. . . ; the various technical departments were "integrated" into ministries under the overall authority of generalist Permanent secretaries, responsible to elected Ministers. Another was to start, however belatedly, training Kenyans to replace the key Administrative cadre. A third was to give new impetus to the desegregation of the services that were formerly run on racial lines. The court system was integrated. The government school system and hospital services became equally open to all races. Fourthly, in the independence constitution, the British set up the Public Service Commission and also a Police Service Commission designed to insulate the appointments process from political and other influences. Lastly there was the constitution. . . .[33]

It was the realization of the complexity of this administrative regime and the roles it had played that led the 1962 World Bank Mission to caution incoming Kenyan African leaders in these terms:

> The demands of an expanding economy for technical, administrative and managerial skills will outrun the speed at which talents can be developed and experience accumulated. Under such conditions, expatriate manpower now in Kenya represents a valuable asset, but one in danger of being lost. If these skilled people should leave Kenya in large numbers during the next few years, it would be difficult, if not impossible, to maintain many of the economic activities on which the present level of output rests. Even if replacements from abroad could be found. . . , to do so would almost certainly inflate the costs of the services and lose the benefit of an extensive knowledge of local conditions.[34]

Notes

1. Vasey, "Development," p. 2.
2. Colony of Kenya, "Industrial Development," 1952. MCI/6/1275, KNA.
3. Colony of Kenya, *Economic Assistance for Industries,* 1956, p. 1.
4. Kenneth Robinson, in *Dilemmas of Trusteeship,* p. 32, wrote: "In the period 1929–1940 . . . expenditure outside the Act was Pounds 19.9 million while advances totalling Pounds 8.8 million were approved under the Act, of which

about Pounds 6.5 million was actually spent in these years. Loans totalling Pounds 8.6 million were also written off under the Act of 1940 but Pounds 5.5 million of this represented the cost of building the Uganda railway in the last years of the nineteenth century."

5. For detailed accounts of the programs undertaken in the 1940s and 1950s, consult, for example, the following: Colony of Kenya, *Colonial Annual Report*; MCI, *Trade and Supplies*; Colony of Kenya, *Economic Assistance for Industries*; *Sessional Paper No. 51 of 1955*; *Development Programme 1954–57*; *Annual Trade Report of Kenya, Uganda and Tanganyika* and *Annual Report of the Department of Economic Coordination*; and *East African Quarterly Economic and Statistical Bulletin.*

6. Board of Industrial Development, "Terms of Reference," 19 June 1956, MCI/6/88, KNA.

7. Board for Commerce and Industry, "Terms of Reference," November 1948, MCI/6/20, KNA.

8. The board was one of the powerful policy instruments in Kenya. It was chaired by the commerce minister. Other ministry officials included the secretary for commerce, and the industrial development officer. Representatives of the supranational state included the economic secretary for the East African High Commission, the chief commercial superintendent of the East African Railways, and the commissioner for customs and excise. See MCI/6/20, KNA.

9. Board of Industrial Development, "First Meeting," 20 June 1956, MCI/6/68, KNA.

10. Cited in Colony of Kenya, "Notes on Industrial Development in East Africa," 1952, MCI/6/1257, KNA. The IDC was also given the task of administering the loans scheme for African industrialists (see Chapter 3 for discussion of this attempt by the colonial state to foster an African business class). See Confidential: Council of Ministers, "A Proposal for the Formation of a Kenya Development Company," 17 October 1962, CS/1/16/35, KNA.

11. Confidential: Council of Ministers, "A Proposal for the Formation of a Kenya Development Company," 17 October 1962, CS/1/16/35, KNA.

12. Notes to the governor by V.A. Maddison, permanent secretary MCI, 10 June 1960, GH/4/441, KNA.

13. See minutes of meetings of the Committee on Duty Drawbacks. MCI/9/554 and MCI/6/694, KNA.

14. Colony of Kenya, *Report of the Committee to Examine the Need for Economic Assistance for Primary and Secondary Industries Excluding Agriculture,* 1955. This important committee was created by notice 919, 29 August 1952. See also Board of Industrial Development, "Criteria," 1956, MCI/6/88, KNA.

15. MCI wrote to Kenya Glass Works on 9 July 1954: "Government is . . . interested in ensuring that the industry will develop on the best economic lines to the advantage of East Africa as a whole, but appreciates that as the manufacture is a comparatively new one in Kenya the best technical advice and guidance may not be readily available locally. To assist the industry further, the Government has approached the Foreign Operations Administration of the United States with a view to obtain the services of an American glass expert to pay a brief visit to Kenya and to report on the industry and give advice on techniques and future development plans. The cost of such a visit . . . should be borne by the two companies engaged in the manufacture of glass in Kenya, as they will benefit directly from the advice obtained." MCI/9/554, KNA.

16. Berman, *Control & Crisis,* p. 272.

17. Colony of Kenya, "Industrial Development in East Africa," 1952, MCI/6/1275, KNA.

18. Berman, *Control & Crisis,* p. 270.

19. H.L. Adams, MCI, to Bernard Lewis, Department of Trade, Northern Rhodesia, 7 January 1951. See also H.L. Adams to R.E. Nicholson, economic secretary, Northern Rhodesia, 21 March 1950, MCI/4/5, KNA.

20. Quoted in the *East African Standard,* 9 June 1956.

21. *Financial Times,* "Colonial Survey—I: Progress in Kenya," 25 January 1956.

22. Colony of Kenya, "Industrial Development in East Africa," 1952, MCI/6/1275, KNA.

23. Livingstone and Ord, *Economics for Eastern Africa,* p. 335.

24. Colony of Kenya, "Industrial Development in East Africa," 1952, MCI/6/1275, KNA.

25. *Financial Times,* 25 January 1956.

26. Transport Memo 40. Report to the high commission, 1954. 24. CS/1/16/26, KNA.

27. Transport Memo 45. Commissioner's report, 1956. 10. CS/1/16/26, KNA.

28. C.T. Hutson, chief commercial superintendent, "Railway Rates Increases," 26 June 1957. MCI/6/88, KNA.

29. Submission by EAR&H chief commercial superintendent to the Board of Industrial Development, 28 June 1957, MCI/6/88, KNA.

30. Board of Industrial Development, "Industrial Plots," 12 January 1957, MCI/6/88, KNA.

31. East African High Commission. Administrator's confidential report, 1956. 9. CS/1/16/26, KNA.

32. Vasey to Governor Sir Evelyn Baring, 17 March 1959. *Vasey Papers,* KNA.

33. Republic of Kenya, *Commission of Inquiry (Public Service Structure and Remuneration Commission),* pp. 8–9.

34. Government of Kenya, *The Economic Development of Kenya,* p. 27.

5

The Fall of Institutions:
Case Histories in Corruption

The period following independence in 1963 saw change as spectacular as that outlined in the previous chapter for the decades following World War II—but the change was in the reverse direction: in effect, toward disintegration. This process began almost immediately after independence with an impassioned program of "Africanization" of the civil service. The World Bank's recommendation quoted at the end of Chapter 4, if known about, was ignored, and the strategies of the new state were more in line with the views of the Kenya African Civil Servants' Union, which demanded in 1963 that the Kenya government terminate the services of expatriates and non-Africans. "Kenya has very many Africans with higher qualifications who are ready to replace these people without difficulty," the union said in a press release.[1] And this belief guided official policy for some time. The vice president and minister for home affairs, Mr. Oginga Odinga, was saying in 1964: "We have continued to Africanise at top, almost breakneck speed."[2]

However, the pool of skilled Kenyan Africans was markedly insufficient to replace those who had been released. In the aftermath of the changes, incompetence of severe proportions took over: financial indiscipline, failure to regulate and maintain economic infrastructures, and inability to implement development goals became the norms.

Thus the postindependence period was marked by profound contradictions. On the one hand, as shown in Chapter 2, local capital maintained its progress and steadily increased its capacity in almost all areas of industry; on the other hand, the state apparatus regressed. The new institutions created after independence were hopelessly ineffective, almost from the start. A decline in public administration was to be expected during and after the transition period, but not the almost total collapse and disparagement of national institutions that in fact occurred.

Ironically, as the situation deteriorated, the services of a new set of international expatriates were required to prevent further decline. The

115

numbers of these expatriates, and their role, continued to expand as units of the Kenyan state apparatus—later threatened with total breakdown— repeatedly required rehabilitation. But that is the subject of the next chapter. Kenya now was to be cushioned, by this international help and a mix of local capital and foreign investment. Even when overseas finance contracted substantially in the 1980s, Kenya was prevented from backsliding as far as did most of sub-Saharan Africa. The comparison, however, is hardly complimentary, given the circumstances of the region.

Africanization of the Civil Service

The impact of Africanization can be appreciated by looking at figures showing the limited extent to which Africans had, before independence, entered the more specialized posts in the Kenyan state apparatus. In 1962, out of eighty-nine civil servants in the upper administrative grade of central government (the rank of assistant secretary and above), only eighteen were Africans; of the 374 posts in the provincial administration, from district assistant and above, only 181 were Africans; of three thousand professional and senior technical staff, only 180 were Africans; and of the 1,900 of executive grade, only 381 were Africans. More than 90 percent of administrative and professional grades were Europeans. Of 4,700 staff in the clerical category, 2,600 were Africans; in the secretarial grade, only one out of 418 was African.[3] The executive end of the the civil service was made up of British civil servants. The bulk of the middle and lower ranks were resident Indians. While the 1971 *Ndegwa Commission Report* did not provide specific figures with regard to the Africanization of these posts, it confirmed the wholesale discharge of skilled expatriate personnel, stating: "By 1965 virtually the entire Administrative cadre consisted of Kenyan citizens."[4]

By the late 1960s, most technical and professional expatriates and local Indian professionals had either been compelled to leave Kenya or were recruited by private sector employers who understood their value.[5] More than 150,000 local Indians are reported to have left East Africa between 1968 and 1969, most of them the families of technical and professional men from such fields as accounting, engineering, and medicine, and the upper and middle administrative cadres in the three East African bureaucracies and the East African suprastate apparatus and its associates.[6]

It did not take long for the effects of this squandering of skilled personnel to be felt in Kenya. It was officially acknowledged in 1971 that Africanization meant a "serious dilution of experience and an over-burdening of comparatively young officials near the top. [In] crucial areas important development projects are held up because of lack of qualified staff."[7] It was in this context that the Kenyan state turned to aid-donor countries to provide a new set of expatriates. In fact, as early as 1965, it was revealed in a euphemistic policy statement that while British and resident Indian staff (categorized as expatriates) were being disposed of, foreign experts were being brought in to supplement the rapidly deteriorating Africanized services. The government report stated:

> Kenya has ample numbers of unskilled manpower. . . . But untrained people cannot be used as teachers, planners, engineers, surgeons, doctors, surveyors, architects, managers and administrators. . . . In order to grow rapidly and *to replace expatriates with comparably qualified Kenya citizens as soon as possible, we must employ in the near future large numbers of foreign experts both to assist in planning and carrying out the work that needs to be done.*[8]

It was restated six years later that deficiencies in the civil service "can be met with help of overseas donors and international aid agencies but even that help, welcome though it is, does not match the problem."[9] The following assessment by Leys in 1977 was not well founded:

> One of the most striking changes in Kenya since 1971 was the coming "on stream" of a new generation of technically trained state economic functionaries. The Industrial Development Bank staff were a leading example of this, combining advanced technical (economic and accounting) qualifications with considerable specialised experience, but the pattern was being repeated in other organisations.[10]

The 1980 Waruhiu report reiterated that "considering the present and anticipated demand for professional and technical services, it will be a long time before the country can achieve near-sufficiency in the supply of required personnel."[11]

Collapse of Parliamentary Management of Finances

The first major casualty of the wholesale release of colonial administrative cadres in the 1960s was management of the national finances. An initial indicator of this involved, predictably, the controller and auditor general, a position that was not Africanized until 1969. In 1964, alarmed by a sudden rise of unauthorized disbursement of national funds and a propensity to disregard established procedures and codes of conduct, the controller and auditor general, C.W. Hodges, issued a special report. He stated that

> There has been a breach of the financial sections of the constitution. . . . [T]he Constitution provides . . . [that] ". . . no moneys shall be withdrawn from the Consolidated Fund unless such withdrawal has been approved by the Controller and Auditor General. . . . [A] net total of Pounds 485,540.00 has been issued. . . . [As] there is no statutory authority for

such expenditures, these are in fact illegal. . . .[12]

D.E. Barnett, who replaced Hodges in 1965, was even more insistent in following established policies and procedures. He issued several reports disclosing misappropriation of treasury funds and general mismanagement. In a 1967 statement, for instance, Barnett noted that some public officials "including hon. Members of Parliament, are receiving more than one salary from the Government and statutory Boards."[13] A climax in the relationship between Barnett and the Kenya government came in 1969. He unequivocally refused to authorize government expenditures before parliamentary approval was granted, as was required by the Kenyan constitution. The Kenyatta government's response, which was to become habitual, was to proclaim a constitutional amendment. Section 122 of the constitution, which stated that "no moneys shall be withdrawn from the Consolidated Fund unless such withdrawal has been approved by the Controller and Auditor General," was discarded, along with Barnett himself.[14]

The year 1969 saw other extraordinary episodes in persisting executive sabotage of fiscal management, among them a scheme concocted to enable ministers to receive gratuities back-dated to 1962. This scheme was ostensibly based on the notion that cabinet ministers were being "cheated" as they could not participate in business like other Kenyans.[15] Hence section 2 (a) of the Remuneration (Amendment) Bill of 1969, which stated that:

> Every Minister shall receive a gratuity, at the rate of twenty per centum of the salary . . . payable at such intervals and subject to such conditions as the President may, from time to time, direct. . . . Gratuities under this section shall be payable in respect of services since the 7th April 1962, or the date of the appointment of the Minister concerned whichever is later, and any such gratuity paid prior to 1st of May 1969, shall be deemed to have been lawfully paid.[16]

Besides undermining established administrative practices, this amendment involved, in effect, the official sanctioning of greed. Among voices in the National Assembly distressed by what was evolving in Kenya was that of Mr. Jean Marie Seroney, who termed the amendment "daylight robbery."[17] More important, however, was the fact that the bill transferred more powers from the Kenyan Parliament to President Kenyatta. Other amendments that granted the president more powers included the Local Government (Transfer of Functions) Bill, 1969, which stated that "the President may, by regulations, make such amendment to the Exchequer and Audit Act and the Local Government Regulations, 1963, as may be necessary."[18]

Indeed, 1969 can be said to be the turning point, when President

Kenyatta and the circle around him became "the state." The specific authority that had previously assigned separate roles to a multitude of national institutions was undermined and even eliminated. By 1975, MPs could be imprisoned for taking a view divergent from the official line in the National Assembly, despite parliamentary immunity that protected them from prosecution for what they said. Mr. Martin Shikuku, MP, defended the supremacy of Parliament over the burgeoning presidential powers, suggesting that some politicians were killing Parliament "the way KANU has been killed." His words were supported by only one other MP (the then deputy speaker, Mr. Jean Marie Seroney). Both men were arrested in the grounds of the National Assembly and imprisoned.[19]

Another revealing moment in the presidential supplanting of the rest of the state and its laws was when, in 1975, the Kenyatta regime passed what is known in Kenya as the Ngei Amendment, named after Paul Ngei, a friend of Kenyatta's. Paul Ngei, a cabinet minister in both the Kenyatta and the Moi governments, was ousted from Parliament following a successful petition against him in 1975 in the high court when he was found guilty of an electoral offense. He was also involved in financial scandals, with some of his creditors seeking to auction his properties.[20] The Kenyatta government passed the (Amendment) Bill, 1975, empowering the president to pardon an electoral offense, an amendment that was subsequently used to override the high court's decision, enabling Ngei to regain his parliamentary seat and cabinet post. Worthy of note is the contribution to the parliamentary debates on the amendment by the then vice president, Daniel arap Moi: "I support this amendment because we know that the President is above the law. If we say that the President is above the law, why should we say that he should be denied these new powers which rightfully belong to him?"[21] Mr. Moi was right at least on one count: Kenyatta was, indeed, above bourgeois law that—to him—may have gone home with the colonial regime. Kenyatta was in a world of his own. As Jeremy Murray-Brown aptly remarked: there seemed "to be two governments functioning in Kenya: the official one in Nairobi" and "the real one at Gatundu run by the Kikuyu inner caucus."[22] Leys similarly observed:

> Even the cabinet had little significance.... It met infrequently. Executive power lay elsewhere. The real institutions of the state were Kenyatta and his court ... [which] was based primarily at his country home at Gatundu about twenty-five miles from Nairobi in Kiambu district; but like the courts of old it moved with him, to State House in Nairobi, to his coastal lodge near Mombasa, and his lodge at Nakuru in the Rift Valley. This corresponded to his dual roles of Kikuyu paramount chief and national leader. . . . The inner court consisted of a small group of Kikuyu politicians from his home district of Kiambu: Mbiyu Koinange, his brother-in-law, Minister for the state in the President's Office; Njoroge

Mungai, his cousin, Minister for Foreign Affairs; Charles Njonjo, the Attorney-General. . . . The outer court—those with good access, though in much less constant attendance—consisted of . . . other Kikuyu-Embu-Meru leaders, who between them controlled the bulk of the remaining important ministries.[23]

President Moi's own strategy after 1978 when he came to power was to follow the footsteps of his predecessor, as his "Nyayo philosophy" conveniently put it, and to use constitutional amendments to transfer more powers to himself, the state becoming more and more a mere rubber stamp. Once again, among the immediate targets of this exercise was the controller and auditor general, whose constitutionally guaranteed tenures were scrapped altogether in 1986.[24] The tenure of the attorney general, judges of the high court and the appeals court, and members of the public service commission was likewise dispensed with by the Constitution of Kenya (Amendment) 1988.[25] The controller and auditor general was now restricted to "carrying out post-mortems of financial damage already done," as one commentator put it.[26] And the loss of tenure meant that, even so, the president could now dismiss anyone for doing merely the accounting.

Almost all elements of the state apparatus, including the cabinet and the judiciary, took on less and less meaning. The state was President Moi himself and his inner court comprised of his Kalenjin tribesmen and their Masai allies. In 1989 this group included the head of the civil service and secretary to the cabinet, J. arap Letting (Kalenjin); the energy minister (who was also deputy leader of government business in parliament), Nicholas Biwott[27] (Kalenjin); the vice president (of both government and the party), leader of government business in Parliament and minister for finance, George Saitoti (Masai); the governor of the central bank, E. arap Kotut (Kalenjin); the cooperative development minister, John Cheruiyot (Kalenjin); the executive chairman of the Kenya Commercial Bank, B. arap Kipkorir (Kalenjin); and the minister for local government, W. ole Ntimama (Masai). The outer court, made up of regional chieftains, included Joseph Kamotho and James Njiru for the central province, Peter Oloo Aringo for Nyanza, Shariff Nassir for the coast, and Elijah Mwangale for western Kenya.

A new development in the Moi era was that membership in his court could be inherited: relatives were permitted to acquire political office. The list of MPs who inherited parliamentary seats when their relatives died included Mr. Katana Ngala (from his father, Mr. Ronald Ngala), Mr. Musalia Mudavadi (from his father, Mr. Moses Mudavadi), Mr. Boy Juma Boy (from his father, Mr. Juma Boy), and Mr. Lazarus Amayo (from his brother, Mr. David Amayo). One of the most bewildering inheritances was the 1988 case of twenty-three-year-old Vincent M'Maitsi, who took his father's seat while still an undergraduate student and was immediately given the portfolio of assistant minister for planning and development.[28]

It was hoped that the multipartyism that led to general elections in December 1992 would put an end to this feudal practice.

Meanwhile, as a result of a loss of powers by the controller and auditor general, Parliament, the most important institution of the land, increasingly became corrupted. With regard to members of Parliament, for example, the auditor general reported in the early 1980s:

> In the Reports of previous financial years, concern was expressed over the lack of Financial Control at the National Assembly and particularly over irregularities relating to outstanding interests, salary advances and cash advances issued against I.O.U. Chits. . . . Considering that most of these amounts have been outstanding for a very long time and also some of the debtors are no longer members of parliament it is doubtful whether the outstanding amounts will be recovered.[29]

The human and financial costs of Kenyan official excesses during the postindependence period are probably impossible to calculate. However, the amounts of money unaccounted for suggest the scope of the problem. Official pillaging of state funds is regularly reported by the controller and the auditor general, almost always showing that the amounts of money involved steadily increased, reaching enormous proportions as indicated in Table 5.1. These figures, showing missing funds, do not include losses by government departments through failure to collect taxes, nor do they include losses made by state corporations, a subject to which we return below.

Such sums lost to Kenya through state ineptitude are in the same range as those forgiven by aid donor countries to assist Kenya. For example, France wrote off Kenyan debts of KShs5 billion in 1989,[30] with Germany writing off KShs8 billion. The United States was to write off KShs2.8 billion by 1990[31] (totalling KShs15.8 billion as compared with

Table 5.1 Funds Unaccounted for by National Ministries

Fiscal Period	Amount in KShs
1963/64	9,600,000
1971/72	90,000,000
1974/75	435,000,000
1979/80	1,500,000,000
1984/85	2,900,000,000
1986/87	6,500,000,000
1980/90	15,700,000,000

Source: Republic of Kenya, Controller and Auditor General reports (1964:p.1); (1972: p.1); (1976:p.1); (1980:p.1); (1985–1987:p.2); (1989–1990: p.1)

KShs15.7 billion squandered by Kenya—Table 5.1). It is worth noting as well that the funds being lost were much larger than the monies Kenya needed to finance its balance of payments. In 1989, Kenya sought KShs6.2 billion of aid for this purpose.[32] These observations have not escaped local editorial writers. For example, under the heading, "A tragic comedy we love to stage," a *Sunday Nation* editorial stated in reference to the incompetence of customs and excise:

> On the one hand, the country is tottering under the enormous weight of a Sh6.4 billion deficit, while on the other, the Government's revenue collecting mechanism is unable to collect a massive Sh2.3 billion. The irony may be funny but the ridiculous position in which it places the country certainly is not. The tragedy is that it is the same old story. If someone is not fiddling with figures and manipulating account mechanisms to line his pockets, then it will be some other person's incompetence and neglect costing the country millions in lost revenue.[33]

Ndegwa Commission: Catalyst for Corruption in Public Service

Perhaps no single policy decision in Kenya contributed so much to the decline of fiscal discipline, and to the undermining of the Kenyan state apparatus in general, as that to set up the 1971 Ndegwa Commission. Ironically, it was set up to identify how to "transform the public service from an organisation merely geared to administrating public affairs into an instrument of development management."[34] Among the adopted recommendations of the commission was its now famous endorsement of civil servants' participation in private enterprises. According to the commission, "there ought in theory to be no objection to the ownership of property or involvement in business by members of the public services to a point where their wealth is augmented perhaps substantially by such activities. . . . It is understandable that public servants should have taken opportunities like other citizens."[35] Corruption and conflict of interest in the upper levels of state management was a reality in Kenya before the Ndegwa report, as was indicated in constitutional amendments empowering the national leadership in effect to defraud the treasury at will. What the commission's recommendation did was to spread this addiction to the entire Kenyan civil service.

Growing corruption, in the aftermath of a breakdown of fiscal controls, was now combined with Ndegwa Commission recommendations, so that it became increasingly hard to distinguish politicians/government ministers/civil servants from black businessmen. By the end of the 1970s, it was hardly too much to say that the Kenyan state apparatus had almost ceased to be primarily concerned with the provision of public services. This was conceded officially in 1980 in a report on the civil service that stated:

The dedication that once characterised the Civil Service has been eroded. . . . The Ndegwa Commission Report was misinterpreted on the extent to which they recommended that a civil servant can attend to his private interests while at the same time serving the public. . . . [T]here has been gross neglect of public duty and misuse of official positions and official information in furtherance of civil servants' personal interests. There are officers who live beyond their means and who cannot honourably account for the wealth they have amassed. Where such an officer is senior, the junior officers under him have sought to justify their abuse of office by arguing that if the senior officer can do it so can they. *Indeed, we have found that we are unable to state definitely as the Ndegwa Commission did that—"the vast majority of civil servants seem to be very good."*[36]

Impact of Ndegwa Commission on the Administration

In this environment, the performance of ministries ranged from dismal to total failure. Remarks made in the National Assembly in 1964 indicate how quickly the Ministry of Commerce and Industry, for example, degenerated after independence:

They call it the "Ministry of Commerce and Industry." In this Ministry you find that even the Minister and the Parliamentary Secretary . . . own commercial firms which come under the Ministry of Commerce and Industry. . . . This is not a Ministry.[37]

Through the 1970s and 1980s, MCI could hardly undertake relatively simple tasks, such as the issuing of import and export licenses, or processing applications for investment. At one point it was discovered that the Ministry of Industry (which was then separate from commerce, only to be merged again: a reorganization that happened several times) did not have any assets, records, and documents of its own and was unable to account for its fiscal performance. The Public Accounts Committee ordered it to confer with the Ministry of Commerce with a view to "preparing correct Statements of Assets and Liabilities without any further delay."[38] By the late 1980s, incompetence in the two ministries was rampant: for example, it required as many as thirty approvals within and outside commerce and industry offices to start an enterprise in Kenya, a process that took as long as three years.[39] But corruption and incompetence continued. That no corrective measures were undertaken after the above policy statement is indicated by the fact that presidential intervention was needed in 1988. A local magazine, welcoming the move, commented:

The presidential intervention came as good tidings particularly for the commercial and industrial sectors. . . . The plight of many industrialists when chasing import/export licences has been a sad industrial story.

There have been many cases when industries have had their applications returned with comments like "not a priority," "apply later," or "buy local" without the wildest idea as to how priorities are determined. . . . [S]ome industrialists have resorted to bribery. Indeed, some of the delaying tactics by the Ministry of Commerce officials are read by some in the industrial and commercial sectors as indirect invitation to bribe their way around. . . . [A] major racket has been thriving within the ministry of commerce licensing departments where non-industrialists and fortune seekers secure "licences for sale." Such licences are understood to be priced for as much as 25 percent of the value of the merchandise to be imported and were being used to generally bring in items that have tended to threaten local industries.[40]

As a result of corruption at the commerce ministry, massive quantities of imported goods found their way into Kenya. This practice became almost routine, undermining the home market.

A few examples will demonstrate the impact of this incompetence on local industry. East African Spectre Ltd., a local company with over a hundred employees that manufactures liquified petroleum gas containers, was seriously threatened by illegal imports in mid-1989. A shipment of similar products was imported into Kenya by a fake company under the name of Penrex Products Ltd. East African Spectre wrote to the state complaining of "unscrupulous people"—for which can be read "civil servant businessmen" and those with political connections. The firm's letter stated:

We wish to draw your attention to the importation of 7,000 pieces of Liquified Petroleum Gas Cylinders by Messrs. Penrex Products (see attached copy of Billing of Landing). As you are aware, our company manufactures these cylinders locally and has the capacity to meet the entire Kenyan demand. . . . It is our humble submission that there is no justification in the importation of LPC cylinders into the country because such importation only aims to kill indigenous entrepreneurship which the government has vowed to promote. Our company has proved its worth by paying the loan it received from the Kenya Industrial Estates ahead of schedule, providing employment to a good number of Kenyans, saving the country foreign exchange and embarking on expansion and diversification programmes designed to promote exports. A search at the Registrar of Companies' records revealed that no such company as Penrex Products Ltd. is registered there. It is therefore, most likely that some unscrupulous people are behind this deal.[41]

Ironically, East African Spectre is one of the few African-owned manufacturing enterprises that successfully graduated from government-sponsored programs. (It was also one of the few African companies in the sample of 100 firms studied by the present author.)

The case of Ndume Agricultural Machinery and Equipment Manufacturers Ltd. parallels that of East African Spectre. It is logical in Kenya to support the local manufacturing of farm machinery, and that there was obvious potential is underlined by the presence not only of a dynamic steel industry but also a components manufacturing sector. In 1989, Ndume was such a manufacturer of machinery[42] but their potential was being eroded by the illegal, unscrupulous granting of import licenses for ploughs and harrows. This almost ruined the enterprise and the firm wrote to KAM:

> Our factory employees [sic] 100 men, all Kenyan. We are currently running under capacity.... What do we do to make Government aware that they are actually killing an industry? ...We are told that over 400 ploughs ... were imported recently into the country by one importer alone ... [and] undisclosed numbers by two other importers.... Why import two to three years' requirement in one year? I leave you to guess! Hence we can reasonably assume we will not be making many ploughs in the next two years. Now if this sort of thing is allowed to continue we will have to face the fact that it will be necessary to close the factory. We certainly cannot maintain our level of employment.... We ask you to arrange a meeting with suitable Government officers so that we may present our problems.... We need a clear statement from the Minister that he wishes to have a local agricultural equipment manufacturing industry.[43]

Perhaps the most spectacular case in which a local industry was sabotaged—and in this example actually killed—by the Kenyan state is that of East African Bag & Cordage. The company was incorporated in 1934 as Kenya Sisal Manufacturing Company, but changed its name to Sisal Products (East Africa) Ltd. in 1936, and to East African Bag & Cordage in 1954, as it was serving the whole East African market. In the postindependence era, the company remained a public company with the government actually holding shares in it through the IDB. The government was also participating, through the Ministry of Agriculture, in growing kenaf, a raw material that was to replace imported jute, the principal raw material used by East African Bag & Cordage. The board of directors was almost entirely African. Its workforce (of the company and its subsidiary, Kensack, combined) was 4,100 in 1988. By early 1989, however, it lost almost all its home market when several state-owned sectoral boards (including the National Cereals and Produce Board, and the Kenya Grain Growers Co-operative Union) imported 33 million gunny bags from China and Bangladesh, a quantity large enough to meet their requirements for more than three years.[44] These events outraged the local media. The *Financial Review* stated:

> The saga in imported gunny bags, like ... sugar, textiles and processed foodstuffs before it, is an indication of a serious flaw in the national economic management. As imported bags flood the local market, local manufacturers of similar bags are closing down for lack of buyers, putting

thousands of Kenyan workers out of work. This dubious goal is achieved at the cost of millions of shillings in foreign exchange.... Observers must wonder how long the government can expect the goodwill it enjoys from foreign donors to last if they (the donors) have to, in effect, subsidise the importation of luxury goods to enrich a few Kenyans at the expense of the majority.[45]

An editorial in the *Weekly Review* lamented:

That no one thought about the fate that would befall hundreds of employees and their families if East African Bag & Cordage collapsed, as it was bound to with continued reliance on imports of gunny bags, is a sorry statement indeed about the country's commitment to the development of local industry and the reduction of unemployment in Kenya.[46]

As a result of imports, three thousand workers lost their jobs. The company's subsidiary, Kensack, collapsed, while the kenaf project in which both the government and several hundred farmers in western Kenya were deeply involved, was abandoned. East African Bag & Cordage itself was placed under receivership in 1989. The following year it was bought by a local Indian conglomerate, Polysack (formerly Unisack, another African-operated company that had collapsed due to mismanagement) with Diamond Lalji as managing director.[47]

This situation, in which the state acts against the national interest, seems to prevail in Kenya. In almost all the above examples, at least four stated goals of Kenyan development plans were sabotaged. First, local industrialization was undermined by the giving of an unplanned niche in the Kenyan market to foreign products. Second, it led to enormous under-utilization of the installed capacity of Kenyan manufacturing industries, and its ensuing unemployment. Third, the country's balance of payments and foreign currency difficulties were aggravated, since importers had to pay in non-Kenyan funds for foreign goods. Fourth, with local industries in trouble, the chances of developing export markets were diminished. In addition, in the cases of East African Spectre and East African Bag & Cordage, the so-called indigenization policy was affected: East African Bag & Cordage passed from African to local Indian ownership. The Indians, who almost always become a scapegoat for governmental incompetence and inconsistencies, will likely return the company to profitable operation—and then once more be subjected to Africanization.

The case of the Ministry of Finance and Economic Planning and Development was markedly worse even than that of MCI.[48] It could not execute even routine tasks such as the keeping of records of state investments and loans, or collecting taxes. In *Report of the Public Accounts Committee, 1986/1987* it was pointed out that "as reported in previous years' Reports, Investments Registers maintained by the Treasury are poorly maintained and are in most cases not up-to-date."[49] In respect to loans made by the government, the committee noted that it "has not . . . been possible to confirm the correctness of these figures due to the fact that loan registers . . . are not maintained."[50] The revenue-collecting departments did not fare better. In the controller and auditor general's report for 1982/83 it was stated that the customs and excise department (now under the control of the ministry since the collapse of East African Common Services) failed to collect KShs653 million (on transit goods and incoming imports); KShs202 million (of duty dating as far back as 1975); and KShs156 million (of excise duty on sugar).[51] By the late 1980s the figures had reached the billion shilling range[52] and in 1988/89 was KShs2.3 billion.[53] The situation deteriorated still further, both for the finance ministry and the office of the vice president (and their associated departments, including customs and income tax) as indicated in the 1991 report of the controller and auditor general.[54]

The finance ministry was no better at implementation of development strategies, although the plans it formulated through the 1970s and 1980s were superficially impressive. (Actually, these were largely drawn up by foreign consultants, as is shown below.) As already indicated, the main fiscal measure used to stimulate industrial development and Kenya's exports from the late 1940s to the early 1960s was the Customs Drawback Scheme. Essentially, this refunded duties paid by manufacturers on raw imported materials to make their enterprises more competitive. This fiscal instrument was revived in the 1970s in the Export Compensation Scheme under the provisions of Local Manufacturers (Export Compensation) Act, 1974. In practice, the program was ineffective due to organizational problems—the inconsistencies and incompetence that prevailed in the postindependence civil service. The scheme was subject to sudden changes, including its suspension. For example, despite the importance previously attached to the scheme, as it was considered to be the main "incentive" offered by the state (although it was actually a refund), it was suddenly scrapped as in the 1982 budget. KAM protested, saying:

> It is our considered opinion Mr. Minister that to suspend export compensation abruptly without any alternative will have a detrimental effect on the export momentum established at considerable costs to both industry and the country as a whole.[55]

The scheme was reinstated in the 1983/84 financial year. An additional drawback was that in each government budget, items were arbitrarily added or removed from the eligibility list. Over the years, eligible industrial activities were reduced from two thousand to eight hundred.[56] Meanwhile, import duties on raw materials increased to a range of 40 percent to 80 percent, while the Export Compensation Scheme remained at 20 percent (calculated against the value of exports). Little wonder that Kenyan manufacturers became less and less interested in exporting, saying "it was far more profitable to produce for the local market than sell internationally."[57] As noted above, however, local markets, too, increasingly became hazardous, due to the corruption at MCI that allowed mass importation of products similar to those made locally.

Other schemes formulated by the finance ministry, aimed at stimulating industry and exports, were not implemented at all, or were partially executed but remained either inactive or were subsequently abandoned. These included an Export Credit Guarantee Scheme (to lend exporters working capital required to meet confirmed orders), an Export Credit Insurance Scheme (to protect against nonpayment in an importing country), and Manufacturing-Under-Bond (to promote export processing zones). In regard to plans for introducing export credit and insurance, it was announced in *Development Plan 1984–1988* that "possibilities for the establishment of an Export Credit and Insurance Guarantees Corporation will be investigated and appropriate action taken."[58] However, this was reversed in the next major policy statement:

> Government-financed export credit guarantees have been discussed for some time as a means of overcoming the inherent risk in loans to exporters. . . . [The government] cannot participate either as a source of capital or as a guarantor. It may be possible to attract foreign assistance to get the scheme started.[59]

This position was reversed yet again in *Development Plan 1989–1993*: "Government will set up a consortium of local commercial banks and insurance companies to operate the Export Credit Insurance and Guarantee Scheme."[60]

The discrepancy between policy pronouncement and implementation is also evident in the case of Manufacturing-Under-Bond (MUB), a scheme through which Kenya hoped to become a center for export processing zones. MUB was suggested by KAM as early as 1973, when its executive officer, Mr. T.W. Tyrrell, wrote to Dr. Kiano, the commerce minister, requesting that special processing zones be considered. KAM said these would

> allow Kenya to develop its potential as a manufacturing centre for support of industries in the more developed countries of Europe. . . . Kenya could well take the place of Hong Kong in this respect. Both Hong Kong and Japan have become too expensive for the European industrialist to use as a manufacturing base for components as well as partially and wholly completed garments. Such a development on a joint venture basis, manufacturing entirely for export from raw materials imported or where possible, produced locally, could open means of development in rural areas . . . [by] providing employment and encouraging service

industries . . . as well as increasing purchasing power of these areas. If this suggestion can be implemented then increased exports can be guaranteed. Without it, the laborious processes of obtaining Customs Duty refunds with all the control and restrictions enforced by the Customs and Excise will continue to the detriment of Kenya's development and continuing loss of export markets. . . . Kenya has a large population of young people, [and] an army of unemployed; it must, therefore, be forward looking, outward looking and positive in its policy, so as to be able to obtain maximum return on the employment of all its assets both natural and human. There is nothing new in the proposal outlined, it has been operating in many countries in terms of industrial development. The system has great advantages in its simplicity and positive approach to the export markets.[61]

These proposals did not feature in official documents until more than a decade late—in *Development Plan 1984–1988,* which declared that "manufacturers have already been called upon to register their interest in producing under-bond."[62] This was another false start, however. Two years later KAM wrote to the government:

This association continues to receive inquiries from its members and overseas investors who are keen to invest under the scheme. . . . We have no clear information on the scheme to enable us to respond adequately. . . . May I please request that you advise this association as to when the scheme is likely to be implemented and when the regulations relating to applications and production of goods under the scheme are likely to be made known.[63]

Part of the problem was that no specific institution to administer the scheme existed before the MUB plans were announced. With the creation of the Industrial Promotion Centre in the mid-1980s, MUB could be implemented. The incentives of MUB included the use of serviced industrial sheds, and duty-free imported raw materials, to be used exclusively in the production of goods for export. MUB manufacturers were required to provide employment for over fifty workers, pay a fee of KShs4,000, and export all their manufactured goods.[64] By 1987–1988, several local industrialists established garment-exporting enterprises under the scheme. These included Fine Garments Ltd., Hercules Mills Ltd., and Brother Shirt Factory Ltd. All these companies obtained international contracts. For example, Hercules Mills Ltd., a company with a workforce of ninety people, was exporting garments to the United States by 1989.[65] After barely a year of operation, however, several problems threatened to derail the entire MUB scheme. First, government fees for investing under MUB were increased without warning by 1000 percent from KShs4,000 to KShs40,000.[66] Second, administrative bottlenecks in such areas as customs clearance, the issuing of export licenses, and the Mombasa port facilities, combined to undermine progress of the MUB scheme. One MUB manufacturer, Mr. Bipin Vora, of Hercules Mills, stated:

> Originally, we used to allow one month for the clearance and transpor-
> tation of raw materials to the inland container depot at Embakasi but
> these days, one could wait for even three months from the time a vessel
> carrying the materials registers at the port.[67]

The government-owned *Kenya Times* lamented that "the anticipated
dream of a strong scheme has slowly been fading away as bonded industrialists grappled with increasing overhead costs and expensive delays in
the delivery of raw materials and dispatching of finished goods." The
result was a loss of overseas customers who decided "to push their orders
to 'more efficient' bonded industries in Mauritius and newly industrialised
countries (NICs) in East Asia."[68]

By 1992, the Ministry of Finance had not only failed to become a
viable agency for implementing development plans, it had joined the ranks
of the openly corrupt ministries. This was exemplified by the Goldenberg
International Ltd. scandal and events surrounding the so-called political
banks. The auditor general's 1992 report indicated that Goldenberg International Ltd., which was licensed to export diamonds and gold, was paid
by the Ministry of Finance over UK£10.4 million in preferential export
compensation payments for largely nonexistent export shipments. As the
Financial Times of London reported: "No action was taken . . . [and]
Goldenberg continues to operate freely with official blessing."[69]

In the case of the political banks, the treasury and the central bank
allowed several politically connected but financially insolvent banks to run
up overdrafts worth KShs10 billion. To counter the banks' chronic deposit
shortages, the state-run National Social Security Fund (NSSF) was compelled to replenish their finances with up to KShs9.5 billion in contraven-
tion of Kenyan banking regulations (introduced in the mid-1980s in the
wake of the collapse of most African banks as indicated in Chapter 3).[70]

Deterioration in Local Government

The ministries responsible for maintenance of national physical infrastructures suffered the same fate as commerce and finance. The Ministry of
Local Government and the municipalities countrywide had, by 1969,
declined to the extent that they hardly functioned. This was acknowledged
in the National Assembly by the minister:

> Almost every county council is in financial difficulties and most are on
> the verge of collapse. . . . [The] major reason for the deterioration in the
> administration and finance . . . is incompetence of staff. The coming of
> independence saw the departure of many qualified and experienced

financial officers. It soon became apparent that there was a very serious shortage of accountants in this country and indeed to the present day, this shortage still exists, but steps have been taken to promote a local qualification and provide training.[71]

The decay in local administration went on almost uninterrupted throughout the 1970s. Mombasa, the second largest municipality, containing key port facilities, was taken over by the Ministry of Local Government based in Nairobi in 1976. The city of Nairobi itself—the administrative, commercial, and industrial center of Kenya—managed to survive the 1970s but crumbled in 1983, when it was replaced by a commission appointed by President Moi to serve until the 1992 multiparty elections. This had been predicted in the 1981 report of the Public Accounts Committee, which stated:

> The City Council of Nairobi has only been able to continue operations by illegally diverting funds which were intended for other purposes. They have broken agreements made with the World Bank in relation to the provisions of monies for water development in Nairobi. . . . [T]he finances of the Nairobi City Council are in a mess; the council has violated all financial management regulations, and there is no co-operation between departments and between Councillors and Chief Officers. As a result of all this the Council is on the verge of collapse.[72]

The implication of the deterioration of these administrative units (all under oversight of the Ministry of Local Government) was that key economic infrastructures were not being maintained. By the 1980s matters had degenerated so much that private sector companies began to build and maintain their own roads. The Kenyan municipalities were no longer able to do this. In the Ruaraka industrial area, for example, where industries have been relocating from the congested and run-down Nairobi Industrial Area, industrialists built a tarmac road linking their factories to Mombasa Road, as the Nairobi City Commission had failed to construct an all-weather road. In Kikuyu township outside Nairobi, industrialists constructed a water reservoir and maintained roads in place of the Kiambu County Council. In the main industrial areas, especially the Nairobi Industrial Area, the situation was even worse. The connecting road to Mombasa Road (leading not only to Kenya's port facilities but to Nairobi's Jomo Kenyatta International Airport) became almost impassable at a narrow, worn-out bridge over the Ngong River that had been built in 1941. With only one other access road to the industrial area, Enterprise Road, which was congested and most often in a scandalous state of disrepair, industrialists collected funds to build an additional road. KAM wrote to its members:

> Work has started on the above project [i.e., Lunga Lunga Outer Ring Roads Project], initiated on harambee basis by KAM members with

factories adjacent to Lunga Lunga Road.... KAM members along Lunga Lunga Road . . . agreed to pay . . . towards the construction of the alternative route to Outering Road to reduce volume of traffic during peak hours on Likoni and Enterprise Roads.... We are writing to appeal to you to make your contribution.[73]

The pitiful situation, and the ineffectiveness of the Ministry of Local Government and the Nairobi City Commission in dealing with it, led local industrialists to charge that the Kenya government was engaging in industrial sabotage. Letters to the editors of local papers became the forum for such complaints. Apparently the Kenyan bourgeoisie felt this attracted public attention to their plight better than private representations to the ministries, which were prone to being disregarded. One letter, to the editor of the *Standard,* stated:

The present state of Enterprise Road in the Industrial Area is pathetic and totally unacceptable. This road is a life-line of all industries in the Industrial Area . . . [but] over the years, it has been totally neglected by the City Commission.... The deep potholes cause heavy traffic jams not to mention the untold damage . . . [done] to vehicles and manufactured goods. This is all costing our country a colossal loss in foreign exchange. It is embarrassing when foreign customers visit our factories and have to go through such roads.... [T]his is a clear insult to the industrial progress that our country has made since independence. . . . Does the City Commission care any more or is this some form of industrial sabotage? How many years of agony and misery do the industrialists have to go through before there is some sort of sanity on this road? This is probably the biggest rip-off by the City Commission as far as the rate payers are concerned.[74]

The Ministry of Local Government was by this time (in the late 1980s) increasingly being run from the home village of the minister responsible, Moses Budamba Mudavadi, or "King of Mululu" as he was widely known. Officials in Kenya's municipal councils began to trek to Mululu to present their problems. A local magazine described a meeting between the minister and a mayoral entourage from Kisumu:

Mululu, the country home of the Minister for Local Government and Physical planning, Mr. Moses Budamba Mudavadi, is perhaps the best known of any cabinet minister in Kenya today.... Hardly a week goes by without a delegation paying homage at Mululu.... Mudavadi has also played host to civic leaders from other parts of the country who have preferred to present civic problems to his home than at his Jogoo House office in Nairobi.... Only last weekend, all civic leaders from the Kisumu municipal council were at Mululu on a goodwill visit and Mudavadi, in a characteristic style, answered the various requests put to him by the mayor, Mr. George Olilo, who led the delegation. Mudavadi pledged to assist the municipality in solving some urgent problems. The delegation returned to Kisumu, assured that their mission had been successful.[75]

As the Ministry of Local Government degenerated, charges for its largely nonexistent services continued to rise. This was indicated by various forms of taxes on both Kenyan manufacturing enterprises and their employees. The Local Government Act, 1988, in effect, gave discretionary powers to local authorities to "charge fees for any licence or permit issued under the Act to any person, premises or trade." Further:

> All fees or charges imposed by a local authority may be imposed by a resolution of the local authority with the consent of the Minister and such consent may be given to allow a specified local authority to impose fees by resolution in respect of a specified power.

These powers, given to local authorities and the minister, led to the imposition of all sorts of taxes, some of which duplicated those of the Ministry of Commerce and Industry. These included a local authority service charge, which was paid by both employers and employees (payable to all municipalities in which a company may do business, irrespective of its location). Other demands were for manufacturing licenses, export/import licenses (which are also charged for by the Ministry of Commerce under other legislation), occupational licenses for manufacturing, heavy industries licenses, site value rates, sewerage and water charges, travelling wholesaler licenses, travelling hawker's market cesses, poll rates, land rent, conservancy charges, storage licenses, a training levy, factory registration fees, road tolls, and more. But, though the fees and charges paid to local authorities increased, there was no improvement in services or in the maintenance of roads, water and sewerage systems, and other facilities.

Clearly, there is a weak relationship between policy formulation and implementation in Kenya. The status of national ministries and their handling of projects does not lend support to Hazlewood's thesis that planning "is a serious exercise in Kenya. The plans are not simply window dressing for local consumption. Nor are they, what is not unknown, purely externally oriented documents, drawn up solely to satisfy the requirements of aid donors by technical assistance staff supplied by the aid donors."[76]

Fall of Development Institutions

The state created purpose-made new bodies to enable it to participate directly in commerce and industry, and to implement localization-Africanization-Kenyanization-indigenization of these sectors. The goal was to supplement private sector investments and to assist black Kenyans to enter these sectors. The main institutions created for these purposes were ICDC and IDB: both were to participate in large commercial and industrial projects, either by providing loans, or by entering into joint venture agreements with private investors. Other organizations to assist black Kenyans to enter commerce and industry were KIE—to provide industrial sheds and machinery—and NCC—to provide know-how and financing for African contractors. Both KNTC and JLBs sought to assist black Kenyans in commerce: KNTC was to become the sole distributor of some essential commodities, such as salt and sugar, and would channel them toward Africans, and in the process stimulate entrepreneurship; JLBs were to provide Africans with loans to establish themselves in the market place. ICDC was unique in the sense that it also participated in the commercial sector in conjunction with JLBs by providing loans to black Kenyan traders.

By 1979 the Kenyan state's involvement in the industrial sector through these agencies was considerable: it participated in 176 companies. The state owned forty-seven of them outright, and controlled thirty-six through majority shareholding, ninety-three through minority shareholding.[77] Such statistics led Swainson and Leys to assert that the ICDC "in addition to underwriting the takeover of the commercial sector from noncitizens in the 1970s, became the primary investment agency for industry."[78] Their observations, however, were not accompanied by analysis of the actual workings of these corporations and their parent ministries. Most state projects rarely functioned as a superficial examination suggested. On the contrary, they became a national liability and had little success in extending Kenya's industrial base, generating revenue for the Kenyan state, or creating an African commercial and industrial class, as the Committee of Review of Statutory Boards found in 1979. It warned that Kenya's state corporations constituted a "serious threat to the economy and it is, therefore, a matter of urgency that steps should be taken."[79] The committee had gathered evidence and concluded that these corporations had become "personalised institutions." Its report found "conflict of interest between public responsibilities and private profit or aggrandizement, lack of . . . planning and inadequate financial management and accountability." The economic and social costs of delay in taking action to remedy these serious problems were "simply unacceptable," said the committee.[80]

The impaired condition of most of these corporations led to the setting up of another commission, the Working Party on Government Expenditures. Its report indicated that by 1982, the cumulative investments of the Kenyan government had exceeded KShs18 billion. Remarkably, dividends paid to the exchequer from these investments amounted to a mere KShs2.2 million, instead of the expected return of KShs1.8 billion (i.e., 10 percent) annually. The report further noted that this sum was paid by only six of the state corporations. Almost all the rest were in serious management and financial difficulties.[81] ICDC was said to represent "an extreme though not exceptional example of poor investment."[82] The working party recommended that the government divest itself of these projects; its participation in industry was "inhibiting rather than promoting development."[83]

By 1989, almost nothing had changed in the workings of most state programs. Profits made by ICDC and its sixty-one related companies for fiscal year 1988/89 were KShs50 million.[84] KShs12 million were presented to the exchequer as dividends in 1989.[85] Meanwhile, a staggering KShs400 million was being reported as an accumulated loss by one state corporation alone—Mount Kenya Textile Mills (Mountex).[86] And during the previous year, KShs73.5 million had been spent by the ICDC to rehabilitate nine of its ailing companies.[87] Further, by 1987, the ICDC owed the Kenya government over KShs1 billion, although the two could not agree on a "real" figure and whether this was a loan or a grant.[88]

The Kenyan state finally responded to the pathetic circumstance of almost all the governmental corporations, acknowledging that they neither supplemented private capital's efforts to extend industrial development, nor helped to create an African business class. *Development Plan 1989–1993* said of the ICDC:

> Over time, this scheme experienced serious difficulties. One of the major problems was the financial constraints faced by the ICDC, which undermined its ability to provide loans for the purchase of existing businesses thus hampering its ability to promote the Kenyanisation process it was intended for. Arising from this and other factors, many businesses transferred in this process from non-indigenous to indigenous businessmen reverted to the former through "back door" transactions.[89]

ICDC and IDB (which was in an equally depleted condition) were instead handed over to the International Development Association (IDA) of the World Bank Group for "rehabilitation." So were KIE and the Agricultural Finance Corporation (AFC).[90] Among management personnel provided by the IDA were an assets manager and a liabilities manager, both of whom were attached to the treasury, which as parent ministry of these institutions was itself in a poor condition. In addition, two financial advisors (one a human resources development and operations advisor; the other a systems advisor) were deployed at each corporation.[91]

For KNTC, it was conceded in *Development Plan 1989–1993* that its "monopolistic status led to inefficiencies and unprofitable operations that were subsidised by Government and Kenyan consumers." And the plan added that "under these circumstances, KNTC failed to compete effectively with older and well established non-Kenyan businesses"[92]—an admission that KNTC changed its mandate from creating a black business class to becoming a trading company. Of course, its new objective it also failed to accomplish. The controller and auditor general indicated that

KNTC had incurred losses of KShs531 million by 1987.[93] The JLBs did not fare better as they faced

> numerous problems due to poor management, false accounting, the issue of fictitious loans, etc. As of 1987, the JLBs had loaned out a total of KShs87.5 million covering 30,000 loanees of which, regrettably, 11,000 were in default involving a total of KShs45 million.[94]

KNTC and JLBs were said to be undergoing in-house rehabilitation, while the NCC was scrapped in 1988. When NCC was dissolved, the Kenyan state's contribution to it was KShs198.3 million, which, according to the controller and auditor general, "was mainly to cover operational losses by the corporation."[95] In its lifetime, NCC had managed to establish only one construction company—International Construction Company Ltd.— which ceased to operate in 1978.[96]

Collapse of the Supranational Services

The situation of the East African Common Service Organisation during the 1960s and 1970s was parlous and it collapsed in 1977, ending not only the joint services of key economic infrastructures, but also the most visionary experiment of the colonial era: the common market that incorporated Kenya, Uganda, and Tanganyika (and informally, Rwanda, Burundi, and parts of Zaire and Sudan that bordered on the East African partner countries).

The principal joint services after independence were the East African Railways Corporation (EARC), East African Harbours Corporation (EAHC), East African Airways, the East African Income Department, and East African Customs & Excise. The initial and devastating problem was that they required a substantial technical and professional cadre and this was not available within the African communities. Yet, the three main partner countries were determined to replace the non-African technical and professional cadres and this placed these services in a profound predicament. The East African bourgeoisie became increasingly alarmed. APIEA proposed to the Kenyan government that:

> The Association, through its members, has a wealth of experience and knowledge of the economy, obtained through many years of practical application to business, which could be utilised to the fullest possible extent in assisting economic growth of East Africa. This knowledge is freely available to each of the East African Governments but is being first offered to Kenya where the bulk of our members are domiciled. The scarcity of skilled administrators within the Government service, places an impossibly heavy burden on those who occupy the posts of ministerial permanent secretaries as well as those technical advisers who are pro-

vided from time to time under the terms of technical aid made available by international agencies. It is in support of the permanent civil servant and the technical advisers that this association with its background of local experience and knowledge believes it could be made use of.[97]

Such presentations did not succeed in sensitizing the Kenyan leadership in the complexities of sound economic management, for this was the period when Africanization, self-interest, individual acquisitiveness, and accumulation of political power was the prime concern. Almost all other issues were relegated to a secondary status. The unravelling of the common services continued through the 1960s and early 1970s, and by 1974, the prized tool of economic development in the colonial period, the East African Railway Corporation (EARC), was in dire straits. A letter to the Kenyan government from KAM stated:

> Railways continue to refuse to accept goods for transportation to Tanzania. It is appreciated that the reason for this embargo on transportation is that the Railways wagons have been retained in Tanzania and not returned for further use between the two countries. It is also appreciated that the retention of rolling stock by both Uganda and Tanzania has caused a deteriorating position in freight movement within Kenya by reason of a shortage of rail wagons. This Association would wish to be kept advised of any progress made in improving the position.[98]

But within Kenya itself, EARC had suspended freight and passenger services for lack of spare parts in the latter part of 1974. In 1975, the World Bank came to the rescue and salvaged the corporation for a few more years. New loans (totalling US$32.4 million—to be added to debts of KShs30 million already owed to Britain, and KShs160 million owed to the governments of West Germany and Canada and the World Bank) were issued by the bank while it entered into new agreements that committed the three East African regimes to reviving EARC.[99] But—as the *Weekly Review* noted—the World Bank, "one of the Corporation's more patient financiers," was losing patience with EARC: "and East African Partner States, who are the proprietors, are behaving as if they have lost interest in it altogether."[100]

Among the reasons for this neglecting of EARC by the Kenyan government was also an issue that kept resurfacing even in the aftermath of the rail corporation's collapse: road transportation became favored. Kenya's public servants, politicians, and new state corporations (such as the Kenya National Transport Company—KENATCO, before it collapsed in the late 1970s) sought to enter the transportation business. Between 1972 and 1974, for instance, there was tension between Tanzania and Kenya. The former insisted that the lucrative trade route of Kenya-Tanzania-Zambia, with goods mainly originating in Kenya, was best served by railway—the Tazara Railway linking Tanzania and Zambia was almost completed. Tanzania maintained that rail transport ensured the maximum use of available and less costly facilities and stressed the high maintenance costs of roads. This problem had been experienced before, when Kenya Co-operative Creameries (KCC) sought to move its butter exports to Northern Rhodesia by road in 1956: the Tanganyikan authorities rightly pointed out that this contravened the Motor Vehicles (Restrictions) Ordinance which prevented "private carriers taking goods over roads used by the railway."[101]

However, after independence the Kenyan government remained adamant in insisting on road haulage. Instead of accepting the rail alternative, it offered to share the expenses of maintaining the Tanzanian roads. The offer was declined, and in 1974 Tanzania prohibited the use of heavy trucks (over 18 tonnes) on its roads.[102] This problem resurfaced twice, in 1986 and 1989. In 1986, following the revitalization of Uganda Railways, the Ugandan leadership was determined to use rail to move its coffee crop to the port of Mombasa. Rail was reportedly cheaper and provided better hauling facilities than the poorly maintained roads in both Uganda and Kenya. The Kenyan authorities unsuccessfully pressed for use of the road route, which was worth an estimated KShs16 million per month to Kenyan transporters.[103] In 1989, the issue was replayed in Kenya itself. With its own road system in appalling condition, including the Nairobi-Mombasa road, and with tea and coffee farming threatened by impassable roads,[104] President Moi eventually ordered all transportation of tea to Mombasa to be done by rail.[105]

Kenya's Role in the Collapse of the Common Market

The common market had developed during the colonial period on the basis of several factors, as already noted. Besides the convenience of joint administration and the resulting economies of scale, the much larger regional market was viewed as an incentive to attract local and foreign capital to invest in East Africa. This vision was undermined immediately after independence. Evidently, incompetence and territorial rivalries overrode the benefits of a single market.[106]

Kenya, as the most commercially and industrially advanced member of the community, was expected to play the principal role in preserving the common market and common services. This was the hope of the East African bourgeoisie and of foreign investors (most of whom lived in Kenya) as indicated in a letter from KAM to the commerce ministry:

> If we are to strengthen the Community and effectively demonstrate to not only the present partners but also potential partners and other countries of Africa, that the East African Community is a live and vital body, it is essential that some positive action is taken. . . . As the most

a copy of the Policy Statement of the previous Export Promotion Council
which should serve as a basic guide in respect of . . . the policy of the
Government in relation to export promotion.[108]

Parliamentary debates of the late 1960s also indicated that the importance
of the common market was not understood by Kenya's political leaders.
The anti-common market rhetoric and petty economic nationalism was so
rife in the National Assembly that Speaker Humphrey Slade had to tell
MPs almost ceaselessly not to make allegations against Kenya's East
African Community partners. Mr. Humphrey warned:

You know the Rule to which I refer so often, and it is particularly
important for all of us that we preserve the best possible relations with
our neighbours. Therefore hon. Members must avoid any allegations
that, operating the Treaty within the bounds of the Treaty, our partner
States are doing something wrong or unfair.[109]

The shortsightedness that led to the eventual collapse of the common
market was not limited to Kenya. The Ugandan state restricted imports from
Kenya by 1968. KAM reacted with a letter to Kenya's commerce ministry:

Industry is experiencing considerable difficulty by reason of obstacles
raised through Import Licensing procedure established in Uganda. . . .
[L]icenses are being refused to importers in Uganda of plastic foot-wear,
plastic hollowware and plastic luggage. All these items are manufactured
in Kenya.[110]

The same year saw the introduction by Tanzania of customs posts at its
borders, subjecting vehicles and goods to comprehensive inspection. This
action provoked KAM to protest:

This could have a disastrous effect upon Kenyan goods moving into
Tanzania. This is the type of control that would exist between two
completely dis-associated countries anxious to protect their revenue and

to discourage movement of goods into the country. Surely such a restriction was never envisaged in terms of the East African Treaty for Co-operation, the implementation of the Common Market and a unified customs and excise service.[111]

An expatriate officer in the Kenyan government was to lament in reaction to the Tanzanian action:

We appear to have reached a situation when it is almost more difficult and expensive to consign goods by road between Partner States than it is to consign goods by road to a foreign country outside the East African Community.[112]

The East African bourgeoisie's attempts to persuade the three territorial regimes of the value of the common market turned out to be futile. One of the last appeals—before the common market disintegrated—came from KAM in 1975:

It is well known that the Treaty itself has not been followed by the Partner States and many Articles of the Treaty have been ignored. Differences in political and economic policy have influenced national and individual feelings to the extent that the benefits originally acknowledged have either been discarded or overlooked. . . . The common market must be fully established in a true sense if the objectives are to be achieved. . . . If the Partners are seriously thinking in terms of continuation of the Community, national status as far as economic development is concerned must be superseded by a complete changeover to East African thinking. In considering the advantages of a common market recognition must be given to the market potential that the whole area offers and therefore the ability to attract large scale industries which could not on a national basis be justified as viable enterprises. The necessity to attract such industries is now emphasized . . . by the world crisis caused by inflation which has raised the prices of raw materials and other imported goods to impossible heights. . . . [T]he countries themselves must consider the economies that can be made in the use of all forms of energy by turning to large scale industry rather than collections of small units. . . .[113]

The East African Community, with all its associated services, and the common market came to an end in 1977, after fourteen years of black rule—seventy-five years after the main unit, the railway, was built. A history paper published in 1989 suggests that Kenya appears to have taken a lead in ending the life of those elements that might have been saved. Katete Orwa wrote:

Finally, in January 1977, Kenya took a bold step in breaking up the East African Airways. Tanzania had earlier pleaded with the members of the East African General Assembly to save the airline, and later retaliated by closing all its borders with Kenya. . . . Tanzania explained her action: "If Kenya did not want air, railway and sea links with her neighbours, there should be no reason why she should want a road link with her neighbours." Kenya was thus mistaken in thinking that Tanzania could not block her access to the southern Africa market.[114]

Notes

1. Kenya C.S.U. press release, 1963.

2. Odinga, speaking in the House of Representatives. Official report, p. 2843.

3. Government of Kenya, *The Economic Development of Kenya*, p. 8 and p. 149.

4. Republic of Kenya, *Commission of Inquiry (Public Service Structure)*, p. 9.

5. Examples include Sir Ernest Vasey, the former finance minister in Kenya and Tanganyika, who joined Comcraft, and Mr. T.W. Tyrrell, a former mayor of Dar-es-Salaam, who joined the Association of East African Industries (now Kenya Association of Manufacturers).

6. See the *Daily Nation*, 9 January 1969 and 10 January 1969. See also the US magazine, *Time*, 17 January 1969.

7. Republic of Kenya, *Ndegwa Commission Report*, 1971, p. 9; see also *Waruhiu Report*, 1980, p. 83.

8. Republic of Kenya, *Sessional Paper No. 1*, 1965, p. 20. (emphasis added).

9. Republic of Kenya, *Ndegwa Commission Report*, 1971, as cited in the Republic of Kenya, *Waruhiu Report*, 1980, p. 83.

10. Leys, "Accumulation," p. 183.

11. Republic of Kenya, *Waruhiu Report*, p. 83.

12. Report dated 7 May 1964. See also "Government Admits Constitutional Breach," the *Daily Nation*, 23 June 1964.

13. Minutes of evidence before the Public Accounts Committee, 15 November 1967.

14. In "Endemic Unauthorised Expenditure by Government Ministries," *East Africa Report on Trade & Industry*, April, 1989, Christopher Mulei wrote: "Kenyans can remember the result of the conscientiousness of this expatriate officer [Barrett]. . . . The point seems to be that in the absence of the Auditor General being an officer of the National Assembly, as he should be, there is very little or no control at all over unauthorised expenditure by Government Ministries."

15. Not everyone acquiesced in this myth. Wariithi is quoted in the National Assembly official report, p. 2643, as saying: "Take the argument put forward in this House by the Minister of Social Services . . . that the principle should be supported because the Ministers cannot be in business. . . . This is not even true, because many of them—and this is known, Mr. Speaker, you know it as well as I do—are able to trade . . . in their wives' names. . . . All we have to do is to look around and see what properties they own, how they live, how they dress, and the cars they drive. Of all Mercedes of the Members of the National Assembly, the majority, 90 per cent, are owned by Ministers, in which case I do not accept the view that by not being in business they are worse off."

16. Republic of Kenya, *National Assembly Official Report*, Vol. XVII (Part II), 27 June 1969 to 19 August 1969, p. 2591.

17. Cited in *East African Standard*, 18 July 1969. Mr. Seroney appropriately noted in the National Assembly: "Now a civil servant cannot, in the middle of his contract, draw from his gratuity which he is expecting; he has to wait until he has satisfactorily completed his employment and then as a sort of gratitude he is paid a certain amount when he leaves the service. [T]his particular payment can be paid

any time the Ministers like it and the President agrees. I think it is quite wrong to introduce something confusing like this and call it gratuity." Republic of Kenya, official report, Vol. XVII (Part II), 27 June 1969 to 19 August 1969, p. 2638.

18. Republic of Kenya, National Assembly report, 17 October 1969, p. 1441. In another development, the Electoral Commission lost its independence through the Presidential Elections Bill (1969) which asserted that "the Minister shall appoint a public officer [to] be the supervisor of Elections . . . with the consent of the President who may confer powers or impose duties on any public officer or authority." Republic of Kenya, *National Assembly Official Report,* 24 July 1969, p. 2445.

19. See issues of the *Weekly Review,* the *Daily Nation,* and the *Standard* for the last week of October, 1975. See also *Weekly Review* of 31 May 1976, for a reassessment of the events around the imprisonment of Shikuku and Seroney.

20. Since the 1970s, Paul Ngei had been one of Kenya's most corrupt national leaders. In 1989, when he was a minister for Manpower Development and Employment, his properties were attached for auctioning over debts amounting to KShs16 million owed to Pan African Credit and Finance Company. Ngei told the judge who heard the case: "The only money I owe the respondents is KShs4 million"—*Daily Nation,* 16 December 1989. Ngei, who retained his position in the Moi cabinet, was by no means an exception. The Kenyan media periodically report "deals" involving high-ranking officials. For example, "Tannery Suit Against [Arthur] Magugu" (minister for commerce, 1989), *Weekly Review,* 18 November 1988; "[Elijah] Mwangale Defends Fertiliser Deal" (minister for livestock development, 1989), *Standard,* 9 June 1989; "Minister Sued over KShs242.1 Million Loan" (Willy Rotich Kamuren, assistant minister in the Office of the President, 1989), *Standard,* 17 September 1989; and "The AFC, the main agricultural credit institution in the country is owed a staggering KShs2 billion. . . . Kenyan leaders, including politicians and senior civil servants owe over KShs300 million of this amount," *Financial Review,* 15 February 1988.

21. Report of the debate in the *Weekly Review,* 22 December 1975.

22. Murray-Brown, *Kenyatta,* p. 317.

23. Leys, *Underdevelopment in Kenya,* p. 246.

24. *Weekly Review,* 12 August 1988.

25. This amendment was passed in Parliament without a single member opposing it—and in less than three hours after it was introduced. The *Weekly Review* reported: "Around 3.00 P. M . . . the Bill was introduced in parliament by the attorney-general Mr. Justice Matthew Guy Muli and by 6:00 P. M., it had gone through its third reading without even token opposition. . . . [M]ost [legislators] appeared more jovial than serious in passing the Bill . . . though it touched on one of the fundamental tenets of the country's constitution, involving the independence of the judiciary and the public service from political control." See "Parliament Amends the Constitution with Surprising Alacrity," 5 August 1988.

26. Mulei, "Endemic unauthorised expenditures," 1989.

27. Nicholas Biwott was said to be the second most important person in Kenya, and a close associate of President Moi. Biwott was, reportedly, one of the most corrupted cabinet ministers. He was implicated by Britain's Scotland Yard in the murder of the former minister for foreign affairs, Dr. Ouko, one of the few officials in Moi regime who was respected by the donor community. Biwott was briefly imprisoned in connection with this case. Following his release he became a member of Parliament in the December 1992 general election.

28. A letter to the editor of the *Weekly Review,* 10 November 1989, read: "It has now become common practice that, when a member of parliament dies in office, his son, brother, cousin or even a wife is declared the sole candidate for the

seat, sometimes amid protests which are never listened to. I suggest that the present parliamentary sitting pass a law called parliamentary perpetual succession and inheritance act. The purpose of the act will be that all present members of parliament be declared life MPs, and if any of them dies, he or she should be succeeded by a family member, preferably a spouse or an off-spring." See also *Daily Nation*, 7 November 1989.

29. Republic of Kenya, Controller's report 1982/83, p. 1xv.

30. *Daily Nation*, 16 February 1990.

31. *Kenya Times*, 10 January 1990.

32. *Financial Review*, 24 October 1988.

33. *Sunday Nation*, 5 November 1989. See also *Kenya Times*, 9 November 1989.

34. As described in *Development Plan 1989–1993*, p. 220.

35. Republic of Kenya, *Ndegwa Commission*, pp. 13–14.

36. Republic of Kenya, *Waruhiu Report*, pp. 37–39 (emphasis in original).

37. Mbogoh, in House of Representatives report, p. 1110.

38. Republic of Kenya, report for 1986/87, pp. 144–145.

39. Republic of Kenya, paper on management for renewed growth, 1986, p. 99.

40. *Financial Review*, 1 February 1988.

41. East African Spectre to D.O. Anyango, the minister for industry, 2 August 1989. Company files.

42. Besides Ndume, a number of Kenyan companies manufacture machinery, for both local and export market. These include East African Foundry Works, Marshal Fowler, Steel Structures, and Specialised Engineering Co. Ltd.

43. Ndume letter dated 14 April 1989. KAM files.

44. Even without this villainous act—participating in killing a local industry and throwing thousands of Kenyan workers out of employment—the National Cereals and Produce Board was one of the most fraudulent state bodies in Kenya. Robert Shaw, writing in the *Sunday Nation*, 1 October 1989, under the headline, "Here's a Way Out of the Parastatal Mess," said: "Many of them [state corporations] are bleeding our economy. . . . The best and most notorious example is that of the National Cereals and Produce (NCPB), which accounts for nearly 20 percent of the country's public sector deficits in excess of Shs5 billion."

45. *Financial Review*, 28 November 1988.

46. *Weekly Review*, 24 June 1988.

47. *Daily Nation*, 8 February 1990.

48. The role of this ministry, as well as that of Commerce and Industry, is frequently changed, leading to considerable confusion. Finance and Economic Planning and Development has, at times, been divided to form (1.) the Office of the Vice of President and Ministry of Finance, and (2.) the Ministry of Economic Planning and Development. Then they would again merge. Commerce has also been divided from Industry from time to time, only again to be merged.

49. Page 16.

50. Page 16.

51. Republic of Kenya, *Appropriation Accounts*, pp. vi–viii.

52. *Appropriation Accounts*, p. 7.

53. *Daily Nation*, 3 November 1989. See also *Kenya Times*, 9 November 1989. While the Ministry of Finance and associated departments were thus failing to collect taxes, new forms of taxation were imposed on ordinary Kenyans: the ruling party, KANU, was given powers to impose charges, for example, on cattle, country buses, and market traders. KANU's paramilitary youth wing was the enforcing agency. The rationale for this was explained by KANU's chairman, and the

minister for education, Mr. Aloo Aringo. "Branches are free to raise money through acceptable means," he said. "We want the branches to be as independent as possible and generate their own funds through the means they deem fit." Cited in *Daily Nation,* 24 August 1989.

54. Republic of Kenya, *Appropriation Accounts for 1989/90, Vol. 1,* pp. 7–14.

55. KAM, "A Paper for Submission to the Minister for Finance on 1982/83 Budgetary Measures."

56. KAM, *Export Incentives,* 1989, p. 34.

57. KAM, *Export Incentives,* p. 34.

58. Page 212.

59. Republic of Kenya, *Sessional Paper No. 1 of 1986 on Economic Management for Renewed Growth,* p. 97.

60. Page 156.

61. Letter datad 6 December 1979. KAM files.

62. Page 212.

63. Silas Ita, KAM, to the Ministry of Finance and Planning, 22 April 1986. KAM files.

64. Investment Promotion Centre, *Investors Guide,* 1989.

65. *Kenya Export News,* May 1989.

66. *Sunday Times,* 18 March 1990.

67. Quoted in *Sunday Times,* 18 March 1990. See also *Sunday Nation,* 18 March 1990. The situation facing exporters of horticultural products was no better. Tons of produce went to waste at Kenyatta international airport due to lack of cargo space and storage facilities. *Daily Nation,* 20 December 1989.

68. *Sunday Times,* 18 March 1990.

69. *Financial Times,* 24 March 1993; see also editorial comment in the same issue.

70. *Financial Times,* 24 March 1993.

71. Minister for Local Government, speech reported in the official report (30 September to 5 November 1969), pp. 367–370.

72. Government of Kenya, report on Nairobi city council, p. viii.

73. KAM, "Lunga Lunga – Outer Ring Road Project," 5 October 1988. KAM files.

74. Letter signed "Miserable Industrialist," 5 June 1989.

75. *Weekly Review* 20 May 1988.

76. Hazlewood, *Economy of Kenya,* p. 174.

77. Republic of Kenya, *Review of Statutory Boards Report,* p. 22.

78. Swainson, "Indigenous Capitalism," p. 150. See also Leys, "Accumulation," p. 185.

79. Republic of Kenya, *Statutory Boards,* p. 22.

80. *Statutory Boards,* p. 22.

81. Republic of Kenya, working party report, p. 41.

82. Page 41.

83. Page 43.

84. *Daily Nation,* 22 December 1989.

85. *Daily Nation,* 22 December 1989.

86. All the ICDC and IDB related textile mills were reported to be making enormous losses. Part of the loss by Mountex, one of the most modern textile mills in the country, had to do with the fact that a senior manager "had refused to take up a residential house in Nanyuki, where the company was based, and was operating from Nairobi on a chartered aircraft regularly." *Standard,* 2 August 1989.

87. ICDC, *Annual Report,* 1987/88.

88. Republic of Kenya, *Report of the Public Accounts Committee 1986/1987,* p. 145.

89. Page 161.

90. The AFC, the main agricultural credit institution, in 1988 was owed KShs2 billion in loan arrears and defaults accumulated over twenty-five years. Most of its debtors were politicians and senior civil servants, dubbed "the untouchables" by the *Financial Review.* The untouchables nearly became touchable in 1988, when President Moi announced that anyone who owed money to state institutions such as the AFC would be barred from participating in municipal and national elections. Moi subsequently reversed the decision and the debtors remained untouchable. *Financial Review,* 29 February 1988.

91. *Weekly Review,* 26 October 1990.

92. Page 159.

93. Controller's report for 1986/87, p. 69.

94. *Development Plan 1989–1993,* pp. 159–160.

95. Republic of Kenya, *Report by the Controller and Auditor General 1986/1987,* p. 36.

96. Report for 1979/80, p. xlvii.

97. T.W. Tyrrell, executive officer, APIEA, to the minister for economic planning and development, 11 May 1966. KAM files.

98. KAM to MCI, 15 March 1974. KAM files.

99. *Weekly Review,* 24 February 1975.

100. *Weekly Review,* 24 February 1975.

101. Cited in *East African Standard,* 17 August 1956.

102. See Aggrey Awori, "The Tanzanian Road Ban Revisited," in the *Weekly Review,* 23 March 1975. Hazlewood, *Economy of Kenya,* p. 100, also noted that "Tanzania's complaint was at the damage being caused to the roads, which can be believed when the similar difficulties on the Nairobi-Mombasa road are remembered."

103. *Financial Review,* 7 July 1986.

104. In December 1989, the *Industrial Review* noted, under the headline "Whither Coffee and Tea?": "It is a truism that since their establishment to oversee the operations of tea and coffee, the Kenya Tea Development Authority and Coffee Board of Kenya have ridden rough-shod over farmers. . . . [The] woes of the . . . industry have ranged from non-collection of harvested green leaf . . . impassable roads during the rainy seasons (where all those hundreds of millions of shillings in county cess and other deductions go to is a question the farmers would dearly love to hear answered) and inconsistent payment patterns."

105. A Kenya Railways Corporation advertisement in the *Kenya Times,* 1 December 1989, said: "The Corporation would like to take this opportunity to thank His Excellency the President for giving Kenya Railways to transport tea, and to reassure farmers of our total commitment in making every effort to enable them to reap maximum benefits by transporting their produce in economical and efficient manner."

106. The *Economist,* of London, 9 June 1962, commented: "East African Federation would in itself be a weak thing; 22.5 million poverty-stricken, backward people; a few thousand bickering, yet educated and modern-minded black politicians and administrators and backward-looking tribal groups. Not much—but more than Kenya, Tanganyika or Uganda standing alone could aspire to. Yet, sadly, the chances of joining up the three territories have grown fainter."

107. Letter dated 5 May 1969. KAM files.

108. A.G. Barve, MCI, to the Association for Promotion of Industries in East Africa, 4 August 1965. KAM files.

109. Republic of Kenya, *National Assembly Official Report,* 28 June to 19 August 1969, p. 3221.

110. KAM to MCI, 21 March 1968. KAM files.

111. KAM to MCI, 4 November 1968. KAM files.

112. Mr. O.S. Knowles, MCI, to T.W. Tyrrell, KAM, 7 November 1968. MCI.19/83.Conf/101.

113. KAM to the Office of the President, 29 April 1975. KAM files.

114. Orwa, "Foreign Policy, 1963–1986," p. 235.

6

Reconstruction

The prediction by the World Bank in 1962 that if skilled people left Kenya in large numbers the country would probably not be able to maintain its 1950s' pace of development (see the report quoted at the end of Chapter 4) appears to have been on the mark. In the wake of rapid Africanization and the depletion of skilled personnel, the Kenyan national leadership discovered the mistake too late. A dire need for skilled managerial cadres was officially acknowledged regularly—for example, in *Sessional Paper No. 1* of 1965, in the *Ndegwa Commission Report* of 1971, and in the *Waruhiu Report* of 1980. As previously noted, the Kenya government simply recruited another set of expatriates to fill critical and specialized positions.

By 1983, the lack of specialized skills had become so critical that even the exercise of recruiting badly needed technical and professional personnel was handed over to a European agency, the Intergovernmental Committee for Migration (ICM). This was explained by the Kenya government in the following terms:

> In accordance with an agreement concluded recently with the Government of Kenya, the Intergovernmental Committee for Migration (ICM) has established an office in Nairobi in order to carry out ... programmes for the transfer of ... specialised human resources to Kenya to meet demands for qualified personnel. ... ICM will seek the co-operation of its member Governments in assisting ... experts (nationals of those industrialised countries) to work in priority sectors of the Kenyan economy.[1]

A number of specific cases illustrate extensive attempts by international development institutions to reconstruct elements of the Kenyan state apparatus, particularly the Ministry of Finance and Economic Development, and Commerce and Industry. In the case of the finance ministry, attempts to revive its capacity involved *teams* of expatriates. For example, a twenty-five-person Canadian team (supplied by the Canadian International Development Agency) was stationed in the ministry through the 1970s. Their principal role was to revitalize the planning capacity of the ministry. Before the Canadian team moved in, there was no centralized planning system in the ministry, and, therefore no basic information on national projects in various stages of planning, preparation, financing, and implementation. Previous five-year plans, as a director of the Canadian project noted, were essentially "based on statistical-economic manipulations and with little substance."[2] Canadian experts became responsible for drawing *Development Plan 1974–1978* and for doing the early work on *Development Plan 1979–1884*. They also, the director noted, assisted in "preparation of the Government's response to the oil price increase in the 1975 Sessional Paper *On Economic Prospects and Policies*."

The above effort did not, apparently, help place the Ministry of Finance on firmer ground. It continued to degenerate and this led to more ambitious attempts by the international development organizations to revamp it. In an effort to avert the total collapse of Kenya's tax regime during the late 1980s, UNDP, the World Bank, and USAID established a program of "modernisation of the tax system in Kenya." The agencies provided technical, administrative, and operational assistance to the ministry and to the income tax department. The project was expected to lead to more efficient revenue collection, increased taxpayer compliance, and more reliable internal auditing systems. Help was given in providing training and formulating new tax policies; and computers were installed to help generate and preserve more reliable data.[3] Another effort was made by the Harvard Institute for International Development (HIID). From 1985 this institute had a team of experts providing technical assistance to Kenya's Ministry of Finance "in preparation of tax policy options and possible administrative improvements in their tax systems."[4]

Under the systems introduced, every citizen earning a substantial income was to be assigned a personal identification number (PIN), which would then be entered into a central computer. For the first time since East African income tax collapsed, the source of income, and the specific manner in which it was made, would be recorded, thereby making it possible to track down those avoiding paying taxes. However, the proposed new tax collection system ground to a halt when, suddenly, President Moi cancelled the program, claiming it "would be too cumbersome and would make it more difficult to collect taxes." However, radio reporter Daniel Zwerdling, noting the opposite to be true, attributed Moi's actions to high-level corruption:

> President Moi and other top officials have become rich from their government work. . . . [They] siphon foreign contracts to their private

companies, they sell land that is supposed to be public property ... many of these wealthy Kenyans then bribe key officials to lose their tax files, so that there is no record of what and how they have or have not paid. ... Now that Moi has blocked the [new tax] system, they won't have to worry.[5]

In the development plan area, several international agencies stepped in to activate what they considered to be more feasible plans than the ministry's to help deepen Kenya's industrial and export capacities. As previously noted, plans for export processing zones, mentioned in various development plans since the 1970s, failed to materialize. The only zone functioning by the early 1990s had been developed by private operators—the Sameer Industrial Park, which came on-stream in 1993 with ten factories employing over 650 people.[6] The World Bank was among the leading forces which went to the rescue of the Kenya government's export processing zones and construction of industrial sheds and other facilities in Athi River, outside Nairobi, was well advanced in 1993. Among other schemes was the Kenya Exporter Assistance Scheme (KEAS), also sustained by the World Bank. The objective of KEAS (with a budget of KShs50 million over two years) was to assist Kenyan exporters to exploit markets in the European Community and South Africa. The project had already assisted over forty companies by the end of 1992.[7] An even larger scheme was the Kenya Export Development Support (KEDS), administered by USAID with US$7 million aimed at creating employment and earning foreign exchange through exports. KEDS was aimed particularly at three export oriented sectors, namely, Fresh Produce Exporters of Kenya, the Kenya Association of Manufacturers, and the Horticultural Crop Development Authority. These organizations were to be helped with technical seminars, improved offices, communication equipment, and market information.[8]

The Ministry of Commerce and Industry, too, was subject to numerous attempts at reconstruction. UNDP tried various projects to revitalize its several elements. One of these efforts was designed to revive the ministry's capacity to undertake industrial surveys and compile reliable data, which had not been possible since independence. A letter from the commerce ministry invited KAM to participate:

You may be aware that the Industrial Survey and Promotion Centre was established in my Ministry, with the assistance of the United Nations Development Programme. . . . It was felt that in the view of the nature of the Centre's function . . . there was a need for an advisory committee. . . . I would like to invite you to participate in its deliberations.[9]

To revitalize the Export Promotion Council and its replacement, the Kenya External Trade Authority, which had become dormant in the 1960s and 1970s, UNDP stepped in with a project in 1986. The objective was to attain a sustained increase in foreign exchange earnings. UNDP sought "the expansion and diversification of exports, so as to contribute to the relief of balance of payments constraints and permit the generation of higher levels of production, employment and income."[10]

Small business development also received attention. UNDP (together with the ILO and UNIDO) moved to rescue the government's plan of creating African businessmen. In view of the failure of Africanization, a major policy document, *A Strategy for Small Enterprise Development in Kenya: Towards the Year 2000,* was issued by UNDP and ILO in 1988. The same three organizations were instrumental in organizing the 1990 conference on industrial subcontracting. This effort aimed to foster an environment in Kenya in which small enterprises could be linked to larger manufacturing companies as suppliers.[11] This consortium of international development agencies sought to engender a nonantagonistic relationship between the formal and informal sectors. Such an environment was seen to be imperative if the acrimonious atmosphere of the Africanization period was to be avoided. At the seminar-conference—for which, one of the secondary organizers was the Ministry of Industry—there was a general consensus that if subcontracting was to help industrialization and African capitalism, it should be guided by "a private sector body or organisation" and not a government ministry.[12] By 1993, UNDP and UNIDO had established Kenya Subcontracting and Partnership Exchange. Its objective was facilitating linkage between large and small firms.[13]

The main benefactor for elements of the defunct East African Common Services (especially the Kenya Railways Corporation and the Kenya Ports Authority) was the British government's Overseas Development Administration (ODA). ODA provided personnel to give training, reorganize record-keeping and purchasing policies, and rehabilitate locomotives and cranes.[14] The British aid package hoped to make these parastatals "more commercial." The World Bank (IDA) was also involved in efforts "to bolster management, financial operations and the services" of these state corporations.[15]

As Kenya's revenue base was being seriously eroded by tax-collection failures, the state became increasingly reliant on foreign aid and grants. By the late 1980s, this situation led to the donor community taking a more direct role in Kenya's state apparatus—involving embarrassing prescriptions, made publicly to the state, as to the economic and political course Kenya should take. The donor community's public denunciation of corruption and mismanagement in the Kenyan state apparatus also appeared to be a new trend.

Examples of this mismanagement abound. There was the case of the price of jet fuel. This was incessantly raised, rendering Kenya's two international airports, in Nairobi and Mombasa, the most expensive in the world, with the exception of Kigali in Rwanda, according to the local press.[16] Moi International Airport at Mombasa was also hazardous, due to potholes on its dilapidated runways; it was in such a run-down condition that international airlines had to fly with minimum fuel because the airport's runways could not support planes with capacity weight. They had to fly to Nairobi for refuelling before proceeding to Europe. Flights going in the reverse direction had to remove weight before proceeding to Mombasa. Condor Airlines, a German tourist charter company, had its own crew to inspect the taxiway before its planes landed or took off; and all German airlines were under instructions not to fly to or from Mombasa at night.[17] The situation, combined with abnormally high prices for jet-fuel, led to a humiliating public warning to the Kenyan government by EEC countries: their airlines would find alternative fuelling points on the continent instead of Nairobi; they might even curtail tourist flights into Kenya. The prices for jet-fuel were immediately reduced by 39 percent.[18] To demonstrate to the EEC that corrective measures were being taken, the manager of Moi International Airport was sent on compulsory leave. Japan meanwhile provided a KShs1.3 billion loan for rehabilitation of the airport.[19]

There were other cases. Before the jet-fuel price exposé, the Swedish Embassy had announced that it was ending its financing of a multi-million-shilling rural water development scheme in Embu District. A Swedish statement read: "We have frozen the funding and we have appointed our own auditor to ascertain how much money has been misappropriated."[20] In another case, the British minister for overseas development, Lynda Chalker—later to be Baroness Chalker—publicly demanded to be told what specific authority was responsible for the maintenance of rural roads if Britain was to continue financing their rehabilitation.[21]

Events took a dramatic turn in 1990 and 1991 when donor countries forced the Kenyan government to abandon building a sixty-story office tower (at a cost of KShs4.3 billion) for its ruling party, an action that may have "saved Kenya from itself" according to the *Economist.* The donors "wondered whether spending $200m, including $150m of foreign borrowing, to build a tower for the ruling party was a wise use of money by a country with an income per head of $330 a year."[22] (As a comparison, it may be noted that while KShs4.3 billion was earmarked for building the complex, coffee exports, Kenya's second major export, earned KShs4.7 billion in the previous fiscal year.[23] Tourism, Kenya's number one earner, netted KShs7 billion.) The following year, the donor community, led by the IMF and the World Bank, imposed on Kenya a comprehensive structural adjustment program (SAP). This called for a reduction in personnel in the civil service, the liquidation and/or privatization of most of Kenya's parastatal sector, the devaluation of the Kenyan shilling, and relaxation of the rules regarding repatriation of earnings by foreign investors. Multipartyism, the curbing of high-level corruption, and human rights improvements were made part of the conditionality for a resumption of aid to Kenya.[24] However, project aid—valued at $850 million to $1 billion a year—was not affected. Mostly, the suspension was of budgetary facilities and balance of payments support.[25]

The influence of the donor community in Kenya was by now so decisive that the Kenya government not only succumbed and provided a detailed privatization plan at the November 1991 donor consultative meeting held in Paris,[26] but, most remarkably, it grudgingly yielded to the establishment of multipartyism. This subsequently led to the general elections of December 1992.

Under privatization, all nonstrategic parastatals were to be sold or liquidated. Parastatals considered unprofitable but worth saving were obliged to sign "performance agreements." External consultants would effectively take over their management to rehabilitate them in preparation for future privatization. Each performance agreement included such measures as a reduction in the number of employees and the appointment of a new board of directors to counter past tendencies such as political patronage. Local parastatal managerial personnel would no longer be appointed on political criteria but on executive qualities, approved by the international development organizations and foreign consultants. All Kenya's leading parastatals, including the ICDC, Industrial Development Bank (IDB), National Cereals and Produce Board (NCPB), the Agricultural Finance Corporation (AFC), the Coffee Board of Kenya (CBK), and the Kenya Tea Development Authority (KTDA), were obliged to sign such contracts.[27]

It was generally assumed that most aid programs to Kenya would resume after the 1992 multiparty general elections, since that was one of the key conditions the government had to meet. This was not the case, however. The party that had been in power, the Kenya African National Union (KANU), and the same president, Mr. Daniel arap Moi, won the elections, assisted—and not insignificantly—by an ethnically fragmented opposition.[28] The IMF and the World Bank insisted on still more rigorous implementation of the SAP in such areas as contracting, the civil service, privatization (or liquidation of the parastatals), and devaluation of the Kenya shilling before a full aid package of about $40 million a month to assist Kenya with its balance of payments problems could be resumed. Consequently, a cumulative aid fund of about $480 million was withheld. The EC followed this lead by insisting on conditionality before releasing some 163.5 million ECUs worth of aid under the Fourth Lome Convention.[29] Individual donor countries, such as the United States—a principal donor—adopted the same position.[30] The United Kingdom, too, took this stance, with Baroness Chalker, the British overseas development minister, stating that "Britain can only accept a reinstatement of aid to Kenya if the IMF and the World Bank say the government has carried out reforms along their recommended lines."[31] In reaction to the unyielding position of the donor community, a despondent Moi regime submitted in late February 1993 to some of the measures called for by SAP: the Kenyan shilling was floated and fell by 60 percent;[32] the central bank lost its monopoly in trading and the allocation of foreign currency; regulations on the repatriation of earnings in foreign exchange were eased.[33]

Then the relationship between Kenya and the donor community went through a series of rapid and confusing changes. This happened in March and April 1993. Initially, in reaction of the IMF–World Bank's hardening position, the Kenyan state withdrew from the reform programs altogether, explaining its new "go it alone" stance by charging donors with failure "to reciprocate by providing the necessary resources as to make the reforms successful."[34] In following this new and unexpected course, the Kenyan government was effectively isolated. Domestic and international forces forged a common front in opposition. In supporting the demands of the donor community, the vice chairman of the opposition party Ford Kenya, Mr. Paul Muite, stated that "if pressure is not kept up, mismanagement and corruption will continue."[35] Kenyan horticultural farmers demanded that Kenya reintroduce the IMF–World Bank reforms—otherwise, they said, their sector, which constituted the fastest growing aspect of an otherwise moribund agriculture, might collapse. The chairman of the Fresh Produce Exporters Association of Kenya (FPEAK), Mr. Kasanga Mulwa, stated that as a result of the Kenyan government's inappropriate actions "there may not be any Kenyan flowers reaching Europe or indeed elsewhere."[36] Meanwhile, as a result of the suspension of balance-of-payments loans, the country was increasingly unable to meet the conditions of foreign investors, especially international airlines. They could not repatriate their earnings as the Central Bank of Kenya did not have the required hard currency, a development that saw some airlines threatening to withdraw from Kenya.[37] Barely half a month after the adoption of the "go it alone" stance, Kenya was becoming something of a disaster. By mid-April 1993, airlines—concerned at the lack of foreign currency and the poor maintenance at government-owned petroleum refineries—were cutting back, or re-routing, their flights into Kenya. The principal carriers of Kenya-bound tourists (now the main source of foreign currency for Kenya), including KLM, British Airways, and Lufthansa German Airlines, suspended direct flights, introducing stopovers in Cairo or neighboring Uganda and Tanzania. Some airlines were said to be importing their own fuel.[38]

Mid-1993, the Kenyan state appeared to be having second thoughts about its "go it alone" policy. Unexpectedly, it devalued its currency by 23 percent, and closed twelve so-called political banks to which the state had lent over Shs11 billion (US$234 million)—against "the assets that the government's own analysts say do not exist"—and this development prompted the World Bank to release US$85 million of frozen aid.[39] The *Economist* delicately summed up the resulting pandemonium: "It has been difficult to discern whether Mr. Moi and his ministers are indifferent . . . , or whether they are simply incapable of getting to grips with some basic principles of economics."

Enterprise and Mediocrity

The second part of this book has sought to demonstrate some of the acute shortcomings of the postcolonial state from the perspective of capital accumulation. Ironically, this was not the case in the 1940s and 1950s. In fact, at independence in 1963 Kenya possessed a remarkable state apparatus that had successfully marshalled commercial and industrial development since the 1940s. A common market and a number of key economic infrastructures placed the country in a very favorable position within eastern and central Africa. At hand was also excellent advice in the World Bank Mission report, commissioned by the colonial state in 1962, that urged caution in regard to the staffing of Kenya's administrative regime if the previous accomplishments and the pace of development already attained were to be sustained. The African leadership did not appear to grasp the importance of having qualified personnel: a program of Africanization of the civil service, including the services associated with the East African Community, was initiated. At the same time, the Africanization of commerce and industry was being attempted. Without qualified personnel to oversee the implementation and administration of development plans, the postcolonial agenda was doomed. The stated development objectives were, in practice, almost never met. In the context of a severe deterioration of the state apparatus, international agencies became involved, averting an economic disaster similar to those which befell Kenya's neighbors. The roles and influence of these agencies grew as the Kenyan state's capacity deteriorated. In this way, Kenya still appeared, to outsiders, to be a prudent planner on a continent where political, social, and economic disintegration became the norm. Most observers continued to view Kenya as a success story, basing themselves on superficial analyses of development plans instead of scrutinizing the plans' implementation. More critical reports by pockets of the state, such as those of the controller and auditor general, or specific commissions of inquiry, were, if known about, not taken seriously.

The only plan that was consistently given attention was that of localization-Africanization-Kenyanization-indigenization. This plan was detrimental to national development because, while the state sought to encourage private capital to invest in manufacturing, it also, for example, attempted to force them to appoint African distributors of their manufactured products—yet there was no pool of competent African businesses to undertake this trade. State corporations created to assist Africans were likewise corrupted.

More generally, the state ceased to provide many of the basic infrastructures needed by industry. Many policies and practices actually injured industry while enriching individual Africans. Thus, the rights of some of the most skilled and experienced Kenyans—namely, Kenyan Indians—were abridged, while efforts to create an African business class to replace them ended in failure. No lesson seems to have been drawn from this experience. As the parastatal sector disintegrated and foreign capital substantially divested in the 1980s, the only dynamic commercial and industrial group, the country's Indians, remained subject to official harassment. This was also the case of the African bourgeoisie-in-formation in the *jua kali* sector, although the official attitude toward this segment improved considerably in the late 1980s.

The main contradiction of Kenyan development was, therefore, clear: on the one hand there was an enterprising commercial and industrial class that continued to sustain the economic development of Kenya but remained politically insecure; on the other hand, there was a governing elite whose mediocrity, corruption, and indifference to national needs continued to undermine the accomplishments of the 1950s and early 1960s and failed to translate Kenya's potential into reality. The third participant in this combination was the aid-donor community, that continued to finance Kenya's development process and provided technical personnel to shore up the decaying state apparatus. The mood of the donor community toward Kenya cooled considerably in the early 1990s in an effort to force the Moi government to curb high-level corruption, to improve its human rights record, allow multipartyism, and quicken the pace of liquidation/privatization of the largely ineffective parastatal sector.

Notes

1. Ministry of Economic Planning and Development, 15 March 1983. EPD/A219/01.
2. Saywell article, pp. 1–5.
3. See the *Daily Nation* and the *Standard,* 23 November 1989.
4. HIID report, 1987–1989, p. 78.
5. On National Public Radio, Washington, D.C., 15 April 1993.
6. Republic of Kenya, *Export Processing Zones,* 1993.
7. *Economic Review,* Nairobi, 4 January 1993.
8. *Economic Review,* 4 January 1993.
9. Permanent secretary, MCI, to T.W. Tyrell, executive director, KAM, 6 July 1977. MCI 166/165/01 (94).
10. UNDP Project document, 1986, KEN/86/107, MCI.
11. UNDP, ILO, UNIDO, *Seminar on Industrial Subcontracting,* Nyeri, 4–9

March 1990.

12. KAM report on the seminar.

13. Interview with Mrs. Emma Muchene-Kolaas, manager of the exchange, January 1993.

14. ODA, *Britain and Kenya: Partners in Development,* September 1989.

15. *Financial Review,* 20 July 1987.

16. *Daily Nation,* 13 December 1989.

17. *Sunday Times,* 1 April 1990.

18. *Daily Nation,* 13 December 1989.

19. *Sunday Times,* 1 April 1990.

20. The permanent secretary in the Ministry of Water Development, Mr. S. Mbova, replied: "There are certain things to be done by us which we have agreed upon. . . . I assure you that the Swedes have not pulled out of the project, but we will implement their request." *Daily Nation,* 27 February 1990.

21. See *Daily Nation* editorial, 9 March 1990. Britain had a high profile in rehabilitation projects. Not only did its aid build the Embu-Meru link, it resealed the road and that of the deteriorating Mombasa-Nairobi road in 1988–1989. The British were active in the rehabilitation of the Kenya Railway Corporation, the Kenya Ports Authority, and government Land Rovers (sic!). See ODA, *Britain and Kenya.*

22. *Economist,* 3 February 1990.

23. *Kenya Export News,* December 1989.

24. *New York Times* and *Financial Times,* 27 November and 1 December 1991.

25. *Reuter European Business Report,* "Kenya Announces Economic Reforms," 19 February 1993.

26. SRI International, *Parastatals in Kenya.* Final report prepared for KAM, February 1992, p. 16.

27. *Parastatals in Kenya,* pp. 14–16.

28. The principal opposition parties are Ford Asili (Mr. Kenneth Matiba), Ford Kenya (Mr. Oginga Odinga), and the Democratic Party (Mr. Mwai Kibaki). Ford Asili and the Democratic Party effectively confirmed the division of the Kikuyu of Murang'a and the Kikuyu of Nyeri. Mr. Matiba's party took almost all seats in Murang'a, Kiambu, and Nairobi; Mr. Kibaki won in his home area of Nyeri and neighboring areas. Mr. Oginga Odinga's Ford Kenya could win only in Luoland. President Moi, who failed to win a single seat in the above areas, could carry only Kalenjin regions and those of other smaller ethnic groups around the country. The 1992 multiparty general elections suggest that—vote-rigging notwithstanding—a coherent national political elite hardly exists in Kenya.

29. European Information Service, "EC/Kenya," 27 February 1993.

30. See for example the interview with the United States ambassador, Mr. Smith Hemptstone, in the *Economic Review,* Nairobi, 11 January 1993.

31. Cited in Manoah Esipisu, *Reuter Library Report,* 8 February 1993.

32. "Kenya Shilling Nosedives as Flotation Takes Hold," Reuter Library Report, February 24, 1993.

33. Ibid.

34. Statement by Musalia Mudavadi, Kenya's finance minister, as announced by Kenya Broadcasting Corporation, 22 March 1993.

35. Cited by Agence France Presse, 25 March 1993.

36. Reuter European Business Report, 30 March 1993.

37. Horace Awori, Inter Press Service, 31 March 1993.

38. Manoah Esipisu, Reuter Library Report, 15 April 1993.

39. *Economist,* 24 April 1993.

Conclusion:
A Heap of Contradictions

The account of the Kenyan development process that has been put forward in this book is the result of an attempt to answer a series of questions regarding the role of Kenyan capitalists and the state. In regard to theory, it has asked: Do the contending theoretical perspectives help shed some light on Kenyan and peripheral development processes? In the case of the bourgeoisie, it has asked: What are its main segments and their respective historical origins? What are their respective patterns of accumulation and the decisive moments in their evolution? What are their respective technical and collective organizational capacities, relative to the requirement of further accumulation? In regard to the state, the questions were: What have been the key moments in its evolution? What role has it played historically in providing policy and infrastructure for further accumulation? How was this role affected by the transition from the colonial phase to independence and from Kenyatta's to Moi's government? Finally, this book asks: What do the responses to these questions collectively imply? This chapter recapitulates these responses, highlighting the principal lessons that may be drawn from the Kenyan development experience.

Contending Theories and Research

It is shown in this book that the contending perspectives in the development field have tended to use theories to defend their preferred positions, instead of using the theories as speculative constructs, or historically derived tendencies, that may guide further inquiry into the prospects and problems of social, economic, and political transformation at the periphery. As Lipietz puts it, scholars in this field force concrete situations into "a schema established by some Great Author of the past," while anything that does not fit is "simply lopped off."[1] In the Kenyan case, unfortunately, what was lopped off was, in effect, what mattered most: the Kenyan Indian bourgeoisie, who, as shown in this book, constituted the principal domestic accumulators in almost all phases of Kenya's history.

Highly instrumentalist conceptions were also at work in the case of the Kenyan state—caricaturing it and labelling it an agency of either the British bourgeoisie, white settlers, or Kenyan Africans, depending on the theory adopted. To quote Lipietz again, "when labels make us forget concrete analysis, and when we enter into metaphysical debates . . . we are headed for disaster."[2]

We should agree that "there is no 'fate' condemning a country, because of some feature or other that it has, to a permanent back seat."[3] Only specific inquiries into domestic social actors can establish diverse outcomes at the periphery. There is really no alternative to examination, case by case.

We live in uncertain times that seriously challenge estalished norms and conventional wisdom. Consider, for example, the fact that the most indebted country is the remaining superpower—the United States.[4] The Soviet Union and Eastern European socialist experiments are no more. The poor performance of the former imperial powers—the home of "real" capitalism—as indicated especially by the industrial decline of the United Kingdom, is another case in point. Japanese direct investments have become a critical factor in reviving ailing British manufacturing industries.[5] And some stunning changes are to be found at the so-called periphery, particularly in Asia where new industrial powers (such as the NICs and Southern China) have more or less replayed the Japanese miracle. Taiwan is said to have "the biggest stash [of foreign reserves] of any country in the world."[6] All these developmental changes ought to discourage the tendency ruefully noted in social sciences by Noam Chomsky. "Once you take a position," he observed, "you are supposed to defend it, no matter what happens. It becomes a question of honour not to change or revise an opinion (that is, to learn something)."[7]

The Kenyan Capitalist Class

A principal lesson that may be drawn from a study of the Kenyan development process is the centrality of Kenyan Indian commercial and industrial capitalists—a group that has been largely left out of the existing literature. The origin of the Kenyan bourgeoisie as conceptualized in this book is traceable to precolonial Indian merchant capital based on the East African coast, and to the Indian immigrants who settled in the region during the colonial period. The first important phase in the evolution of this class was between the early 1900s and the Second World War, when the East African home market took form. The second phase was the conversion of merchant capital into industrial capital, a transformation that was encouraged by the isolation of East Africa from its traditional suppliers of goods during the Second World War. This forced the Kenyan state to regard homegrown manufacturing activity as a viable alternative. The third, and perhaps most decisive, phase in the rise of the Kenyan bourgeoisie was the creation of national ministries from the late 1940s up to independence. The establishment of the Ministry of Commerce and Industry, in particular, and its implementation of a number of development schemes to stimulate local accumulation, was important; and with institutional support and a conducive state, local capital also became better organized through bodies such as the Association of Chambers of Commerce and Industry of Eastern Africa and the Association for the Promotion of Industries in East Africa. Kenyan and East African capitalists moved from commercial and merchant activity to manufacturing in relatively large numbers, thereby considerably expanding the pool of the Kenyan industrial bourgeoisie.

The fourth phase was the postcolonial period and Kenyan Indian capitalists continued to play a leading role in industrialization. The motivation now, however, was not conducive policies but rather the need to escape from the commercial arena in the face of legislative attempts to Africanize it. Manufacturing was considered to be relatively safe from African takeovers due to the complexity of its technical, managerial, and capital requirements. Kenyan Indian commercial capitalists therefore placed their capital in the manufacturing sector, which led to another round of industrialization in the 1960s and 1970s.

European and African segments of the bourgeoisie that have been the chief objects of the debates on Kenyan development were never central to the accumulation process. Both tended to lack a tradition in business generally. Of the Kenyan European businessmen, only an extremely limited number were entrepreneurial material. They were predisposed to look to the state to provide both financial backing and technical assistance through state agencies. This dependence on the state proved to be a major weakness, notwithstanding instrumentalist conceptions that the Kenyan state acted as agency for European settlers. The transfer of state power to Africans after independence saw an almost instant collapse of the European segment of domestic capital—with notable exceptions, such as the Block family. The Blocks kept most of their holdings, not selling them until 1989–1991.

African capitalists followed a remarkably similar pattern. Their initial widespread attempt at business was from the mid-1940s to the early 1960s when a relatively large number of Africans entered the retail trade. Most of their pooled funds came from World War II–related earnings. This activity proved to be premature, however, and most of these enterprises could not be sustained—even though, contrary to widespread belief, the colonial state sought to assist them. The various state-sponsored schemes created in the aftermath of the collapse of African businesses did not lead to substantial success. The second key phase in this development began after independence, when the Kiambu-based Kikuyu, then in control of the state, headed most state finance corporations. This avenue led a number of Kikuyu businessmen into commerce and industry in the 1960s and 1970s and some Kikuyu enterprises looked promising. Several development institutions, some of them dating back to the colonial period, sought to provide African businessmen with capital, technical assistance, and industrial sheds and machinery. These schemes, however, fared worse than during the colonial period, mainly because the agencies responsible were as lacking in technical skills as the African businessmen they were supposed to sustain. The loss of state power following the demise of the Kenyatta regime in 1978 was apparently decisive in leading to the collapse of almost all the major Kikuyu enterprises—a close parallel to the case of the European capitalists after 1964.

The lessons to be drawn from the Kenyan experience are thus both positive and negative. The country has obviously not experienced an economic decline on the scale of most sub-Saharan Africa countries. One of the factors that accounts for this success is the fact that the Kenyan national leadership, though seeking to create an African business class, did not underestimate the historical role of the Kenyan Indian bourgeoisie. They did not squander the resources represented by Indian skills and capital as did their Ugandan and Tanzanian counterparts. Thus, while prone to use the Kenyan Indians as scapegoats, especially during periods of economic difficulty, the Kenyan political elite has tolerated them. Meanwhile, the fertile ground from which African capitalists may eventually emerge, the *jua kali* sector, has received less attention. The bias has been toward businessmen in the public sector, notwithstanding the fact that they have been discredited by their inability to survive in the market on their own.

The Kenyan State

The principal impression gained by studying the contemporary Kenyan state is essentially negative. It can, in fact, be said that the leading obstacle to further accumulation is the postcolonial Kenyan state. Beginning as a transplanted apparatus administered by the British colonial service, the state was expanded considerably from the late 1940s up to the early 1960s. This period can be seen as a phase of spectacular industrial development, notwithstanding the political struggles during the Mau Mau revolt. The presence of an institutional regime and conducive policy was vital.

The succeeding decade saw a number of contradictions that still affected the workings of the state in the 1990s. An ambitious but authoritarian Kikuyu-dominated regime attempted a policy of Africanizing both the public and private sectors. This policy became "Kikuyization" in practice alienating other ethnic and racial groups who felt cheated from sharing the fruits of independence. The policy also clashed with industrialization plans, since it interfered with private manufacturing capital, attempting to force it to hire Africans either as managers or as retailers of its products. The outcome was disastrous, particularly for the public sector. The pool of non-African administrative personnel was depleted within a year or two. It soon became apparent that another set of expatriate cadres was urgently needed. By the late 1960s, some key elements of the Kenyan state apparatus had collapsed altogether, and the remainder was barely functioning. This led to the consistent soliciting of technical and administrative expertise from the international donor community.

Accession to power of the Kalenjin-led coalition of small tribes in 1978 marked another stage in the retrogression of the Kenyan state. The initial preoccupation of the Moi government was to consolidate itself, a lesson well learned from the Kenyatta regime. In the case of the Kalenjin and their associates, this was done at the expense of the Kikuyu, who now lost most of their positions in the state apparatus. The loss of these positions profoundly affected their performance in the private sector. Financing and contracts from the state were no longer forthcoming, and most of their businesses collapsed. By 1990, the Kikuyu did not hold a single high-level position of political substance—not the vice presidency, nor a major ministry such as finance or defense, nor a chairmanship of a leading institution such as the central bank.

Thus, the Kenyan state is in effect a heap of contradictions. A coherent national political elite hardly exists either in government or in opposition. The Kikuyu-led coalition essentially disintegrated after the demise of the Kenyatta government. The Kalenjin-led coalition systematically undermined the former Kikuyu establishment. Since 1990, the latter's attempts to challenge the Moi government have met with little success, mainly because it lacked credibility outside its tribal confines. The Kikuyu could not, therefore, mobilize the rest of Kenyan society. The rise of multipartyism and the general elections of 1992 well demonstrated this: not only did Kikuyu-led political parties fail to rally the non-Kikuyu electorate they themselves fragmented on geographical grounds. The historical rivalries between the Kikuyu of Murang'a and the Kiambu on the one hand, and their Nyeri counterparts on the other hand, proved still to be strong. Thus Ford Asili, led by Mr. Kenneth Matiba, could succeed electorally only in Murang'a and Kiambu; the Democratic Party, led by Mr. Mwai Kibaki, carried the Nyeri region. Likewise the Luo-dominated political party, Ford Kenya, could find strength only in Luoland. Moi's KANU retained the "smaller tribes" around the country.

Meanwhile, the state as an agent of development remained in question. Most of its elements consistently declined, or even collapsed, to exist only in name. It is this vacuum that the international financial institutions have attempted to fill. The partnership between the Kenya state and its international handlers went through some modifications. The donors adopted a harsher tone in the 1990s, ostensibly to get the former to behave more accountably.

Prospects of sustained development in Kenya remain precarious. On the one hand, a still quite dynamic private sector is led by a Kenyan Indian bourgeoisie with a proven record and the technical capacity to place Kenya on a far more promising path; supplemented by a substantial but declining segment of foreign capital. The problem with this combination is that the Kenyan Indians remain politically insecure: they are still regarded as foreigners. For the African segment, it is, if anything, the *jua kali* sector that shows promise, and not the discredited public sector, the would-be businessmen who thrive on the basis of the "colonizing" elements of the state apparatus.

On the other hand there is an unsteady political elite and a declining state apparatus that is unable to provide a stable political environment and strategic framework for development by providing enabling policies. This is a profound difficulty for the Kenyan development process, for there is hardly a case where a country successfully transformed itself without consistent policies on the part of the state. Recent experiences of the NICs and the RICs show that the role of the state was indispensable, notwithstanding the neoliberal orthodoxy that identifies the "market" as the engine of their transformation. The World Bank's views are in the latter category:

> Thus policies of the successful countries have been generally supportive of industrialization and commerce but have avoided directing that support at any particular sector or method. Decisions about what activities and what processes could be effectively and profitably built up are left to individual firms, which succeed or fail as their decisions prove to be correct or incorrect.[8]

A large body of literature establishes the fact that the reality of the newly transformed areas was strikingly different from neoliberal views of the World Bank.[9] In his assessment of the South Korean case, for example, Kwan Kim describes how the national leadership of the early 1960s,

> learning from neighbouring Japan's experience, saw the need to build an industrial base. . . . To pursue the policy objective for industrialisation, it was felt necessary that the state, given the initial weakness of the private sector, had to play a leading role in formulating and implementing trade and industrial policies. The basic strategy to develop industry called for targeting a few sectors of the economy that were expected to perform well in international markets. Those firms entering them would be granted special incentives.[10]

Thus, besides providing a strategic policy framework, the state mobilized and allocated resources and undertook to build heavy industries—steel mills and chemical industries—because the Korean entrepreneurial class was too weak to do this. Kim notes that the closest historical parallels— "although far from being exact"—might be the developmental state of Bismarck's Germany or Meiji's Japan in the late nineteenth century. Both of these states provided basic materials and heavy capital investment because their capitalist classes were either too weak or too cautious.[11]

Some leading mainstream economic historians have already acknowledged the fact that the state was an important player in the transformation process, at least in a minimal sense, to provide "public goods" such as roads, railways, and other large-scale infrastructural installations whose administration and costs are beyond the range of individual capitalists. However, according to Charles Kindleberger, where domestic entrepreneurs were weak or in short supply, the state's involvement in the economy was much greater, as the private sector alone was "expected to perform badly."[12] In fact, as Alexander Gerschenkron notes, historically, the more backward the country's economy

> the greater was the part played by special institutional factors designed to increase supply of capital to the nascent industries and, in addition, to provide them with . . . better informed entrepreneurial guidance; the more backward the country, the more pronounced was the coerciveness and comprehensiveness of those factors.[13]

The Kenyan experience confirms this pattern. In the period from the Second World War to 1963 when the Kenyan state pursued more consistent policies that encouraged both domestic and foreign capital to invest in Kenya, a spectacular commercial and industrial development took place in a remarkably short time. This experience confirms the fact that there can be no substitute for the state in capitalist development (just as there can be no substitute for a domestic accumulating class). Nor is it likely that international financial institutions (which are currently attempting to reconstruct elements of the Kenyan state and force the adoption of reforms) can become a surrogate for a national interventionist state that conceives and implements a consistent program of development. The fate of Kenya, therefore, hangs on the rise of this historically important social agency.

Notes

1. Lipietz, *Mirages*, p. 4.
2. Lipietz, *Mirages*, p. 28.
3. Lipietz, *New Economic Order*, p. 24.

4. See for example Gilpin, *Political Economy,* 1987.

5. See Daniels article, "EC–Japan," p. 283.

6. *Economist,* 1 May 1993.

7. Cited in Lipietz, *Mirages,* p. 1.

8. World Bank report, 1981, p. 25.

9. See for example Deyo (ed.), *Asian Industrialism,* 1987; and Foster-Carter's article, 1985. For Mauritius's attempts to join the ranks of the NICs see Bowman, 1991. For surveys of China and Malaysia see the *Economist,* 28 November and 4 December 1992 and 17–23 April 1993 respectively.

10. Kwan S. Kim article, 1991, p. 10.

11. Kwan S. Kim article, pp. 4–5.

12. Kindleberger, *Economic Development,* p. 383.

13. Gerschenkron, *Economic Backwardness,* p. 354.

Appendix:
Sample of Author's Questionnaire

The Role of Local Entrepreneurs in Kenyan Development
(Questionnaire strictly confidential)

Name of firm: ....

Address: ....

Main Products: ....

Name of Entrepreneur or Manager: ....

I. *Establishment of the firm:*
    (i)   Key stages in the growth of firm:
          (a)   First steps to set up firm were in 19................
          (b)   Firm began to operate in 19.....................
          (c)   Firm began to produce in 19....................

    (ii)   Original source for investment came from:
          (a)   Small-scale trade
          (b)   Import and export
          (c)   Loan from local private commercial banks
          (d)   Loan from overseas private financing
          (e)   Loan from government development institutions
          (f)   Grants from aid-donor sources
          (g)   Personal savings
          (h)   Combination of (–) and (–)

II. *Expansion of enterprise:*
    (i)   Growth of the firm:
          (a)   Estimate of original amounts was KShs...........................
          (b)   Funds invested after initial investment came from:

1. Reinvestment from the income of the same firm
2. Loan from local private commercial banks
3. Loan from overseas private financing
4. Loan from government development corporations
5. Grants from aid-donor sources
6. Personal savings

(ii) The plant is currently valued at:
  (a)   Whole plant in KShs. ....
  (b)   Buildings .... %
  (c)   Machinery .... %
  (d)   Inventory .... %

III. *Production and utilization of the plant:*

(i) Plant operates at:
  (a)   Full capacity (day and night shifts)
  (b)   One shift (day or night)

(ii) Reasons for underutilization (one shift):
  (a)   Lack of imported raw material
  (b)   Lack of domestic raw material
  (c)   Lack of demand for products manufactured
  (d)   Unavailability of supervisors
  (e)   Unavailability of experienced labor force
  (f)   Unavailability of technicians
  (g)   Government regulation

(iii) Reasons for investment in manufacturing:
  (a)   Was in trade but prospects were poor
  (b)   Manufacturing more profitable
  (c)   Government policy to encourage industry
  (d)   Belief in importance of industry
  (e)   Family member was already in industry

(iv) Reasons for entry into this particular line:
  (a)   Was trading in the same line
  (b)   Looked profitable
  (c)   Availability of raw material
  (d)   Existence of market
  (e)   Government encouragement
  (f)   Opportunity to buy an existing firm
  (g)   Industry more prestigious

(v) Reasons for choosing location:
  (a)   Near raw materials
  (b)   Near market

    (c)   Near to important infrastructure
    (d)   Government policy, i.e., rural industrialization
    (e)   Incentives to locate, i.e., serviced lots
    (f)   Incentives to locate, cheap land
    (g)   Close to sister companies

(vi) Ownership of facilities:
    (a)   Firm owns buildings
    (b)   Firm rents from private sources
    (c)   Firm rents from government

(vii) The following changes have taken place:
    (a)   Establishment of new units
    (b)   Expansion of original units
    (c)   Improvement of design or layout of plant
    (d)   Installation of improved machinery
    (e)   Introduction of new products or activities
    (f)   Important changes in marketing arrangements

(viii) Future investment plans are:
    (a)   Magnitude of investment in next two years
         KShs...
    (b)   Magnitude of investment in next five years
         KShs...

(ix) Potential obstacles to future investments:
    (a)   Financial constraints
    (b)   Foreign exchange
    (c)   Bureaucratic red tape
    (d)   Lack of government permission
    (e)   Political instability
    (f)   Stiff competition
    (g)   Technical know-how
    (h)   No serious obstacle

IV. *Financing of industrial expansion:*
  (i) Financial sources for further expansion:
    (a)   Fully self-financed
    (b)   Largely self-financed
    (c)   All borrowed
    (d)   Partially borrowed

  (ii) If finance to be borrowed, it will come from:
    (a)   Private commercial banks
    (b)   Development corporations
    (c)   Foreign sources

V. *Organizational form of the firm:*
- (i)   Firm is organized in the following form:
  - (a) Private limited
  - (b) Public limited
  - (c) Government
  - (d) Cooperative
  - (e) Partnership

- (ii) The controlling share in firm (51%) or more is by:
  - (a) Individual
  - (b) Family
  - (c) Partnership
  - (d) Stockholders

- (iii) Investment decisions are made by:
  - (a) Owner
  - (b) Family
  - (c) Partners or one of them
  - (d) Board of directors

- (iv) Financial decisions are made by:
  - (a) Owner
  - (b) Family
  - (c) Partners or one of them
  - (d) Board of directors

- (v) Sales decisions are made by:
  - (a) Owner
  - (b) Family
  - (c) Partners or one of them
  - (d) Board of directors

- (vi) Actual operation of the firm is managed by:
  - (a) Owner
  - (b) Member(s) of the family
  - (c) Partner(s)
  - (d) Manager (local)
  - (e) Manager (expatriate)

VI. *Technical know-how and technological transfer:*
- (i) Source of technical know-how for the firm:
  - (a) Through import business
  - (b) Family members educated abroad
  - (c) Local people outside educated overseas
  - (d) Travelling abroad
  - (e) Expatriate technicians

   (ii)   Source for technological transfer:
- (a)   Presence of multinational corporations
- (b)   Local research and development

  (iii)   Presence of multinational companies:
- (a)   Enhances local technological advancement
- (b)   Hinders local technological advancement

  (iv)   Firm keeps up to date with developments in its industrial line through:
- (a)   Technical journals
- (b)   Suppliers of machinery
- (c)   Suppliers of raw materials
- (d)   Travelling abroad
- (e)   From business associations

VII. *Character of the market:*
   (i)   Products of the firm are aimed at:
- (a) Local market .... %
- (b) Export into PTA.. %
- (c) Export into non-PTA Africa... %
- (d) Export to Asia (except Japan).. %
- (e) Export to Europe, North America, and Japan................. %

   (ii)   Reasons for not exporting:
- (a)   Local market satisfactory
- (b)   Lack of foreign currency in PTA
- (c)   Lack of foreign exchange to buy inputs
- (d)   Similar products produced in the PTA
- (e)   Protectionism in industrial countries
- (f)   Stiff competition from elsewhere
- (g)   Lack of incentives from government
- (h)   Bureaucratic red tape

  (iii)   Export Compensation Scheme:
- (a)   Is effective in stimulating Kenyan exports
- (b)   Does not make a difference because:
  - 1   ....
  - 2   ....
- (c)   Would stimulate exports if:
  - 1   ....
  - 2   ....

VIII. *Role of government policies in industrial development:*
   (i)   Main benefits from government policy to firm are:
- (a)   Financing through development corporations

      (b)   Tax concessions
      (c)   Land concessions
      (d)   Physical facilities
      (e)   Labor policies, i.e., control of wages
      (f)   Labor policies, i.e., industrial training
      (g)   Technical help
      (h)   Provision of infrastructure
      (i)   Provision of foreign exchange

(ii)   Main difficulties as a result of government policies:
      (a)   Lack of imported raw material
      (b)   Lack of imported machinery
      (c)   Poor labor policy
      (d)   Bureaucratic red tape and delays
      (e)   Lack of protection from imports
      (f)   Price controls
      (g)   High taxation

IX. *Management and labor relations:*
  (i)   Firm belongs to employers' association because of:
      (a)   Benefits from other employers' experience
      (b)   Common front to trade unions
      (c)   Lobby government for desired policy
      (d)   Firm belongs to:
          1. Kenya Association of Manufacturers
          2. Federation of Kenyan Employers
          3. Chamber of Commerce and Industry
      (e)   The most useful organ for manufacturers is:
          1. KAM; 2. FKE; 3. KNCCI
      (f)   Why? ....

(ii)   Firm's employees:
      (a)   Current number of employees
      (b)   Current number of supervisors (local)
      (c)   Current number of expatriates

(iii) Trade unions are:
      (a)   Active at the plant
      (b)   Useful in building up industries
      (c)   Not recognized at the plant
      (d)   Harmful to industrial development

(iv) Wages:
      (a)   Total wage bill per year in KShs
      (b)   Other employee benefits

(v) Efficiency of labor at the plant is:
   (a) Increasing rapidly
   (b) Increasing slowly
   (c) Remaining same
   (d) Decreasing slowly

(vi) Industrial training for employees is provided by:
   (a) Government
   (b) Firm
   (c) Combination of both of the above

(vii) Labor at the plant is:
   (a) Very stable
   (b) Average
   (c) Unstable

(viii) The number of industrial disputes have been:
   (a) In the last year ....
   (b) In the last two years ....

X. *Role of entrepreneurs in Kenyan development*
   (i) Kenyan industrial development pace is:
      (a) Better than most African countries
      (b) Closing gap with NICs
      (d) Very slow and prospects poor

   (ii) Kenya industrial development is enhanced by:
      (a) Presence of local entrepreneurs
      (b) Good political climate
      (c) Efficient bureaucracy
      (d) Large pool of Kenyan experts
      (e) Presence of multinationals

   (iii) Kenyan industrial development is hampered by:
      (a) Lack of initiative by entrepreneurs
      (b) Bureaucratic red tape
      (c) Labor inefficiency

   (iv) Entrepreneur or manager's background:
         Which community do you belong to?
      (a) Local African
      (b) Local Asian
      (c) Local European
      (d) Local Arab

   (v) When did your family first come Kenya?

(vi) Highest education achievement
    (a)   Where?

(vii) To become a successful industrialist, the
      following is important:
    (a)   Formal education
    (b)   Training on the job
    (c)   Initiative

(viii) Background before entering manufacturing:
    (a)   Trader (local)
    (b)   Manufacturer: large? medium? small?
    (c)   Real estate developer
    (d)   Wage-earner

(ix) Occupation:
    (a)   Of Father...
    (b)   Of Grandfather ....
    (c)   Likelihood for your children ....

Bibliography

Books and Journal Articles

Amin, Samir, *Unequal Development.* Monthly Review Press, New York, 1976.
———, "The Agricultural Revolution and Industrialization," in Hamid Amara and Bernard Founou-Tchuigoua, *African Agriculture: The Critical Choices.* Zed Books, 1990.
Anonymous authors, *Independent Kenya.* Zed Press, London, 1982.
Anyang' Nyong'o, Peter, "State and Society in Kenya: The Disintegration of the Nationalist Coalitions and the Rise of Presidential Authoritarianism, 1963–1978." *African Affairs,* Vol. 88, 1989.
Bauer, Peter, *Economic Analysis and Policy in Underdeveloped Countries.* Duke University Press, 1954.
Beckman, Bjorn, "Imperialism and Capitalist Transformation: Critique of the Kenya Debate," *Review of African Political Economy,* No. 91, 1980.
———, "The Post-Colonial State: Crisis and Reconstruction." *IDS Bulletin,* Vol. 19, No. 4, 1988.
Berman, Bruce, *Control & Crisis in Colonial Kenya.* James Currey, London, 1990.
Bloch, M., *The Historian's Craft.* Manchester, 1954, pp. 27–28.
Blomstrom, Magnus, and Bjorn Hettne, *Development Theory in Transition.* Zed Press, London, 1984.
Brett, E.A., *Colonialism and Underdevelopment in East Africa.* NOK Publishers, New York, 1973.
Cardoso, Fernando, and Enzo Faletto, *Dependency and Development in Latin America.* University of California Press, 1979.
Cockcroft, James, Andre Gunder Frank, and Dale Johnson, *Dependence and Underdevelopment.* Anchor Books, Garden City, New York, 1972.
Coughlin, Peter, "What's Going On in the Glass Manufacturing Industry?" *Industrial Review,* Nairobi, February 1989.
Coulson, Andrew, *Tanzania: A Political Economy.* Oxford University Press, 1982.
Cowen, M.P., "The British State and Agrarian Accumulation," in Martin Fransman (ed.), *Industry and Accumulation in Africa.* Heinemann, London, 1982.
Daniels, Gordon, "EC–Japan: Past, Present and Future" in Juliet Lodge (ed.), *The European Community and the Challenge of the Future.* St. Martin's Press, New

York, 1989.

Deyo, Frederick (ed.), *The Political Economy of the New Asian Industrialism.* Cornell University, Ithaca, 1987.

Dilley, Marjorie, *British Policy in Kenya Colony.* Frank Cass, London, 1966.

Dos Santos, T., "The Crisis of Development Theory and the Problem of Dependence in Latin America," in Henry Bernstein (ed.), *Underdevelopment and Development.* Penguin Books, 1981.

Ehrlich, Cyril, "Economic and Social Developments Before Independence," in B.A. Ogot and J.A. Kieran (eds.), *Zamani: A Survey of East African History.* East African Publishing House, Nairobi, 1968.

Evans, Peter, *Dependent Development.* Princeton University Press, New Jersey, 1979.

Foreign and Colonial Compiling & Publishing Co., *British East Africa: Its History, People, Commerce, Industries, and Resources.* London, 1909.

Foster-Carter, Aidan, "Korea and Dependency Theory," *Monthly Review,* Vol. 37, No. 5, October 1985.

Frank, Andre Gunder, *Capitalism and Underdevelopment in Latin America.* Monthly Review Press, New York, 1969.

———, *Lumpenbourgeoisie: Lumpendevelopment.* Monthly Review Press, New York, 1972.

Gerschenkron, Alexander, *Economic Backwardness in Historical Perspective.* Harvard University Press, 1962.

Gilpin, Robert, *The Political Economy of International Relations.* Princeton University, 1987.

Gregory, Robert G., *India and East Africa: A History of Race Relations Within the British East Africa (1890–1939).* Clarendon Press, Oxford, 1971.

Hailey, Lord Malcolm, *An African Survey: A Study of Problems Arising in Africa South of the Sahara.* Oxford University Press, London, 1938.

Hazlewood, Arthur, *The Economy of Kenya.* Oxford University Press, London, 1979.

Henley, John S., "Discussion Note on Chapter 9," in Martin Fransman (ed.), *Industry and Accumulation in Africa.* Heinemann, London, 1982.

Hill, M.H., *The Permanent Way: The Story of Kenya and Uganda Railway.* East African Literature Bureau, Nairobi, 1949.

Himbara, David, "Myths and Realities of Kenyan Capitalism," *Journal of Modern African Studies,* Vol. 31, No. 1, March/April 1993.

———, "Kenyan Domestic Capitalists and the State," in Bruce Berman and Colin Leys, *African Capitalists in African Development.* Lynne Rienner, Boulder, 1993.

Hirschman, Albert, "The Search for Paradigms as Hinderance to Understanding," in Norman Uphoff and Warren Ilchman (eds.), *The Political Economy of Development.* University of California Press, Berkeley, 1972.

Hollingsworth, Laurence, *The Asians of East Africa.* Macmillan, London, 1960, p. 28.

Holthham, Gerald, and Arthur Hazlewood, *Aid and Inequality in Kenya.* Overseas Development Institute, London, 1976.

Huxley, Elispeth, *White Man's Country: Lord Delamere and the Making of Kenya,* Vol. I & II. Chatto and Windus, London, 1935.

Kamau, J., "Problems of African Business Enterprise," Center for Economic Research, University of Nairobi, *Discussion Paper No. 6,* 1965.

Kaplinsky, Raphael, "Capitalist Accumulation in the Periphery: Kenya," Martin Fransman (ed.), *Industry and Accumulation in Africa.* Heinemann, London, 1982.

———, "Capitalist Accumulation at the Periphery: the Kenyan Case Re-examined." *Review of African Political Economy, No. 17,* 1980.

———, (ed.), *Readings on the Multinational Corporations.* Oxford University Press, 1978.

Kennedy, Paul, *African Capitalism: The Struggle for Ascendency.* Cambridge University Press, Cambridge, 1988.

Kenyatta, Jomo, *Facing Mount Kenya.* Mercury Books, London, 1961.

Kim, Kwan S., "The Korean Miracle (1962–1980) Revisited: Myths and Realities in Strategy and Development," Working Paper #166, the Helen Kellogg Institute for International Studies, Notre Dame, November 1991.

Kimambo, Isaria N., "The Economic History of the Kamba 1850–1950," in B.A. Ogot (ed.), *Hadith 2.* East African Publishing House, Nairobi, 1968.

Kindleberger, Charles P. , *Economic Development.* McGraw Hill Books, New York, 1958.

Kitching, Gavin, *Class and Economic Change in Kenya: The Making of an African Petite Bourgeoisie.* Yale University Press, New Haven, 1980.

———, *Development and Underdevelopment in a Historical Perspective.* Methuen, London, 1982.

———, "Politics, Method and Evidence in the 'Kenya Debate'," in Henry Bernstein and Bonnie K. Campbell (eds.), *Contradictions of Accumulation in Africa: Studies in Economy and State* (Vol. 10, Sage Series on African Modernisation and Development). SAGE Publications, Beverly Hills, 1985.

Langdon, Steven, "The State and Capitalism in Kenya," *Review of African Political Economy,* No. 8, 1977.

———, "Industry and Capitalism in Kenya: Contributions to a Debate," in Paul Lubeck (ed.), *The African Bourgeoisie.* Lynne Rienner, Boulder, 1987.

Leakey, L.S.B., *The Southern Kikuyu Before 1903.* Academic Press, London, 1977, p. 479.

Lerner, Daniel, "Modernisation: Social Aspects," *International Encyclopedia of the Social Sciences,* D. Sills (ed.). Macmillan, New York, 1968.

Levi, Werner, "Third World States: Objects of Colonialism or Neglect," *International Studies Quarterly,* No. 17, June 1973.

Leys, Colin, *Underdevelopment in Kenya.* University of California Press, Los Angeles, 1975.

———, "Capitalist Accumulation, Class Formation and Dependency: The Significance of the Kenyan Case," *Socialist Register,* 1978.

———, "What Does Dependency Explain?" *Review of African Political Economy,* No. 17, 1980.

———, "Accumulation, Class Formation and Dependency," in Martin Fransman (ed.), *Industry and Accumulation in Africa.* Heinemann, London, 1982.

———, "The Kenya Debate Ten Years On," Kingston, 1991.

Leys, Norman, *Kenya.* R.R. Clark, Edinburgh, 1924.

Lipietz, Alain, "Marx or Rostow?" *New Left Review,* No. 132, 1982.

———, *Mirages and Miracles: The Crisis of Fordism.* Verso Press, 1987.

———, *New Economic Order.* Oxford University Press, New York, 1992.

Livingstone, I., and H. Ord, *Economics for Eastern Africa.* Heinemann, Nairobi, 1980.

Long, Norton, "Politics, Political Science and the Public Interest," *PS: Political Science and Politics,* Vol. XXIV, No. 4, December 1991.

Lubeck, Paul, "The African Bourgeoisie: Debates, Methods, and Units of Analysis," in Paul Lubeck (ed.), *The African Bourgeoisie.* Lynne Rienner, Boulder, 1987.

Macgoya, Marjorie, *The Story of Kenya.* Oxford University Press, Nairobi, 1986.

Mahmood, Mamdani, *Politics and Class Formation in Uganda.* Monthly Review Press, New York, 1976.

Mahmoud, Fatima, *The Sudanese Bourgeoisie: Vanguard of Development.* Zed Press, London, 1984.

Mangat, J.S., *A History of the Asians in East Africa c. 1886 to 1945.* Oxford University Press, London, 1969.

Marris, Peter, and Anthony Somerset, *African Businessmen.* Routledge & Kegan Paul, London, 1971.

McDermitt, P. L., *British East Africa or Ibea.* Chapman and Hall, 1893.

McGregor-Ross, W., *Kenya From Within.* George Allen & Unwin, London, 1927.

Miller, Norman, *Kenya: The Quest for Prosperity.* Westview Press, Boulder, 1984.

Moon, Thomas T., *Imperialism and World Politics.* Macmillan, London, 1930.

Muller, Maria, "The National Policy of Kenyanisation of Trade: Its Impact on a Town in Kenya," *Canadian Journal of African Studies,* Vol 15, No. 2, 1981.

Mungeam, G.H., *British Rule in Kenya 1895–1912.* Oxford University Press, London, 1965.

Muriuki, Godfrey, "Kikuyu Reaction to Traders and British Administration 1850–1904," in B.A. Ogot (ed.), *Hadith 1.* East African Publishing House, 1967.

———, *A History of the Kikuyu 1500–1900.* Oxford University Press, London, 1969.

Murray, Robin, "The Chandarias: The Development of a Kenyan Multinational," in Raphael Kaplinsky (ed.), *Readings on the Multinational Corporation in Kenya.* Oxford University Press, Nairobi, 1978.

Murray-Brown, Jeremy, *Kenyatta.* George Allen & Unwin, London, 1972.

Ogot, B.A. (ed.), *Hadith 5: Economic and Social History of Kenya.* East African Publishing House, Nairobi, 1975.

Ohlin, Goran, "Development in Retrospect," in Albert Hirschman et al., *Toward a New Strategy for Development.* Pergamon Press, New York, 1979.

Onimode, Bade, *Imperialism and Underdevelopment in Nigeria.* Zed Press, London, 1982.

Orwa, Katete, "Foreign Policy, 1963–1986," in W.R. Ochieng (ed.), *A Modern History of Kenya 1895–1980.* Evans Brothers, London, 1989.

Robinson, Joan, *Economic Philosophy.* Aldine, Chicago, 1962.

Robinson, Kenneth, *The Dilemmas of Trusteeship: Aspects of British Colonial Policy Between the Wars.* Oxford University Press, 1965.

Robinson, Ronald, and John Gallagher, with Alice Denny, *Africa and the Victorians.* Doubleday Anchor Books, New York, 1968.

Rostow, W.W., "The Take-off into Sustained Growth," A.N. Agarwala and S.P. Singh (eds.), *Economics of Underdevelopment.* Oxford University Press, 1958.

Sandbrook, Richard, *The Politics of Africa's Economic Stagnation.* Cambridge University Press, Cambridge, 1985.

Saywell, John T., "York University Kenya Project," in Tom Pinfold and Glen Norcliffe (eds.), *Development Planning in Kenya.* Geography monograph No. 9, Toronto, 1980.

Seers, Dudley, "The Congruence of Marxism and Other Neoclassical Doctrines," in Albert Hirschman et al., *Toward a New Strategy for Development.* Pergamon Press, New York, 1979.

Sender, John, and Sheila Smith, *The Development of Capitalism in Africa.* Methuen, London, 1986.

Shivji, Issa, *Class Struggles in Tanzania.* Monthly Review Press, New York, 1976.

Sorrenson, M.K.P., *Origins of European Settlement in Kenya.* Oxford University

Press, Nairobi, 1968.

Swainson, Nicola, "The Rise of a National Bourgeoisie in Kenya," *Review of African Political Economy,* No. 8, 1977.

———, "Against the Notion of a 'Comprador Class'—Two Kenyan Case Studies," paper presented at the Second Bi-Annual Conference of the African Association of Political Science, Lagos, 4–8 April 1979.

———, *The Development of Corporate Capitalism in Kenya 1918–77.* Heinemann, Nairobi, 1980.

———, "Indigenous Capitalism in Postcolonial Kenya," in Paul Lubeck (ed.), *The African Bourgeoisie.* Lynne Rienner, Boulder, 1987.

Tandberg, G.G., "Duka-Wallah: The Backbone of the East African Economy," in S. Pandit, *Asians in East and Central Africa.* Panco Publications, Nairobi, 1963.

Van Zwanenberg, R.M.A., with Anne King, *An Economic History of Kenya and Uganda 1880–1970.* Macmillan Press, London, 1972.

Vasey, Sir E.A., "Development: Economic and Political Planning in Kenya," a paper read to the Economics Club of Kenya, 21 July 1955, *Vasey Papers,* KNA.

Wanjui, J.B., *From Where I Sit: Views of an African Executive.* East African Publishing House, 1986.

Warren, Bill, *Imperialism Pioneer of Capitalism.* Verso Editions, London, 1982.

Waters, Robert, and David Blake, *The Politics of Global Economic Relations.* Prentice Hall, Englewood Cliffs, 1992.

Theses, Research Documents, Reports, and Correspondence

Agence France Presse, "Kenya's Economic Prospects Bleak," 25 March 1993.

Awori, Horace, "Kenya: Airlines Threaten to Pull Out," Inter Press Service, 31 March 1993.

Balala, "African Businesses," in House of Representatives official report, Vol. III (Part II), 28 July 1964 to 1 October 1964.

British Broadcasting Corporation, *Summary of World Broadcasts,* 22 October 1990.

Chandaria, Indravadan, "The Development of Entrepreneurship in Kenya," B.A. thesis, Department of Economics, Harvard, 1963.

Daily Nation, Nairobi, Kenya. Various issues.

East African Royal Commission 1953–1955, *Report* (O.H.M.S., Cmd 9475), London 1956, pp. 65–194.

East African Trade and Industry, "Special Report on the Madhvani Group," Nairobi, March 1972. Also various other issues.

Economist, London. Various issues.

Esipisu, Manoah, "Fuel Shortage in Kenya Forces Airlines to Divert Flights," Reuter Library Report, 15 April 1993.

Financial Review, Nairobi, Kenya. Various issues.

Government of Ontario, *Competing in the New Global Economy: Report of the Premier's Council,* Vol. 1, 1988.

Harden, Blaine, "Kenya and the Cult of the 'Big Man'; Western Pressure Could Help Stop the Rot," *Washington Post,* 9 December 1990. Final edition.

Harvard Institute for International Development, *1987–1989 Biennial Report.*

Hayes, Stephen, "Ivory Coast's Sad Story," *Christian Science Monitor,* 9 April 1993.

Hill, Merynn, director of the Kenya Farmers' Association, to Mr. E.A. Vasey, 8 March 1945. *Vasey Papers,* KNA.

Industrial and Commercial Development Corporation, *Industrial and Commercial Development Corporation: Role and Activities,* 1989.

International Labour Office, *Employment, Incomes and Equality: A Strategy for Increasing Productive Employment in Kenya,* ILO, Geneva, 1972.

International Monetary Fund, *Surveys of African Economies,* Vol. 2: Kenya, Tanzania, Uganda, and Somalia. Washington, D.C., 1969.

Kamau, J., "Problems of African Business Enterprise." Centre for Economic Research, University of Nairobi, *Discussion Paper No. 6,* 1965.

Kenya Association of Manufacturers, "Industries Issued with Quit Notices," 1975. KAM files.

———, *Rural Industrialisation,* 1988.

———, *Export Incentives for Kenyan Industry,* 1989.

———, *Government Controls and Their Impact on the Manufacturing Sector,* 1989.

———, *Members' List and Industrial Index Incorporating Industrial Maps of the Major Cities and Townships.* Various issues.

———, *Report on Industrial Sub-contracting Seminar Organised by UNDP in Collaboration with UNIDO, ILO, and the Ministry of Industry,* March 1990. KAM files.

———, *Parastatals in Kenya: Assessment of Their Impact and Action Plan for Reform; Final Report,* February 1992.

Kenya Industrial Estates Ltd., *Financing and Promoting Indigenous Entrepreneurship Since 1967,* 1989.

Kenya Times, Nairobi, Kenya. Various issues.

Kiano, Dr. J.G., (speaking on Industrial Development Bill, 1964), House of Representatives official report, Vol. III (Part II), 28 July 1964 to 1 October 1964.

Kibaki, Mwai, National Assembly official report, Vol. XVII (para II), 27 June 1969 to 19 August 1969.

Mbeo-Onyango, MP, National Assembly official report, 30 September 1969.

Mbogoh, MP, (in debate on budget speech), House of Representatives official report, Vol. II (13 December 1963 to 18 March 1964).

Morara, A.N., K–Map, "Linking Industry for Faster Development," paper presented at the UNDP, UNIDO, and ILO conference, *Seminar on Industrial Subcontracting,* Nyeri, 4–9 March 1990.

Mulei, Christopher, "Endemic Unauthorised Expenditure by Government Ministries," *East Africa Report on Trade & Industry,* April 1989.

Mwaura, Z.N., "Kenya's Industrialisation Strategy," a paper presented at Kenya's Industrialisation Strategy Conference, Nyeri, 4–8 August 1986.

Oduya, speech in House of Representatives official report, 23 September 1964.

Odinga, Oginga, speech in House of Representatives official report, Vol. III (Part II), 28 July 1964 to 1 October 1964.

Overseas Development Administration, *Britain and Kenya: Partners in Development,* September 1989.

Reuter European Business Report, "Kenya: Horticulture Farmers Want IMF Reforms Back," 30 March 1993.

Standard, Various issues.

Vasey, E.A., "Development: Economic and Political Planning in Kenya," a paper read to the Economics Club of Kenya, 21 July 1955, *Vasey Papers,* KNA.

Wariithi, speech in House of Representatives official report, Vol. II, 13 December 1963 to 18 March 1964.

———, speech in National Assembly official report, Vol. XVII (Part II), 27 June

1969 to 19 August 1969.

Wanyeki, Karanja, letter to the editor, *Weekly Review,* 25 October 1976.

Weekly Review, Nairobi, Kenya. Various issues.

World Bank, *The African Capacity Building Initiative: Toward Improved Policy Analysis and Development Management,* Washington, D.C., 1991.

————, *The Economic Development of Kenya: A Report of An Economic Survey by the International Bank for Reconstruction and Development,* 1963.

————, *World Development Reports.* Washington, D.C., 1981 and 1988.

————, *Sub-Saharan Africa: From Crisis to Sustainable Growth.* Washington, D.C., 1989.

United Nations, *Survey of Economic and Social Conditions in Africa, 1987–1988,* New York, 1991.

————, *Debt Equity Conversions,* New York, 1990.

————, *World Investment Report: Transnational Corporations as Engines of Growth,* New York, 1992.

United Nations Development Programme, *A Strategy for Small Enterprise Development in Kenya,* 1988.

————, "Project Document: Export Development, Diversification and Promotion," 1986, KEN/86/107, MCI.

UNIDO (United Nations Industrial Development Organisation), *Kenya: Sustaining Industrial Development Through Restructuring and Integration,* New York, 1988.

Zarwan, John Irving, "Indian Businessmen in Kenya During the Twentieth Century," Ph.D. thesis, Yale University, 1977.

Zwerdling, Daniel, "Kenya's President Blocks New Tax Collection System." Report on National Public Radio, Washington, D.C., 15 April 1993.

Kenya National Archives

Colonial Office, London, Circular 217 from the secretary of state to the governor of Kenya, 27 August 1941.

Colony and Protectorate of Kenya, Circular 24 on the formation of the Ministry of Commerce and Industry, 25 March 1948. MCI/2/3, KNA.

————, *Report of the Committee to Examine the Need for Economic Assistance for Primary and Secondary Industries Excluding Agriculture in the Colony,* 1956.

————, *Report on the Working of the Civil Service Commission from 1st January to 30th June, 1955,* Nairobi, 1955.

————, Circular 18, Civil Service Commission, 24 December 1954.

————, *Sessional Paper No. 51 of 1955,* Nairobi, 1956.

————, *The Development Programme 1954–57,* Nairobi, 1956.

————, MCI, "The Objectives of the Board of Industrial Development," MCI/6/88, KNA.

————, *Colonial Annual Report* (various issues), Nairobi.

————, J.S. Stirton Report on Rural Industries, 15 June 1945, MCI/6/1833, KNA.

————, "Mombasa Surveys," OP(EST)/1/465, KNA.

————, "Notes on Industrial Development in East Africa," 1952, MCI/6/1257, KNA.

————, Confidential: "A Proposal for the Formation of a Kenya Development Company," Council of Ministers, 17 October 1962. CS/1/16/35, KNA.

————, Report on Rural Industries, 15 June 1945, MCI/6/1833, KNA.

————, Executive Council, minute 552, "Formation of Commercial Companies by Africans," 9 September 1950. MCI/6/675, KNA.

East African High Commission, Transport memo 40, report by the commissioner of transport, H.C. (1954) 24, CS/1/16/26, KNA.

———, Transport memo 45, report by the commissioner of transport, H.C. (1956) 10, CS/1/16/26, KNA.

———, Confidential: report by the administrator, H.C. (1956) 9, CS/1/16/26, KNA.

———, *Annual Trade Report of Kenya, Uganda and Tanganyika* (various issues), Nairobi.

———, *Annual Report of the Department of Economic Coordination* (various issues), Nairobi.

———, *East African Quarterly Economic and Statistical Bulletin* (various issues), Nairobi.

———, Submission by the chief commercial superintendent to the Board of Industrial Development, "The East African Railways & Harbours Corporation and Economic Development," 28 June 1957. MCI/6/88, KNA.

———, East African Industrial Council, *Progress Reports,* 7 February 1954. MCI/9/554, KNA.

East African Railways and Harbours. Chairman, the Kenya Glass Works Ltd., to the chief commercial superintendent, 9 July 1959. MCI/9/554, KNA.

East African Royal Commission 1953–1955, *Report* (O.H.M.S., Cmd 9475), London, 1956.

Government House, Kenya Civil Servants' Union press release, 18 July 1963, GH/4/766, KNA.

———, Letter from Messrs. Stephen, Gillitt & Co. to Mr. H.M. Kanja, a Kikuyu businessman, 25 November 1946, MCI/6/782, KNA.

———, Speech by Sir Evelyn Baring, governor, to the Kenya African Civil Servants' Association, 11 April 1953, GH/4/766, KNA.

———, Speech by Sir Henry Moore, governor, to the Association of Chambers of Commerce and Industry of Eastern Africa, October 1944, MCI/4/5, KNA.

———, Correspondence between R.J. Metha, president of the Association of Chambers of Commerce and Industry of Eastern Africa and A.T. Lennox-Boyd, secretary of state for the colonies, 1957, CS/1/16/35, KNA.

———, Confidential: Council of Ministers, "A Proposal for the Formation of a Kenyan Development Company, 17 October 1962, GH/4/952, KNA.

———, Notes to the governor by V.A. Maddison, permanent secretary for commerce and industry, 10 June 1960. GH/4/441, KNA.

———, Letter from J.P. Gaynord, secretary, East African Tanners' Association, to the director of veterinary services, 27 November 1956, OP/1/759, KNA.

———, Letter from K.D.S. MacOwan, director of veterinary services, to the secretary, East African Tanners' Association, 6 December 1956, OP/3/759, KNA.

Government of Kenya, *The Economic Development of Kenya: Report of An Economic Survey Mission by the International Bank for Reconstruction and Development,* Nairobi, 1962.

Ministry of Commerce and Industry, "Industrial Development in East Africa," 1952, MCI/6/1275, KNA.

———, *Trade and Supplies* (various issues).

———, Board of Industrial Development, MCI/6/1275, KNA.

———, Minutes of the Board of Industrial Development, MCI/6/68, KNA.

———, Board of Industrial Development, "Criteria for the Granting of Assistance to Industry," 27 October 1956, MCI/6/88, KNA.

———, Letter from G.P. Henderson for the secretary for commerce and industry to the manager, Kenya Glass Works Ltd., 9 July 1954, MCI/9/554, KNA.

————, Board of Industrial Development, "Industrial Plots," 12 January 1957, MCI/6/88, KNA.

————, Letter from H.L. Adams to Bernard Lewis, Department of Trade, 7 January 1952, MCI/4/5, KNA.

————, Letter from H.L. Adams to R.E. Nicholson, economic secretary, Northern Rhodesia, 21 March 1950, MCI/4/5, KNA.

————, Letter from R.P. Chandaria, director, Kenya Aluminium & Industrial Works Ltd. to the member for commerce and industry, 10 November 1953, MCI/6/694, KNA.

————, Minutes of the Ad Hoc Committee on Drawbacks of Customs Duty, Nairobi, 17 November 1953, MCI/6/694, KNA.

————, Minutes of the Ad Hoc Committee on Drawbacks of Customs Duty, 5 December 1955. MCI/6/694, KNA.

————, P.C. Harris, assistant secretary, report on the conflict between the East Africa Industries and the Muljibhai Madhvani Companies, 10 June 1960, MCI/6/697, KNA.

————, Company profiles and applications for drawback rebates, 1952, MC1/6/462, KNA.

————, Letter from L.N. Madhvani, Kenya Sugar Ltd. to MCI, Kenya, 12 December, 1954, MCI/9/678, KNA.

————, Correspondence between G.P. Henderson for Commerce and Industry and the manager, Kenya Glass Works Ltd., 9 July 1954, MCI/9/554, KNA.

————, Speech by Oginga Odinga at the opening of the Ramogi House, Kisumu, MCI/6/783, KNA.

————, Board of Commerce and Industry, report of the Working Party on Assistance to African Traders, 22 May 1955, MCI/6/821, KNA.

————, Letter from the Federation of Indian Chambers of Commerce and Industry of Eastern Africa supporting "Credit to Africans," to the Minister for Commerce and Industry, 10 January 1956, MCI/6/782, KNA.

————, Letter from J.G. Courtenay-Bishop, Department of Trade and Supplies, to Miss M. Paterson, secretary for commerce and industry, on the Amendment of the Credit to Africans (Control) Ordinance of 1948, 28 February 1957, MCI/6/782, KNA.

————, "Manual of Instructions for Boards and Committees Established to Make Loans to African Traders, Artisans and Industrialists," MCI/6/1275, KNA.

————, V.A. Maddison, "Progress Report on the Scheme of Assistance to African Industrialists, Artisans and Businessmen," 11 September 1956, MCI/6/782, KNA.

————, V.A. Maddison, 29 June 1959, minutes on C/TRDS/Central/Vol D/, MCI/6/1275.

————, Letter from the Association of Chambers of Commerce and Industry of Eastern Africa to the chief secretary, Kenya Government, 21 August 1945, MCI/4/5, KNA.

Ministry of Local Government, Confidential: report on loans to employers, *Monthly Report,* May 1955, CS/1/16/11, KNA.

————, Letter from the commissioner for local government to all town clerks, clerks to county councils, presidents of African district councils, 15 August 1955, MLG/3/144, KNA.

Registrar General, Letter from the provincial commissioner, central province, to chief secretary on "Trading Licences," 15 November 1946, MCI/6/782, KNA.

————, "African Companies," 12 October 1950, MCI/6/789, KNA.

————, Law Courts, "African Companies," 23 June 1949, MCI/6/788, KNA.

————, "Report on African Companies," 23 June 1949, MCI/6/788, KNA.

————, "Report on African Companies," 12 October 1950, MCI/6/789, KNA.
Secretariat, Confidential: notes of a meeting held in the secretariat on 17 March
    1947 to discuss division of responsibility between the member for agriculture
    and the member for commerce and industry, MCI/4/5, KNA.
————, Monthly ministerial reports. MCI/6/1275, KNA.
————, Letter from Van Scharrel & Stephen Advocates to A. Hope-Jones,
    economic and commercial advisor, 23 August 1946, MCI/6/782, KNA.
————, Letter from A. Hope-Jones, economic advisor, to Messrs. Stephen and
    Gillitt & Co., 27 November 1945, MCI/6/782, KNA.
————, "The African in Business": memorandum for meeting of provincial com-
    missioners," February 1950, MCI/6/782, KNA.
————, Report by chief native commissioner on Ramogi House, Kisumu, 6
    November 1950, MCI/6/783, KNA.
————, Secret letter from the Office of the District Commissioner, Nairobi, to the
    chief secretary, 29 December 1944, MCI/6/782, KNA.
————, Confidential report on African businesses, by E.H. Windley, ag. chief
    native commissioner, 25 July 1953, MLG/3/144, KNA.
Treasury, Report by the ministerial working party on credit for Africans.
    Treas/4/4797, KNA.

Contemporary Kenya Official Documents and Correspondence

Government of Kenya, House of Representatives official report (various issues),
    Nairobi.
————, *Report of Controller and Auditor General, 1965/1966,* Nairobi, 1966.
Ministry of Commerce and Industry, A.G. Barve to the Association for Promotion
    of Industries in East Africa, 4 August 1965, KAM files.
————, Letter from C.O. Kamidi to Silas Ita, KAM chief executive, 15 October
    1984. Ind 170/01E (44).
————, Engineering & Construction Division, "A Position Paper to FEAC [sic]
    on the Importation of the Completely-Knocked-Down (DKD) Kits into
    Kenya." 10 January 1989.
————, Letter from Dr. J.G. Kiano, the minister, to T.W. Tyrrell, KAM, 13 June
    1974, MCI/CONF 75/01(154).
————, C.N. Kebuchi, to the chairman, Kenya Association of Manufacturers, 3
    August 1971. MCI/CONF 73/02 (246).
————, Letter from G.M. Matheka, permanent secretary, to all manufacturers, 29
    November 1973, MCI/CONF 73/01 (143).
————, Mwamunga, E.T., the minister, press release, 1981 (month and day not
    indicated).
————, Letter from J.G. Shamalla, permanent secretary, to KAM, 3 October 1980,
    TS.45/04/ (46).
————, Letter from L.N. Kabetu, permanent secretary, to KAM, 6 April 1976,
    MCI/A 93/9/01 (84).
————, G.N. Kebuchi to KAM, 3 August 1971. MCI/CONF 73/02 (246).
————, G.N. Kebuchi to all manufacturers, 3 August 1973, MCI/CONF 73/02
    (246).
Republic of Kenya, *Official Records of the National Assembly* (various issues),
    Nairobi.
————, *Sessional Paper No. 1, 1965, African Socialism and its Application to
    Planning in Kenya.*

————, Development plans (various issues), Nairobi.

————, Various reports of the controller and auditor general, Nairobi.

————, Public Accounts Committee reports (various), Nairobi.

————, *Commission of Inquiry on Public Service Structure and Remuneration,* Nairobi, 1971.

————, *Commission of Inquiry (Public Service Structure and Remuneration Commission) or Ndegwa Commission,* Nairobi, 1971.

————, *Review of Statutory Boards,* Nairobi, 1979.

————, *Trade Licensing Act 1980,* 1972.

————, *Report of the Civil Service Review Committee,* Nairobi, 1980.

————, *Working Party on Government Expenditures Report,* Nairobi, 1982.

————, *Report and Recommendations of the Working Party on Government Expenditures,* 1982.

————, *Report of Judicial Commission Appointed to Inquire into Allegations Involving Charles Mugane Njonjo,* 1984.

————, *Sessional Paper No. 3 of 1985 on the Acceptance and Implementation of the Recommendations of the Civil Service Salaries Review Committee,* 1985.

————, *Sessional Paper No. 3 of 1985,* Nairobi, 1986.

————, *Sessional Paper No. 1 of 1986 on Economic Management for Renewed Growth,* Nairobi, 1986.

————, *Industrial Registration Act,* 1987.

————, Regulations of the Industrial Registration Act, 1987, *Legal Notice No. 437,* 21 October 1988.

————, *Directory of Industries 1986 Edition,* Central Bureau of Statistics, June 1988.

————, *Kenya Gazette Supplement Acts, 1988,* Nairobi, 1988.

————, *Economic Survey 1990,* Nairobi, 1991.

Index

Absorbent Cotton Industries Ltd., 54
Accumulation: capital, 9, 23, 31*n1*, 43, 80, 106; local, 159; patterns of, 51-59, 65-66, 93
Addly, F.J., 97
Africanization, 9, 36, 85, 86, 115, 133-136, 137, 154; of civil service, 116-117; failure of, 10, 92; governmental inability to promote, 63-64; impact on Indian capitalists, 59-67; program disintegration, 62-65
Aga Khan community, 37
Agricultural and Industrial Holdings Ltd., 95
Agricultural Finance Corporation, 135, 152
Agriculture, 12; dependence on Indian-dominated sectors, 41; European dominance of, 40; white settlers in, 36, 38, 40
Aid, foreign, 12-13; suspension of, 13, 151-152, 154
Akamba Handcraft Industries Ltd., 84
Akamba peoples, 21
Alliance Hotels, 96
Amalgamated Saw Mills, 97
Amayo, Lazarus, 120
Amin, Idi, 53, 54
APIEA. *See* Association for the Promotion of Industries in East Africa
Aringo, Peter, 120
Arusha Declaration, 67
Association for the Promotion of Industries of East Africa, 58-59, 67, 136, 159. *See also* Kenyan Association of Manufacturing.
Association of Chambers of Commerce of Eastern Africa, 58, 159
Awori, Moody, 96

Banking, 39, 42, 85-86; Indian domination of, 34*n51*, 37
Banks, 105; political, 88, 130, 153

Baring, Sir Evelyn, 44, 57
Barnett, D.E., 118
Biwott, Nicholas, 120, 142*n27*
Board of Industrial Development, 82, 105, 110
Botswana: manufacturing exports, 11*tab*; monocommodity economy in, 11
Bourgeoisie, 4; consolidation of indigenous, 18; Indian merchant origin, 7; industrial, 18; national, 21, 29; petty, 22
Boy, Boy Juma, 120
British American Tobacco, 96
British East African Association, 37-38. *See also* Imperial British East Africa Company
Brother Shirt Factory Ltd., 129
Burundi, 12, 136
Business Finance Company, 88

Canadian International Development Agency, 148
Capital: accumulation, 9, 23, 31*n1*, 43, 80, 106; Asian, 8, 23, 33*n40*, 68; collective organizations, 51-59, 58-59, 66-67; domestic, 6, 9, 23, 159; foreign, 4, 9, 18, 19, 59, 70, 75, 105, 155; formation, 4; industrial, 22, 30; in informal sector, 91; international, 17; local, 17, 59, 70, 105, 115, 138; manufacturing, 24; merchant, 21, 30, 37-38, 43-51, 159; metropole, 24; private, 106, 135, 161; sectoral organizations, 70; settler class, 5
Capitalism: industrial, 9; merchant, 9; origins of, 17-31
Capitalists, Kenyan African, 5; creditworthiness of, 86; establishment of manufacturing firms, 47-50*fig*; historical perspective, 75-97; impact of traditional values on, 89, 90; lack of commercial skills, 6, 10, 59, 77, 78, 84, 88, 89, 115;

185